Main

W9-CDV-081

memory

AT WORK IN THE CLASSROOM

Strategies to Help Underachieving Students

This item no longer
belongs to Davenport
Public Library

DAVENPORT PUBLIC LIBRARY
321 MAIN STREET
DAVENPORT, IOWA 52801-1490

memory
AT WORK IN THE CLASSROOM

Strategies to Help Underachieving Students

FRANCIS BAILEY and KEN PRANSKY

 ASCD | Alexandria, Virginia

DAVENPORT PUBLIC LIBRARY
321 MAIN STREET
DAVENPORT, IOWA 52801-1490

ASCD®

1703 N. Beauregard St. • Alexandria, VA 22311-1714 USA
Phone: 800-933-2723 or 703-578-9600 • Fax: 703-575-5400
Website: www.ascd.org • E-mail: member@ascd.org
Author guidelines: www.ascd.org/write

Gene R. Carter, *Executive Director;* Richard Papale, *Acting Chief Program Development Officer;* Stefani Roth, *Publisher;* Laura Lawson, *Acquisitions Editor;* Julie Houtz, *Director, Book Editing & Production;* Deborah Siegel, *Editor;* Sima Nasr, *Graphic Designer;* Mike Kalyan, *Production Manager;* Keith Demmons, *Typesetter;* Kyle Steichen, *Production Specialist*

Copyright © 2014 ASCD. All rights reserved. It is illegal to reproduce copies of this work in print or electronic format (including reproductions displayed on a secure intranet or stored in a retrieval system or other electronic storage device from which copies can be made or displayed) without the prior written permission of the publisher. By purchasing only authorized electronic or print editions and not participating in or encouraging piracy of copyrighted materials, you support the rights of authors and publishers. Readers who wish to reproduce or republish excerpts of this work in print or electronic format may do so for a small fee by contacting the Copyright Clearance Center (CCC), 222 Rosewood Dr., Danvers, MA 01923, USA (phone: 978-750-8400; fax: 978-646-8600; web: www.copyright.com). To inquire about site licensing options or any other reuse, contact ASCD Permissions at www.ascd.org/permissions, or permission@ascd.org, or 703-575-5749. For a list of vendors authorized to license ASCD e-books to institutions, see www.ascd.org/epubs. Send translation inquiries to translations@ascd.org.

Printed in the United States of America. Cover art © 2014 ASCD. ASCD publications present a variety of viewpoints. The views expressed or implied in this book should not be interpreted as official positions of the Association. All referenced trademarks are the property of their respective owners.

All web links in this book are correct as of the publication date below but may have become inactive or otherwise modified since that time. If you notice a deactivated or changed link, please e-mail books@ascd.org with the words "Link Update" in the subject line. In your message, please specify the web link, the book title, and the page number on which the link appears.

PAPERBACK ISBN: 978-1-4166-1757-0   ASCD product # 114005

Also available as an e-book (see *Books in Print* for the ISBNs).

Quantity discounts: 10–49 copies, 10%; 50+ copies, 15%; for 1,000 or more copies, call 800-933-2723, ext. 5634, or 703-575-5634. For desk copies: www.ascd.org/deskcopy

Library of Congress Cataloging-in-Publication Data

Bailey, Francis (Francis M.)
  Memory at work in the classroom : strategies to help underachieving students / Francis Bailey and Ken Pransky.
      pages cm
  Includes bibliographical references and index.
  ISBN 978-1-4166-1757-0 (pbk. : alk. paper) 1. Learning, Psychology of. 2. Remedial teaching. 3. Memory in children. I. Pransky, Ken. II. Title.
  LB1060.B35 2014
  370.15'23--dc23
                                2013043880

23 22 21 20 19 18 17 16 15 14   1 2 3 4 5 6 7 8 9 10 11 12

To my two daughters, Sela and Leah. Your presence in my life has been a sweet blessing.

—FB

To Hilary Russell, one of the most dedicated and skilled educators I've ever met— and who I'm also lucky enough to be married to!

—KP

memory
AT WORK IN THE CLASSROOM
Strategies to Help Underachieving Students

ACKNOWLEDGMENTS

We would like to thank the many people who have informed and inspired this book. We are greatly indebted to researchers in psychology, anthropology, cultural studies, and education who have conducted the research and constructed the theories of memory and learning drawn on in our book. We would also like to thank our encouraging and talented editors, Deborah Siegel and Laura Lawson. We would like to give a special thanks to Jeanne Chin for using her significant computer talents to create the book's graphics.

This book benefitted from the feedback, criticism, and engagement of many readers over the last two years. In particular, we would like to thank Dave Martin, Elka Todeva, Molly Lim, Joanna Oleet, Torie Weed, Anastasia Pickens, Amy Faeskorn, Joan Zukas, Jo Mackby, and Jeongsun Bang.

Francis would like to express his gratitude for financial support from the University of Kentucky and the interest and enthusiasm for the book's subject matter among classroom teachers he has had the good fortune to work with and his many graduate students.

Ken would like to thank his long-time colleague and friend, Deb Zacarian, for encouraging him to pursue his interests, and Cecelia Buckley at the Collaborative for Educational Services in Northampton for her support. He also wants to acknowledge the long list of teachers who opened their classrooms to him and collaborated with him around supporting their struggling learners.

PREFACE

Ken writes:

In the early 1990s, I was several years into being an English as a Second Language teacher at an elementary school in a small, relatively affluent western Massachusetts town. While I was pretty successful teaching students from families associated with the five colleges in the area and students who were from professional families, I was increasingly dissatisfied with my work with the children of Cambodian refugee families who were being settled in the area in large numbers. The school had creatively organized around supporting the students and their families, and while the students were making academic gains, they were not achieving like other populations of English learners, let alone other students at the school. As the population in the town grew more economically and culturally diverse, other pockets of underachievement began to develop. I had been trained in cutting-edge ESL techniques and was well-versed in the progressive pedagogy of the school, but felt I was still missing something important. I knew I needed to think outside the box—but I didn't know the nature of the box I was in.

Francis writes:

I bumped into Ken at a party in the early 1990s. He was an acquaintance from our days as graduate students at The School for International Training, and I was now a doctoral candidate in education at the University of Massachusetts. Ken told me of the academic struggles of some of his Cambodian American students. I told Ken about sociocultural theory, and we discussed the connections among language, learning, and culture. In particular, we spoke about my interest in Vygotsky and the sociolinguist James Gee, and his conception of thinking and doing as a part of the communities in which we live and work. While Ken and I had both lived and taught abroad, and thinking about culture is part of the air an ESL teacher breathes, thinking about learning itself as fundamentally a cultural (as opposed to mainly intellectual) process struck a chord with Ken. He invited me to observe his classes, and a collaboration was born.

Over the next two decades, we worked together to try to better understand the many ways struggling learners can be mismatched with the U.S. school system and the cultural assumptions that underlie schooling in the United States. We conducted classroom research and wrote articles, and Ken wrote a book on working with culturally and linguistically diverse learners who struggle academically, based in large part on the journey we had taken together. Ken has since become a coach and trainer focusing on helping teachers better meet the needs of struggling learners, and Francis's career as a teacher educator has ever since been grounded in the realities of children struggling to make sense of language, culture, and schooling.

But how did we, with our passionate interest in culture and language learning, end up writing a book about memory and cognition? We realized that a better understanding of the brain was the next step for us to take in order to understand and respond to the needs of struggling students. Ken had already been trained in a cognitive education program,[1] which was quite successful with his struggling students, and it opened up new horizons for us to explore together. We have come to realize that language/culture and cognition are two wings of the same bird. When both are intentionally accounted for in teaching, learning has a chance to soar.

Our explorations have led to the conclusion that understanding the role that memory plays in learning is something that would benefit every teacher. We try to explain memory systems in straightforward terms and connect them to learning principles, instructional strategies, and teaching techniques. We use classroom scenarios to ground the discussion of memory, learning, and classroom practices in the realities of academically struggling students. We review relevant classroom research and also draw our own inferences for applications to classrooms. Our choice of what to address out of the myriad possibilities in this fascinating field is guided by one principle: it must have a clear and direct link to academic learning, and a discernible payoff for classroom practice.

This is a book about the brain and learning, but we focus on memory systems. These connect us directly to the neurology and physiology of the brain, such as neurons, neurotransmitters, and white and gray matter. However, that level of knowledge can rarely be used to help us make decisions in our classrooms or plan lessons, so we try to focus on what is most practical for classroom teachers. For example, while the brain's production of dopamine is integral to the process of learning, we do not describe how that system works, but instead focus on what at the cognitive level stimulates the brain to produce it. Although the various brain regions are quite specialized in their role in learning, we do not identify which brain regions are responsible for what learning, but rather describe ways to structure activities to get those areas of the brain to engage.[2]

One of the challenges of exploring cognitive research is that while much has been learned about human cognition in the last few decades, it is still an area of active research. It's a complex and messy field with multiple models and interpretations. But there are nuggets to glean. The research and theories that resonated most with us were developed by cognitive psychologists who propose that humans create internal representations of experience as we learn. We draw on these representations to process future experiences and to direct behavior. Most of this literature is written by psychologists who are eager to share their insights with educators but know little about classroom learning. So they provide general, mainly theoretical guidance that does not translate easily to classroom practices. And they often use complex, technical language that is challenging to wade through unless you yourself are a cognitive psychologist. One thing we have tried very hard to do is write a book that communicates directly to you, our teaching colleagues, in the context of classroom practice.[3]

Finally, humans are social beings, and we learn in context. The problem is that education tends to be a rather compartmentalized field. There are the brain specialists, and there are experts in the social and cultural influences on learning. But the mind is the nexus that connects our inside to the outside context. So while the main focus of the book is the learner's "inside," we cannot ignore its connection to the context of learning. The social and cultural contexts of learning are the most relevant environments for us as teachers, and for our students as learners. Because so many struggling learners are from diverse cultural communities, we realize that any attempt to understand learning that focuses mainly on culture or the brain, but not both together, is missing a vital connection. We want to tie the insights from these two powerful fields together into a coherent whole. Our goal is to write the book that we wish we'd had when we were struggling to make sense of things long ago. We believe that our intentional coupling of these two fields makes this a more valuable book for the realities of practicing teachers.

We are very excited to share a perspective on teaching and learning that infuses important cognitive science research on memory systems with issues of culture and language, one that is practical and can directly support the achievement of struggling learners. We hope you find it as enjoyable and helpful to read as we found it enjoyable and educational to research and write!

---

1. The Feuerstein Instrumental Enrichment program.
2. The models and theories of cognition that we draw on are grounded in research in the cognitive sciences, and our understanding of memory and learning is informed by this work.
3. We often use "we" as a pronoun throughout the book to mean "us and you, our teacher colleagues." One other pronoun note: we alternate "he" and "she," as the third-person singular pronoun when referring to an unnamed student.

INTRODUCTION

The primary goal of this book is to help classroom teachers figure out how to support learners—*especially* struggling learners—through a focus on human memory. By developing a deeper understanding of learning and learners, we can teach more effectively. We also have to understand classroom learning as a process that plays out in a social and cultural context. Each chapter is a balance between science's new insights into human memory, filtered through the lens of how learning is also a cultural process, and how this informs classroom learning and instruction. We can harness this knowledge to gain fresh insights into the challenges faced by students who struggle academically. Each chapter provides a set of practical classroom strategies that address pressing issues in the education of our school-age children.

By exploring the different dimensions of memory and their implications for the social and individual dimensions of teaching and learning, this book can serve as a primer for all of us who would like to better understand why our struggling students continue to underperform academically, and how we can enrich our classroom teaching to better address their educational needs.

What You Will Learn in This Book

Through the study of research on learning and memory, we encourage teachers to take on the role of "learning specialist" with a particular focus on students who are academically underperforming. The book provides classroom teachers with the opportunity to deepen their understanding of both the central role that memory plays in academic learning and the (sometimes surprising) role that culture plays in memory formation and use. We present a framework for looking at learning as a social and cultural process, as a way to connect the reality of learners as neurobiological individuals to their equally important reality as social and cultural beings.

Using real-life teaching examples, the book highlights a set of specific classroom learning challenges that students (and teachers) face. We analyze these challenges from the perspective of the memory systems that play the central role in classroom learning. At each major point about memory systems, practical classroom applications accompany new insights into memory and learning. When appropriate, these are described as to how they apply to more than one grade level, and there are examples from both elementary and secondary levels throughout the book. The final chapter argues for the importance of teachers advocating for and teaching in ways that are consistent with the needs of academically challenged learners.

Chapter 1: Why Learn About Memory?

Teachers are overwhelmed as it is, so why add one more thing to our load? This chapter explores the importance of teachers becoming learning specialists, attuned to the leaning needs of our most vulnerable learners. We connect the dots as to why it is so important to take the time to understand memory systems in relation to learning, in spite of all we have to do, to better reach and teach our struggling learners.

Chapter 2: Five Core Memory and Learning Concepts

As classroom teachers, we are well trained in terms of curriculum and teaching methods, but often don't know enough about the process of learning itself. However, if we understand the functional and neurological characteristics of memory and learning, it will help us better understand the nature of classroom learning and avoid misunderstanding the source of many challenges that students face. The five core concepts introduced in this chapter sketch out the parameters of the physical nature of our memory systems and guide our understanding of the cognitive realities of classroom learning.

Chapter 3: Why Do the Cultural Roots of Learning Matter So Much?

Many culturally and linguistically diverse learners struggle in our classrooms, in spite of best practices and new training and programs. Low-income students struggle even if they are from the "mainstream culture." This chapter explores diverse communities of learners and highlights the social roots of human memory and learning. A sociocultural framework is introduced to help understand and respond effectively to the struggles that many academically underachieving students face.

Chapters 4: Working Memory: The Doorway to Learning

Ever wonder why students seem to forget so much of what we thought they'd learned? The key is working memory.[1] Working memory is central to learning, as it is where we initially process new information about what we're learning, focus attention, and manipulate information. It is closely connected to the conscious mind. It's the gateway for all learning. It is in working memory, for example, that reading comprehension takes place and mental math is processed. Chapter 4 shows how working memory plays a decisive role in all learning—if the classroom environment is not attuned to working memory, then learning will be impaired.

Chapter 5: Executive Functions

Academic learning depends on the ability to independently interpret, strategize, and problem solve—what are called executive function skills. The problem for many struggling students is weak executive function skills, so their learning is built on a house of sand, no matter how we teach our lessons. Executive functions[2] work closely with working memory in the regulation of attention and decision making to support academic learning. In this chapter, we explore some key executive function skills needed for successful academic learning.

Chapters 6 and 7: Semantic Memory

Semantic memory[3] is our storehouse of facts about the world: world capitals, the year we were born, the molecular formula for water, our child's face, the texture of oatmeal. It is stuffed full of all the accumulated knowledge of our own years on the planet, not to mention whatever we take from the store of human knowledge formed over millennia, and stored (semipermanently) in our semantic memory. It is semantic memory that stores our knowledge of words—their meanings, pronunciations, and spellings—and how they are related to other words and concepts. Much of schooling is directed at enriching the knowledge stored in semantic memory. Chapter 6 examines important features of semantic memory that impact classroom learning. In this chapter, we also discuss another long-term memory system, procedural memory,[4] and its role in issues of literacy development and second language learning. Chapter 7 explores the cultural roots of semantic memory organization, as well as a set of important cognitive skills closely connected to semantic memory organization.

Chapter 8: Episodic Memory

Think of an important event that you experienced in your life. Perhaps you remember the birth of a child, or the day you graduated from college or were married. Vivid personal memories of both daily events and important events in our lives, complete with images, sounds, and feelings, are stored in episodic memory.[5] It records our everyday lives—where we were, when the event happened, what we did and said, what we were wearing, who we talked with. While semantic memory stores facts, episodic memory records our sensory impressions of our lives. We explore the role that this form of long-term memory plays in classroom learning in Chapter 8.

Chapter 9: Autobiographical Memory

Over time, students develop a sense of themselves as students: good at math, bad at spelling, interested in art or science, and especially good or not at reading. This self-image strongly impacts academic performance and is formed in autobiographical memory.[6] When students are independent, confident, and motivated, there's a much stronger likelihood of academic success than if students are always dependent on us, lack confidence, and feel that any efforts they make will go for naught. An understanding of autobiographical memory provides an opportunity for us to develop a new awareness of our role as classroom teachers in creating positive learner identities, a key indicator of our effectiveness as teachers.

Chapter 10: Practice

It is essential that students take initial classroom learning and transform it into stable, productive, long-term development. They do that through practice. In this chapter, we explore a number of issues related to maximizing student practice, including the importance of helping struggling learners figure out effective ways to practice.

Conclusion

The sad reality is that despite an endless parade of new teaching methods, curriculum reform, and educational policies, the academic gap of middle-class/affluent and lower socioeconomic students continues to grow. Many of our struggling students come from diverse communities, with non-literacy-oriented and culturally disrupted learners. We advocate for teachers as *learning specialists* to focus on understanding the source of struggling students' academic challenges and ways to help students become better learners especially in light of the Common Core. This includes advocating for classroom practices that are aligned with the functioning of human memory and the ways children learn.

---

1. Baddeley (2007).
2. Barkley (2012).
3. Grossman and Koenig (2002).
4. Paradis (2009).
5. Draaisma (2004).
6. Baddeley et al. (2009).

WHY LEARN ABOUT MEMORY?

Wouldn't it be great to walk into a classroom full of students and feel like you really knew how they learned? To feel confident that the lessons you designed worked in sync with the way the brain works? To pinpoint problems in the learning process to help struggling students learn better?

We all want to do the best we can for our students. We spend hours and hours planning wonderful lessons, but we know that not all students benefit equally from our hard work. We agonize over students who struggle in our classrooms. We receive professional training in program after program—both what our districts make us do and what we do ourselves—to try to make the learning process work well for all students. But it still doesn't. So what are we missing?

The central idea of this book is that if we knew more about how the brain actually works in the process of learning, we would become more flexible, skillful, and successful teachers—and our students would be more successful learners. One of the challenges of teaching is that classroom teachers cannot focus on only one dimension of a learner: We must teach to the whole student—their cognitive, emotional, and social selves. We must balance their complex needs and unique characteristics with our curricular goals. This book shows the importance of memory in learning and how social learning affects memory and the complex learners we work with.

In spite of the many serious challenges of being public educators in this day and age, we are fortunate because we now know so much more about the human brain. Until recently, that was a door that was closed to us. But now that door is at least partly open, and we can begin to explore and use what we find on the other side. Cognitive science is transforming the way we understand our brains and offers many insights into how the memory system is integrally connected to the process of learning. With decades of research to draw upon and many new research tools to use, cognitive researchers have much to offer us in our work with students.[1]

Much of cognitive research has been done in controlled research settings, and reading about it can often feel like wading through a swamp. But we educators must find practical ways to use the information emerging in cognitive science. This book is written by educators for educators to harness this emerging knowledge of the human brain and memory systems in the service of our students and our profession. *In particular, this perspective will enable us to work more successfully with populations who struggle in our classrooms for whatever reason, including many low-income students, English language learners, special education students, and others.*

For all too long, our field has operated like the enchanting logic employed by a character in this Iranian story:[2]

A neighbor of Mullah Nasruddin's woke up early one morning and went outside to stretch in the early light. He noticed the Mullah at his doorstep, throwing rice all around.

"Good morning, Mullah. And may I ask, what on earth are you doing throwing rice around like that?"

"Keeping away the lions," said the Mullah.

"Don't be silly," said the man. "There are no lions around here!"

"Aha!" said the Mullah, wagging a finger and smiling. "It works!"

Many things do work in the classroom—but not always for the reasons we think. We are barraged with "best practices," new programs, new movements in education, all claiming to have *the* answer to how to overcome inequalities. But the fundamental questions we address throughout this book are, How can a clearer understanding of memory and the brain help us understand teaching and learning? And how can this knowledge help us reach and teach struggling students?

Memory: Central to Learning

Knowledge and memory are inseparable—if you are in the knowledge business, then you are also in the memory business. An efficient memory system is a requirement for all learning, in or out of the classroom. At times, children do not seem to be learning what we want them to learn—and their memory systems are at the heart of that, too. We believe that it is crucial for teachers to understand *why* effective practices are effective for many students, and also why they may not be so effective for others. The key to understanding teaching and learning processes, including the breakdowns that sometimes happen, can be found by better understanding memory.

Consider the following scenarios. Do they resonate with your experiences as a teacher or remind you of other situations where you wondered, "What is going on?!"

Scenario #1: A teacher in 2nd grade is leading a discussion in a science unit on mammals. The teacher is focusing students on the physical traits that all mammals have in common. In the classroom discussion, one child begins to talk about her pet dog and why she likes to play with it. The teacher notes that this child usually approaches school subjects from her own personal experience and is slow to keep up with the flow of classroom learning. The teacher thinks, "Why can't this child stick to the topic?"

Scenario #2: A 5th grade student from Southeast Asia is being referred for a possible learning disability. His academic progress has been slow, although it doesn't seem to be an issue of language, as the student has pretty strong oral communication skills in English. In the testing, nothing specific shows up. The child is given an exercise to choose one object from a set of three or four objects that does not belong with the others. The very first item has pictures of a knife, fork, and cake. The student looks confused. When gently pressed for an answer, the student says, "I don't get it." The tester explains the directions again. The student says, "But they all belong together!"

Scenario #3: A 9th grade algebra class has a number of students who constantly get overwhelmed and confused. They seem to forget how to solve the kinds of problems they once seemed to know, they mix up terms and concepts, they skip steps, and they get low scores on tests after they seemed to know the material. No matter what the teacher does, these students almost always have the same kinds of issues, unit by unit by unit.

This book examines situations like these from the perspective of memory to help us understand why these situations occur, how to understand them, and how to work with them.

We all know teaching consists of many roles: lesson designer, curriculum specialist, instructor, assessor, psychologist, counselor, and even surrogate parent at times. One role that we urge teachers to take on through this book is that of "learning specialist." We find it ironic that while there can be no learning without the learner, out of all the factors we have to juggle in our various teaching roles, we may know *least* about the mechanics of learning! Many of us have been trained in schools of education and our school districts in teaching methodologies, curriculum mapping, assessment, using test data . . . but how learning is a function of the memory system? Not so much! Yet memory is a key system we need to troubleshoot when problems in learning arise.

So What Is Memory, Anyway?

In which of the following activities do you think memory plays a role?

- Driving a car and talking with a friend in the passenger seat
- Reading and understanding a news story
- Hearing a new word and being able recognize it and use it later
- Retracing one's steps to find a lost item
- Describing specific details about an important personal event from the distant past
- Adding the numbers 12, 3, and 5 together
- Recognizing the face of a loved one
- Describing what you did yesterday
- Knowing that the capital of Massachusetts is Boston

Memory plays a role in all of these activities. For many of us, memory is synonymous primarily with just "remembering" a past personal experience or "memorizing" some new information. So it may come as a surprise that human memory plays such a central role in learning. *Memory is the label we use for cognitive processes that are central to our lives and sense of who we are, and they cross the boundaries of all types of activity in our lives.* We draw on various elements of our memory systems for *all* thinking, and *all* learning.

Memory is fundamental to our humanity and identity. Who would we be without our memories of past events and people in our lives? How would we survive without the ability to remember where we have gone and what we did in the past? How would we learn without the ability to store information away and retrieve it when needed? As humans evolved, we developed memory systems that allowed us to store and retrieve information necessary to take care of basic survival needs, such as gathering food, reproducing, and responding to danger by fleeing or fighting.

We also developed memory systems that are central to human cultural evolution. Our ability to learn and manipulate cultural symbol systems and their meanings has provided the social knowledge and organization that underlie modern life. With the development of language, which is also intimately connected to the memory system, humans gained the ability to work skillfully in the abstract realm of thought, a skill that is highly prized in schools.

Every day in classrooms, students struggle to learn the vast ocean of knowledge that sweeps over them. New concepts, images, names, dates, and formulas roll in. Some students float to the top and swim around happily, others flounder and struggle, while yet others sink like stones. If we reflect on this honestly, we notice that who swims, who flounders, and who sinks is pretty predictable, all things being equal.[3] But don't we all want to know how to help all students float and swim, not only the students who are most likely to do so anyway? After all, we should measure our effectiveness as teachers not by the achievement of the strongest swimmers (who are likely to achieve, with or without us), but by the achievement of those who need us most. When we work with the most academically challenged students in our schools, such as English language learners or students with individual educational plans, we have the most to gain from understanding how the memory system impacts learning, and how to adapt our instruction to reflect those realities. *Understanding how memory works can help us get all students to swim!*

---

1. Medina (2008); Dehn (2008); Sousa (2011); Ambrose et al. (2010).
2. Shah (1972).
3. It is well established that poverty, race, cultural background, and linguistic diversity are all predictors of academic underachievement of U.S. public school students (Hochschild, 2003; Kozol, 1992; Spring, 2011).

FIVE CORE MEMORY AND LEARNING CONCEPTS

This chapter establishes five core realities about memory and the hardwiring of the brain that define learning at the physical level. It's important to ground our understanding of human learning in the realities of neurological and physiological processes.[1] This understanding pulls back the curtain on educational philosophy and methodology and allows us to shine a light on learning "the way it is," based on how our brain works, at least to the degree that early 21st century science allows. We refer to these five elements throughout this book.

1. Learning Means the Efficient Functioning of the Memory System

Without memory, learning would be impossible. The very act of thinking[2] cannot happen without engaging our brain's memory system. To a large degree, the process of learning means

1. Creating a representation of some type of information;
2. Storing that representation in long-term memory;

3. Being able to retrieve that representation to interpret reality and solve new problems.

In order to make meaning of the world around us and problem solve (e.g., apply math to a story problem, interpret a poem or graph, write an essay), all the components of our memory systems need to be working in sync. So, one of our primary roles as teachers must be helping students shape their memory systems to the demands of the school curriculum. We must also shape the focus and flow of the school curriculum to our students' memory systems. The memory systems explored in this book are represented in Figure 2.1.

Figure 2.1 | **Human Memory Systems**

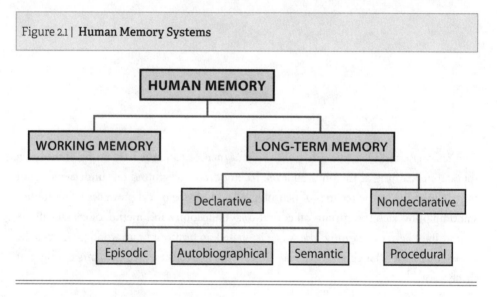

2. Memory Is a Physical Process

The brain is continually being shaped through experience. When we learn, a physical change takes place in our brain. Our ability to be lifelong learners, to continue to update our memory systems, is termed "neuroplasticity."[3] Anyone can learn at any time. Understanding the physical side of the learning process can help us become better learning specialists in the classroom.

Our brains have a system of neurons—billions upon billions upon billions of them— linked together through a web of connections through axons (the armlike parts that send information to other neurons by electrochemical means) and dendrites (the fingerlike part of the neuron that receives information from other neurons). Data signals pass from neuron to neuron—the axon of one neuron meets the dendrite of another. There are actually tiny gaps between neurons, and signals jump these gaps aided by complex chemical processes. (See Figure 2.2.)

Figure 2.2 | **Neuron Diagrams**

When we learn, our neurons are bombarded with all kinds of input, clamoring for their attention, sort of like being on the floor of the New York Stock Exchange at peak trading hours—it is lively and cacophonous! Sometimes the loudest shouts are "Yes, yes, go for it!" and we choose it, at other times, "No, no, not that!" and we let that go. So, neurons can either send data along the neural web or inhibit the data. In fact, one of the main processes of learning is inhibiting unwanted information and selecting desired information. The things we exclude do not make it into our neural network and cannot be stored for future use. Successful learners are successful in part because they can select the right information to pass along and store. Conversely, this is a key obstacle for many struggling learners.

What to focus on, what to let pass? It seems easy enough, but when that curricular tidal wave is rolling over our struggling learners, their instinct is to grab onto the closest, most obvious, easiest thing—the problem is, that's not always the best one to grab onto.

As neurons get activated during learning, their axons get coated with goopy white brain matter, called a myelin sheath.[4] The more a neuron gets activated about a particular piece of learning, the more goopy coating its axons get, which facilitates faster information transfer and protects that particular connection. The more we use a connection, the faster it gets triggered as well. While our parents always told us that practice makes perfect, it actually happens that *practice makes goop* (while it also makes permanent).

One other relevant thing to note about myelination is that it prevents the brain from "pruning" unused or rarely used connections.[5] Our brain does periodic "desktop cleanups" with neural networks. It does a lot of dendrite pruning when children are very young, and as we get older, it prunes away some neural connections. Myelin is a signal to the brain to "leave this connection alone." (See Figure 2.3.)

Figure 2.3 | **Neuron and Myelination**

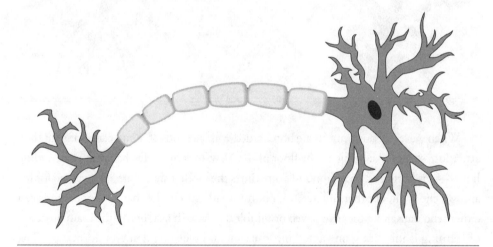

Firing and Wiring

We retain information learned through stimuli and responses.[6] This concept is famously expressed by Canadian psychologist Donald Hebb (1949) as "*neurons that fire together, wire together.*" When we notice something in our environment, we automatically link that object or event to a network of internally stored information. When a child encounters a dog and hears the word "dog," she begins to build an association between the word and the animal. Over time, the network of neurons that constitute the child's representation of a specific animal will become densely connected to the verbal label "d-o-g."

The physical nature of learning and the brain's plasticity has profound implications for us as educators. It makes us question commonly held perspectives of early childhood and human development that view children as permanently limited if they have not attained the requisite developmental, behavioral, cognitive, and academic milestones by certain ages. For example, we may view a child who cannot read well at age 13 as not having the *capacity* to learn to read well. *Research in cognitive science and education is now showing us that this view actually limits us; it limits our view of children and what they can do.* As we understand our memory system, we gain new tools to make a deeper and more long-lasting impact in our work with students who struggle, helping them to become more flexible and considered learners in their future.

We should note that sleep loss, poor diet, and lack of exercise impair the generation of neurons in the brain. Many of us have students who, unfortunately, experience these conditions, so it is important to acknowledge the special challenge these students face in learning. Armed with this information, we can advocate for the pace of our instruction to be decided by our students' learning needs. But we must also advocate for the importance of helping accommodate these needs in school programs—such as having food available for students, resisting the reduction of recess time in favor of more on-task content learning time, or building more physical movement into the school day. These things may not be what politicians, bureaucrats, and district administrators think learning entails, but our kids' brains know better.

3. Our Brain Learns Best Through Multiple Pathways

Throughout most of human history, we learned through direct experience, when almost all our senses were engaged. Our brains evolved to prefer multisensory experiences for learning. Now, with schooling and literacy having taken on an increasingly important role in our cultural learning practices, we have forgotten how our brain is built, and we create learning experiences that do not build on the brain's preferred ways to learn. But we have all experienced how hands-on learning usually sticks best, and how students typically enjoy it more.

Each part of the brain is dedicated to a specific set of tasks: sensory processing, motor activity, and verbal and mathematical processing centers. For example, the brain's web of neural interconnections allows us to take visual information and integrate it with our language system so that we can talk about what we see, and so that we can reach into our long-term memory to recall a vacation we took to the mountains in Idaho in July and tell our family and friends about it when we get back to New England in August—or write in response to the prompt "What did you do during your summer break? Be sure to be as descriptive as you can."

Networks of Representations

The way our brains prefer to learn explains how information is stored once it gets into our memory system. Information is stored in diffuse networks linked to multiple regions of the brain, as language, nonverbal images, feelings, sounds, sensations, and smells.[7] For example, here's a common tool:

This image activates neuron clusters in both your visual processing system and in the motor system that would activate in order to use the hammer. This allows you to both re-create an image of the tool in your brain as well as know how to use it. This neural network is also linked to the word "hammer," which in turn is also linked to the concept and word "tool." The flip side of saying that a student has "learned something" in our classroom is saying that a new neuron network has been forged across a range of regions of the brain, all connected up in semantic memory. So, for example, as we read, images and other mental sensations are created along with our processing of word meanings.[8]

Teaching with a Multisensory Perspective

As Judy Willis, a neurologist and classroom teacher, notes, "By stimulating several senses with the information, more brain connections are available when students need to recall that memory later on. This means that the memory can be retrieved by more than one type of cue" (2006, p. 10). For example, having students listen to a video of a scientist talking about a concept, and then having them read about the same topic along with visual representations (such as pictures, graphic organizers, or charts), provides three pathways to learning the new concept and helps to build networks that facilitate long-term storage and retrieval. Then if we engage students in actively manipulating that information (sorting and categorizing the information, problem solving, experiments, projects), we add new possibilities of sense connections. Visuals, role-plays, manipulatives, and realia not only are more fun for students to engage with than verbal lessons but also allow them to grab onto learning in many different ways. All our lessons should involve at least two learning channels.

4. We Do Not Experience Reality Directly

Knowledge is a representation stored in long-term memory and is often termed "schema." A schema is essentially a network of neurons that gets activated based on what we experience in our environment or something we think about. To say you "know" or "know how to do" something means that you are able to access the relevant representation and activate it. Once you have activated the precise schema, you are able to use it to carry out daily plans, solve a problem, or learn something new.

An astonishing insight regarding learning comes from a deeper understanding of the connections between raw input from our environment—a thunderclap, an utterance from a teacher, a sentence from a book—and the "knowledge representations" we store in memory. By the time we are conscious of experiencing something happening around us, our brain has already processed the initial sensory information, activated the relevant schema, and created a new knowledge representation of the experience. We use that knowledge representation to think with and respond appropriately. In fact, whenever we are thinking, learning, or acting, we are manipulating schemas stored in long-term memory.

The sensory world does not have a direct pipeline into our memory system. The various centers of the brain are interconnected and process information at *really* high speeds,[9] so it seems like we are reacting to an external stimulus. But we relate to reality through the lens of our own mental constructs about the world, through words, concepts, images, feelings, likes and dislikes, and our *interpretation* of experience rather than the direct experience itself. Students are not just information-processing devices—computers—neutrally taking in and storing our instructions, but rather are making sense of, interpreting, and shaping our instruction based upon their own internal schema. *Student learning is fundamentally determined more by what goes on inside the learner than on our instruction pouring in from the outside.*

This highlights three elements of instruction that we should be sure to incorporate in order to teach in sync with the realities of the brain: backgrounding, uncovering misunderstandings, and monitoring learning.

Backgrounding

Many of us already use "background-building" activities. Students are usually asked to focus on something they learned earlier in that school year or in a previous year, or on something they learned outside school that is related to the new material in some way. Indeed, from a memory system perspective, it is important to have some kind of schema-activating activity prior to any lesson. By engaging learners in extended talk about a topic, we wake up those neuron clusters in long-term memory associated with the topic.

However, it is usually a mistake to assume that all of our students have "learned" material from a previous month or year at school to the point that it is readily retrievable now. Have they *really* moved the new information into long-term memory storage and integrated it into existing networks of information? It is quite likely that many students will only have a vague recollection of it. In addition, we all have students who, for any number of reasons, were not at our school when those lessons were taught.

So we also advocate putting students in touch with their real-life experiences outside the classroom. All learners have knowledge and experiences from their home and community lives, and we can almost always find something to connect to. Whenever possible, we need to help students get in touch with information that they know best: their own lives.

There are parallels between real life and almost anything we learn at school.[10] Some examples: we could use a discussion of fights with friends on the playground to learn about the American Revolution, because conflict is conflict; we could talk about planning for a party before we turn students' attention to the value of pre-writing. What real-life connections could you help students make to (see our suggestions at the end of the chapter)

- Inferencing?
- Multiplication?
- The scientific method?
- Manifest Destiny?

As we think in this way more and more, it becomes easier to see these connections.

Learning occurs because there is background to build on. All students can get excited talking about their lives, and that shared experience becomes the baseline of what the new learning is built on. Then students are walking into a lesson that otherwise they may have little or no interest in with more interest and desire to learn. It stimulates more of a feeling of "Hey, I know this already!" instead of "Yuck, another hard, boring thing I have to learn and will be bad at."

By making efforts to connect "inside school" to "outside school," we also help students to develop semantic memory systems fully integrated with the fabulous cultural resources and cognitive tools that they have inherited from their ancestors. We will be revisiting this topic of background grounding frequently throughout the book, as it is so important to the efficient functioning of the entire memory system.

Uncovering Misunderstandings

Students may have "faulty" background knowledge. We all have created misunderstandings about things, which form the (faulty) baseline for our new learning. The longer a misunderstanding persists, the harder it is hard to shake.

Once Ken was working with some students on a book about the fires that raged through Yellowstone in 1988. The book was about the controversy that ensued—should the fires be put out or not? The author stated directly on the back cover that the book was about the controversy, not taking a position on which side was right. But after reading and processing that with the students, Ken asked as a comprehension check, "So, does the author think the fires were good or bad for Yellowstone?" All the students instantly replied, "Bad!" Why? Even though they had ostensibly "understood" the back cover statement about the book, the year before in 4th grade they had all been through a fire safety unit where the message was quite clear: *Fire is dangerous and bad!* That past learning would have formed the faulty baseline for the comprehension in the present text if Ken had not lucked out by asking them a follow-up question that required them to apply what they apparently had "clearly understood" just seconds before in the conversation. There can never be too many comprehension checks or attempts to pin students down about what they actually understand.

Monitoring Learning

We have to create opportunities for students to demonstrate their real-time learning, which can be evaluated on an ongoing, formative assessment basis. With frequent check-ins, we have a better chance to head off misperception, misinformation, and poorly processed ideas at the pass. Not only are turn-and-talk, Think-Pair-Share, learning log reflections, and other ongoing assessment techniques helpful for students to get time to take stock of and solidify their learning, but if we *actively attend to* what students are saying or writing during such activities, we can see how accurate their fledgling understanding is.

5. Honoring the Limbic System

The limbic system[11] is the brain's center of emotional control. The thing to realize about emotion is that it is a form of intelligence in its own right. Emotions like anger, fear, or joy are the result of our limbic system's assessment of our environment. The limbic system draws on the knowledge representations we've stored in long-term memory to make sense of context and come to a conclusion about what our priorities for action should be, based upon how we are feeling. Without the limbic system assigning a high priority to what is being taught, or if we sense a threat in the environment or even feel generally uncomfortable, we will simply not activate our memory systems for learning.

For example, if we are forced to go to a professional development (PD) workshop by our district about a topic we do not find engaging or important, and the presenter just reads off the slides, our limbic systems rebel, and we retain very little of the content—we might even get surly! Feelings of anxiety, fear, disconnection, confusion, and anger all make the limbic system tell the brain to hunker down in "protect" or "disengage" mode.

Similarly, if our classrooms feel to students like that PD feels to us, their learning won't happen, either. If students think that we don't like them, or that other students don't like them, or that they are just bad at school, or that everything moves too fast, or for any other reason, their emotional response makes it very unlikely that they'll engage their memory systems successfully in learning. Without positively engaging our students' limbic systems, we are unlikely to be able to teach them successfully, however wonderful or built on "best practices" our lessons are otherwise.

Or maybe a student's limbic system is still engaged with something that happened in the home, or on the street, or on the bus. It is *so* important to ensure a safe, welcoming, and open classroom environment. Otherwise, we are just slamming the door shut on even the *possibility* of some (or even many) of our students' being able to learn.

Acute stress causes us to produce hormones that make us go into "hunker down mode."[12] Learning becomes problematic and it gets hard to think straight because our limbic system is on such high alert. At that point, neither working memory nor our long-term storage systems work as optimally. Many children, sadly, grow up in a very stressful environment and come to school fighting an uphill battle with their stress hormones. In Chapters 3 and 5, we will see that this directly impacts their ability to learn independently. Knowing this makes creating a warm, welcoming, and stress-free classroom so important, and we need to take the time to make it happen.

Teaching Point

The more we know about something, the better we can make use of it. That's the spirit behind the value of becoming a learning specialist. As we learn more about the physiological and neurological realities of learning, we can teach in ways that honor these truths. In the same way, students can make use of this information: everything we need to know, they can benefit from knowing, too.[13] We highly recommend trying it out!

For example, if they know that without tapping into background, learning won't happen, there is at least the possibility that they will try to tap into it independently, and maybe be more proactive about asking if they don't know much about a subject or text. If they learn about myelination, it's an easier sell in reply to "We did this already—why are we doing it again?" to say, "But remember, practice makes goop!" Each of the core concepts in this chapter can be fodder for lessons where students learn about how they learn. The class can physically act them out after they learn about them, sing songs about them, or draw their own pictorial representations, cartoon, or learning flow chart.

The same can be done with the different memory systems (working memory, long-term storage systems) when we get to those. By learning how their brain is working as they learn, what makes learning easier and what complicates it, students can become better learners, more able to advocate for themselves individually and as a class.

What's Next

Before we explore each section of the memory system in greater detail, we first take up, in Chapter 3, the social and cultural context in which schooling occurs. Although it may seem counterintuitive, important elements of our memory system—which we just described as a physical and neurological process in this chapter—are profoundly affected by culture. In order to fully appreciate the workings of memory and the struggles of many learners, we need to establish learning as a social and cultural process.

OUR BACKGROUND GROUNDING IDEAS (from page 19)

- **Inferencing**
  We could ask students, "Have you wanted to ask your mom and dad for something, but when you go to ask them, something about them makes you think, 'Whoa, now's not the time!'?" Or, "Have you ever done something your parents asked you not to do, and just by looking at them, you know just how they feel about it?" *All kids "read" expressions of parents, teachers, friends, etc.*

- **Multiplication**
  We could ask students how many of them eat cookies or chips, how many of their parents buy gas for the car or how basketball shots turn into points. *There are many examples of things that kids know well that come in packages or groups, or that are calculated more than one at a time.*

- **The Scientific Method**

  We could ask students what they do if they ask their parents for something and their parents say no. Do they ask again another time, in a different way? Or, how do they figure out how to beat levels in a video game? *Kids hypothesize and make adjustments to what they do through what they've experienced throughout their lives.*

- **Manifest Destiny**

  We could ask, "How many of you have a bigger brother or sister who comes into your room anytime they want, even takes your things, but you aren't allowed into their room without getting permission first"; or, "If you're the older brother/sister, is it that way for your younger brother/sister?" *There's unfairness (at least the perception of it), and the abuse of position because one has the means to do so, in every child's life.*

---

1. Gluck et al. (2008).
2. The brain does initially process sensory information from our eyes, ears, nose, skin, and tongue (somewhat) independent of long-term memory. However, quite early on in sensory processing, a long-term memory schema is engaged to help identify and make sense of new environmental input. Conscious thoughts such as naming an object or event, comparing two things, forming an opinion, and interpreting language require access to long-term memory (LeDoux, 2002).
3. Feuerstein et al. (2010).
4. Armstrong (2008).
5. Vanderhaeghen & Cheng (2010).
6. Tulving (1985).
7. Pinker (1997).
8. Sadoski & Paivio (2001).
9. Measured in one-thousandths of a second.
10. Egan (1997).
11. LeDoux (1996).
12. Bibok, Carpendale, & Müller (2009); Blair et al. (2011); Buckner & Kim (2012); Fernald et al. (2011); Herbers et al. (2011); Hughes & Ensor (2009).
13. Armstrong (2008).

WHY DO THE CULTURAL ROOTS OF LEARNING MATTER SO MUCH?

The primary focus of this book is helping classroom teachers to support their struggling learners. We all have students who struggle to learn content and develop literacy and other academic skills, despite our best efforts. In this chapter, we explore the social nature of learning because this perspective provides important insights into the learning challenges faced by culturally and linguistically diverse students.

As teachers, we need to keep in mind a learner's dual nature as both a neurobiological device and a cultural being.[1] To maximize our teaching influence, it is essential to understand how students use their brains to learn, and equally important to appreciate the ways that the brain and learning are shaped through social interaction. An understanding of how memory systems work during the learning process, combined with an understanding of the social and cultural roots of learning, gives us a powerful framework for better understanding and working with culturally and linguistically diverse students, many of whom struggle academically in our nation's classrooms.

Three Core Social Learning Concepts

In this chapter, we describe three key concepts as they relate to learning as a social activity. We will return to them throughout the book.

1. Memory Is Socially and Culturally Constructed

The brain is designed to interpret reality based on the knowledge representations we have stored in long-term memory. Our students are always constructing their own interpretation of classroom lessons based on their knowledge representations, and these are heavily influenced by culture. Culture shapes our everyday cognition: categorizing, reasoning, comparing, and so on. This social learning concept and our five core brain-and-learning concepts form the nexus that connects our inside (our brain) with the outside (the society and culture in which we live). We should never lose sight of the fact that learning is a social process.[2]

Imagine a family with a 5-year-old child visiting a local zoo. They are standing in front of the elephant cage. The parents and child are talking. About what? What they see: the elephant. The parents are using language to focus the child's attention on certain features of the elephant— maybe how the trunk looks like a snake, the ears like huge fans, and so on. And on the drive home? More talk, about what they saw. Though the child experienced many things at the zoo, the conversations about the elephant and other aspects of the zoo trip will directly shape many of the child's memories of her zoo trip. Around dinner that night, the child may recount the trip again through direct questioning by the parents: *What did we see first? What did the elephant do with his trunk? What did you like the best?* In this way, the child collaboratively constructs a coherent narrative about the visit to the zoo with her parents. She also develops categories of knowledge for elephants and other animals, trips to the zoo, the importance of asking questions, and the characteristics of experience she should pay more or less attention to.

Direct experience of the world (that is to say, as direct as it can ever be, given our reliance on internal knowledge representations) is not the primary way that we learn. Family, friends, teachers, and others mediate young children's learning experiences through talk and interaction, and orient them to the world and their place in it.[3] Children are trained to notice and remember certain kinds of experiences, interpret them, tell stories about them, and draw conclusions about them. Over time, these experiences become a child's knowledge base, the foundation of his or her conception of the world. The interactions that children experience with others help shape their knowledge, their ways of thinking, and their uses of language, in ways that may or may not echo school expectations.

While the zoo scenario is probably very familiar to many of us, all parents in all communities do not highlight similar aspects of experience. If we are the parents of a child in a

Southeast Asian village where elephants are work animals, for example, we may direct our child's attention toward those characteristics of the elephant that are functionally important, such as how the trunk lifts large logs, and the neck is big enough to ride on—that is, if we talk about it at all. For us in this setting, an elephant is a local beast of burden with an important role to play in the local economic life of the village. *But even if we did go to a zoo and see an elephant, whatever we talked about would likely not shift to the kind of conversation the parents and child had in the first scenario.* We may not ask them what they liked best or what they think about any of the animals. Through hundreds of such conversations, this village child stores information about elephants and other phenomena in their environment that highlight their function within the social and economic world of the village. The child also comes to understand that adults lead discussions.

Children are socialized by parents, community members, teachers, and even peers to particular ways of using language and organizing memory.[4] These experiences shape their developing memory systems in ways that directly impact later learning in school and beyond. In short, memory is socially organized.

2. Our Students Come from Two Distinct Communities of Learners

There are two distinct orientations to the process of learning, and almost all of us will have students from both orientations in our classrooms:

Literacy-oriented students:[5] The students who seem most successful at school learning often have an orientation to literacy practices that serve them well in classroom learning and testing situations. They often have parents or guardians who are more formally educated, and they develop various linguistic and cognitive skills at younger ages that privilege them in our classrooms. They are the parents and child in the first zoo scenario.

Indeed, there is ample evidence that shows that children from literacy-oriented communities achieve at much higher levels than children from communities where parents are less formally educated. The following graph (Figure 3.1) represents data from the National Assessment of Educational Progress (NAEP). The scores of 8th grade students whose parents had at least bachelor-level study after high school far outperformed students whose parents' formal education stopped at high school, and they outperformed students whose parents did not finish high school to an even greater degree. Note that these achievement gaps held relatively steady over 13–15 years.

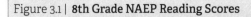

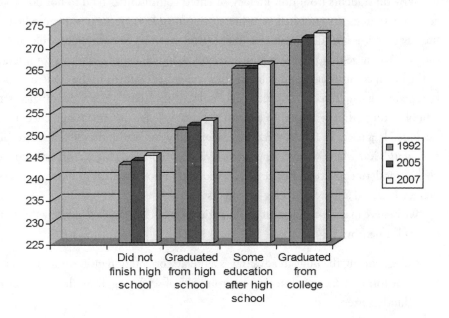

Figure 3.1 | **8th Grade NAEP Reading Scores**

Parents who have formal education are typically in sync with the requirements of school achievement. So they are more likely to parent their children in ways that instill the skills their children will need to achieve academically. A literacy orientation cuts across the lines of race, culture, ethnicity, and language. School curricula are usually created with these students in mind.

Non-literacy-oriented students:[6] What we term "non-literacy-oriented" students are born into communities that are less oriented to formal schooling. Parents and families want their children to do well in school. However, they lack the expertise that literacy-oriented parents have of the linguistic and cognitive skills that schools require of children—they were not as successful in school, or maybe didn't have the opportunity to attend school all the way to graduation, or come from a community where formal schooling was not for everyone and not an essential element of their society. This community was illustrated in our second zoo scenario. We want to stress that the linguistic practices of communities and families that are less literacy oriented are not less valuable. Their children have the same intellectual potential and the same learning capacity as literacy-oriented students.

Why do students from non-literacy-oriented communities tend to not do as well in academic settings? In a nutshell, non-literacy-oriented learners are not as enmeshed in the literacy practices found in modern technological societies. For example, while they typically use language that may be rich in vocabulary and language structures for interacting in their own communities and cultures, they are not as oriented to the academic vocabulary, grammar, and discourse needed in school settings. To be independently successful in school settings, they will need to expand their knowledge of, and competence in, using academic language. In fact, to become academically successful, they will have to adopt a new worldview where written language plays a central role. This is a primary curricular goal of modern education. Figure 3.2 lists several important areas of difference between literacy-oriented and non-literacy-oriented students.[7]

We believe that we can disrupt the historic cycle of underachievement by this population of learners by

- Recognizing the built-in advantages a literacy orientation gives some children in the formal, academic learning environment of schooling, from the time they enter kindergarten; and
- Systematically and intentionally helping struggling learners develop the same set of skills.

This book suggests ways to accomplish this goal.

While less facility with literacy-oriented skills is certainly not the only reason that children from non-literacy-oriented communities perform less well in school, it is one of the key factors, and perhaps the least well understood. Many educators and researchers have described how mere immersion in a schooling environment does not necessarily (or even usually) enable students to develop academically oriented cognitive skills if they do not already possess them.[8]

The proof is in the pudding: if it were otherwise, by high school, all children would be equally proficient as learners in school, and this is demonstrably not the case, as any high school teacher would attest. And it's often the same children in high school who struggled in earlier grades. Given this situation, if we teach the same way to all students in our classroom, we are often missing the academic needs of non-literacy-oriented students, one of whose primary needs in a school setting is to intentionally develop the cognitive, linguistic, and cultural skills that literacy-oriented students *already* have, and upon which typical classroom instruction and the curricula are built. Throughout this book, we explore the connections among literacy-oriented skills, our memory systems, and learning.

We can use Figure 3.2 to assess how literacy oriented particular students are. Students' literacy orientation can be thought of as placement on a continuum along the dimensions outlined in the figure. Figure 3.2 should be interpreted within the context of what we typically expect from students in the grades we teach. In addition, we should try to learn as much as we can about the cultural backgrounds of our students, which may give us a more accurate perspective on our students vis-à-vis this chart. It is also important to note: *This is not intended as a proscriptive view of students that we use to sort students before we have seen them perform in the classroom.* Rather, it is a way to help guide our thinking as we see students who struggle academically, so we know what we have to explicitly teach them beyond the content curriculum.

Figure 3.2 | **Literacy Orientation vs. Non-Literacy Orientation**

Non-Literacy Orientation	**Literacy Orientation**
Limited ability to independently use written texts, such as dictionaries, references, and subject-matter texts to mediate learning	More ability to independently use written texts such as dictionaries, references, and subject-matter texts to mediate learning
Limited metalinguistic awareness (i.e., an understanding of language as a system, which can itself be analyzed as an object of study)	More metalinguistic awareness
Limited metacognitive awareness at younger ages	Greater metacognitive awareness at younger ages
Limited ability to independently use knowledge of multiple functions and genres of literacy: academic, economic, etc.	More skillful at independently using knowledge of multiple functions and genres of literacy
Limited ability to independently and skillfully use a variety of written texts (i.e., scientific models, theories, novels, histories, news stories, etc.)	Able to independently and skillfully use a variety of written texts

continued

Figure 3.2 | **Literacy Orientation vs. Non-Literacy Orientation** (*continued*)

Non-Literacy Orientation	Literacy Orientation
Often less willing to independently persevere in learning challenging content that is not seen as valuable or of immediate personal interest, especially as students get older	More apt to independently persevere in learning challenging content that is not seen as valuable or of immediate personal interest, especially as students get older
Smaller and less sophisticated knowledge of vocabulary (for English language learners, this includes in their first language)	Larger and more sophisticated knowledge of vocabulary (for English language learners, this includes in their first language)
Less developed grammatical complexity in oral and written language (for English language learners, this includes in their first language)	More developed grammatical complexity in oral and written language (for English language learners, this includes in their first language)
Typically less confident as an independent, self-directed learner in academic settings, needing more teacher direction	Typically more confident as an independent, self-directed learner in academic settings, needing less teacher direction

There is one other significant group of learners to discuss: culturally disrupted learners. This is slight rephrasing of a term[9] coined by an eminent Israeli psychologist, Reuven Feuerstein, to indicate children (or adults) who have had a sustained, serious interruption in the normal child-rearing practices of their community. We regard Feuerstein as particularly important because he has developed a cognitive education program that is highly effective with non-literacy-oriented and culturally disrupted learners, called the *Feuerstein Instrumental Enrichment* (FIE) program.[10] FIE is now used extensively in over 60 countries worldwide and is based on a coherent, well-integrated theory of learning that has been validated by recent discoveries about how the brain works.[11]

Cultural disruption may occur in both literacy-oriented and non-literacy-oriented communities. As we've noted, parenting is built on interactions between families and children in culturally appropriate and comfortable ways, and children learn how to learn based on these interactions. Therefore, circumstances that interrupt these interactions or change them over long periods may have a negative impact on children's cognitive development. For example, war or prolonged civil strife, alcoholism, long-term family stress, severe poverty, or even too much TV-as-parent when children are very young are all circumstances that can lead to cultural disruption if sustained over long periods, and these conditions can affect children's cognitive development whether they are born into a poor household or a very affluent one. The consequences of long-term cultural disruption strongly impact the efficient functioning of memory systems required for classroom learning. By understanding the underlying needs of these learners and how their memory systems have been affected, we will become much more effective in our work with them.

Figure 3.3 lists a number of classroom interventions we can use to support non-literacy-oriented and culturally disrupted learners within the curriculum and also help them develop literacy-oriented skills.

Figure 3.3 | **Classroom Modifications for Non-Literacy-Oriented and Culturally Disrupted Learners**

Non–Literacy Oriented	Culturally Disrupted
In addition to what the curriculum requires of us:	Everything from the left, and also more help with
More vocabulary work	Focus and attention
More concrete learning tasks	Impulsivity control
More visuals	Finding relevance and value
More practice opportunities	Comparison and categorization
More homework support	Using language precisely
More breaking down content	Problem solving
More wait time	Generalizing learning
More talk opportunities	Cause-effect reasoning
More reflection time	Persevering
More help making connections	Goal setting and organization
Building strong relationships	
Helping students become independent	

3. Quality Learning Interactions Are Predicated on Mediated Learning Experiences

One other key concept we draw on from Feuerstein et al. (2006, 2010, 2012) is called the mediated learning experience.[12] *In a nutshell, mediated learning experiences (MLEs) are culturally grounded learning interactions between a more competent guide and a learner that are defined by particular characteristics.* The quality and quantity of MLEs children have in their developing years shape their cognitive capabilities at school. Yet we know because of neuroplasticity that there is no "cap" on a person's capability: everyone can always learn to improve their performance.

For example, the parents in the two zoo scenarios earlier are mediating their children's perception of the elephant in culturally appropriate ways through their discussion of the elephant; by the parents' use of language, each child's own relationship to the elephant is channeled in a certain direction. They each help their child understand the elephant beyond just what their five senses tell them. Through many such interactions in a child's life, cultural knowledge is transmitted from adult to child. The lack of these interactions is one reason that students with minimal MLEs are referred to as "culturally disrupted."

There are three essential qualities of a Mediated Learning Experience that *must* be present for the interaction to be an MLE. Figure 3.4 illustrates these three qualities.[13]

In addition to those three factors, MLEs are different from other types of typical teacher-student interactions in two important ways. The first is that a more competent person interposes him-/herself between the learner and his/her experience in order to help the learner interpret the experience (and create knowledge representations) beyond what he would otherwise have been able to do on his own, such as the parents at the zoo. The mediator also intervenes between the learner and his response, which allows for a range of options that would likely be unavailable to the learner working on his own.

The second aspect of an MLE that makes it different from teaching is that *the real goal is not to learn information, but for the learner to become a more competent, flexible, and adaptable thinker.* An assessment question of a *teaching* interaction would be "Has the student learned *x*?" The "assessment" question of an *MLE* is "Will the child be even a tiny bit better off as an independent thinker or problem solver tomorrow because of this interaction now?"

For example, Joey wanted to hang out with Ezra during recess but just ended up bothering him. Ezra got frustrated and said something mean. Joey got angry and wanted

Qualities of Mediation	The Mediator ensures that ...
Meaning	The interaction or learning goal has meaning and value to the learner.
Intentionality/reciprocity (alignment[14])	• His/her interaction and the task are molded to the learner. • The learner adapts him-/herself to the mediator and the task. • Interest and motivation are roused as needed. • The goal of the interaction is becoming a better learner.
Transcendence	The interaction is grounded in what the learner knows and connected to future learning and problem solving.

Figure 3.4 | **Three Universal Qualities of Mediated Learning Experiences**

to punch Ezra. The adult at recess sees this develop and is just interested in controlling their behavior, so he marches both children to the office where they might be told not to behave that way again, or their parents will be called. In contrast, an adult mediating here would help Joey think through the consequences or repercussions of acting on that impulse and help him figure out a more productive way to respond to mean words. Once Joey was calmed down, the mediator would also try to help him see how bothering people might not be a great way to make friends, and they might talk about the kinds of behaviors he might try next time to get the results he wants. The mediator would help Ezra see the direct connection between mean words and someone wanting to punch him, and they might brainstorm alternatives to getting so frustrated at someone that he just gets mean, and also maybe generate some empathy for Joey as someone looking for a friend. We can see that there was *alignment, transcendence,* and *meaning* present in this interaction, that the mediator tries to help both children see how they could reinterpret what caused the problem as well as how to respond differently, and both children are learning how to handle these situations better in the future.

Many of us instinctively would mediate here instead of just try to control the children's behavior. We often fall into the mediator's role quite easily when there's a behavior-related issue. We are advocating that it is productive to apply the mediator's role to classroom learning situations where a student is struggling, as quite often it is not the curriculum itself that poses the real challenge, but something within the child that is not up to the learning challenge.

Say it's a math lesson. A student is trying to wrap his head around two-digit multiplication. He keeps forgetting how to line up the numbers, and because he has very little confidence as a learner, he gives up. A teacher might try to figure out some new way to help. Maybe the teacher would give the student graph paper so that he can write numbers in the little squares, which would be an external scaffold that helps the student line the numbers up correctly. A great teaching intervention, no doubt.

However, a teacher/mediator would identify the student's lack of skill in organization and lack of confidence as the *real* issues and create an MLE around one of those two things. Then the teacher/mediator might segue to the graph paper strategy, and it would be used as the concluding point of transcendence: next time he's doing this kind of math, what could he do to make his life easier?

The main goal in this scenario is *not* that the student can end up being more accurate with two-digit multiplication—although, of course, it's important that he eventually become so. The main goal is that the student has some capability to ramp up his confidence even to a tiny degree, or recognize that organization is the challenge and have a strategy to recognize and deal with it. The incident would be something to refer back to at some future time when the student experienced a similar difficulty, and he could ground his new MLE in this past incident when the student was able to change his behavior to effect a more positive outcome.

In this book, we use "teaching" to indicate a focus on learning the formal school curriculum and "mediation" when the focus is on learning how to learn and thinking skills. We teach when we address learning in the information/school curriculum, but we need to mediate when we want to help students develop skills in learning. Figure 3.5 lists the basic differences between teaching and mediation.

Figure 3.5 | **Teaching Versus Mediation**

Teaching	Mediation
Oriented toward learning of content	Learning process oriented
Focused on here and now	Future oriented
Learner viewed in terms of content and curriculum	Learner viewed in terms of learning
Emphasizes techniques, methods, best practices, programs	Emphasizes flexibility based upon learner needs

Feuerstein writes that children who have had fewer mediated learning experiences are often more impulsive, tend to be less flexible thinkers, remain egocentric longer, and have what he terms an "episodic grasp of reality." That means that their relationship to experience is less generalized and coherent, so learning becomes more disconnected and difficult to sustain. According to Feuerstein, the following are some characteristics that *well*-mediated learners apply in learning and problem-solving contexts. Culturally disrupted learners often lack these traits to a greater or lesser degree. Well-mediated learners

- are flexible and adaptable problem solvers;
- have a sense of self as interconnected with the world;[15]
- have well-developed spatial and temporal (time) concepts;
- can generalize learning to new contexts and problems;
- understand the need for planning;
- understand the need for logical evidence;
- can more easily take the perspective of others;
- exhibit stronger control of the attention system;
- engage in spontaneous comparisons;
- engage in accurate and precise labeling.

Teaching Point

The three essential elements of mediation—transcendence, meaning, and alignment—can form the structure of quality classroom lessons that are also in sync with how memory systems work. While mediation ideally happens with individual learners, we can strengthen our classroom instruction by intentionally harnessing the power of transcendence, meaning, and alignment. It is important to note that these core elements of mediation do not change K–12. Each lesson element below will be reinforced and described in more detail in the book as it relates to memory (the chapter it is in is in parentheses after the first sentence in each section).

1. *Take whatever time is needed at the start of a new subject or unit to ensure that students find meaning and value in the new learning, and periodically check on how students are doing in terms of their motivation to put forth effort* (Chapter 5). In doing this, we mediate meaning and alignment. If we are teaching 9th grade biology to a group of disconnected, disempowered students, this might entail a conversation about what brings us together in this moment to learn about a subject that doesn't seem to have much connection to their lives. We certainly would need to know why we thought it was worth their time and effort! If we have no answer for that, we are just verifying their feelings that it really doesn't have any connection to them. We might talk about how the food we eat affects our body's systems, what diet our students typically have in their home, what kind of fast food is accessible in their neighborhoods, and what kind of discussion they might have with family members about this subject. However we do it, the class discussion should be a *student-centered* discussion, not subject centered.

2. *Helping students connect to their background experiences is essential* (Chapters 2–10). By helping students connect the new learning to their lives outside school, we mediate transcendence, one element of which is connecting present learning to past experience. This is more than just reminding students of something they (supposedly) learned about the subject in the past at school. We suggest multiple ways to do this in the chapters to come.

3. Whenever possible, *we should start lessons in a motivating, thought-provoking, or exciting way* (Chapters 4 and 5). This begins to mediate our intention, which in this sense is to help students be present in the moment and rouse the energy they need to learn. In a classroom, we'd like this to be something connected to our content or lesson,

but if it seems like student energy really needs rousing, or the content itself will initially not be compelling enough, this can mean using humor, surprise, or even silliness to get our class "with us" in the moment! Another aspect of alignment in this sense is building off strong relationships with students. So, talking about something we did with a friend or family over a weekend, and asking students about what they did, is another way that helps engage students emotionally and cognitively. Younger children are usually very eager to learn whatever we seem eager for them to learn, but as they get older, we have to be more intentional about orienting ourselves to their diverse lives and motivations.

If it's a chemistry class, we could have some chemicals mixed together spewing smoke as kids walk in. If it's an upper elementary class studying prerevolutionary American history, we could start, "Okay everyone, if you think knowing about the past is important, stand over against that wall. If you think it's a boring waste of time, stand over at the wall by the window."

4. *Setting clear goals is essential for struggling learners* (Chapter 5). When we do this, we also mediate alignment among curriculum goals, classroom activities, and our learners.

5. *It's essential to teach only when students are paying attention* (Chapters 4 and 5). In doing so, we mediate alignment. Although it seems self-evident to state this, so many of us start teaching when some students are clearly not attending! Striking a chime, starting to speak very softly, doing something startling like suddenly saying loudly, "Oh no!" and when the students say, "What? What?" saying, "Just making sure you're with me"— anything that grabs student attention. We learn what we pay attention to, and so we all must become adept at capturing, and maintaining, learner attention.

6. *We need to create multiple opportunities for students to actively respond to, and practice, the new learning* (Chapters 2 and 10). When we do this, we mediate alignment. Many ways to do this will be shared in the book.

7. *At the end of lessons, we should give our students time to reflect on their learning (process and content) and connect the learning of that day to future possibilities.* In this way, we round out mediation of transcendence (Chapter 10). We recommend that every lesson end five minutes before the bell (or however periods are marked at your school) to afford students time for this reflection. Prompts such as "What did you learn today that you can use tomorrow?" or "Is there any way that you learned better today than yesterday?" are just as valuable (if not more so) as "What did you learn today?" If you

give students a sentence starter, avoid "I learned . . ." and instead have students complete "I learned that . . ." If students just write "I learned math today," it doesn't really tell us anything.

We are sure most teachers do some, many, or even all of these elements of a mediated lesson, at least some of the time. A central idea of this book is that struggling learners, many of them non-literacy-oriented or culturally disrupted students, require opportunities to focus on learning and thinking skills for their own sake. If we structure all our lessons around these principles every day, we powerfully help mediate student learning at all times and in all subjects. Even if you already have a number of ideas for each of these lesson elements, we think you will finish this book with a deeper appreciation for how they connect to memory and learning.

Conclusion

The cultural roots of learning matter because learners come into our schools from differing communities, with differing orientations to literacy and schooling. Unless we are aware of what some of these differences are in our classrooms, and how to mediate them in sensitive and productive ways, just knowing more about the memory system will not be enough. The five brain-and-learning principles in Chapter 2 in conjunction with the three social learning principles in this chapter provide the conceptual framework for understanding many of our students who struggle academically. Within this framework, we explore in the upcoming chapters powerful teaching approaches to address their learning challenges.

---

1. Frawley (1997).
2. Vygotsky (1978; 1986); Feuerstein et al. (2010).
3. Feuerstein et al. (2010).
4. Rogoff (2003); Gauvain (2001).
5. The perspective on literacy orientation developed in this chapter is grounded in sociocultural perspectives on literacy use and learning (Bloome & Bailey, 1992; Delpit, 1996; Heath, 1983; Gee, 1990; Purcell-Gates, 1995; Perry, 2012).
6. The term "non-literacy-oriented students" is a term of convenience to identify a group of students in our schools who often struggle academically. The term is not meant to suggest a deficiency, but it

does highlight a way to conceptualize the root challenges that many struggling students face in our schools. The relative degree of orientation toward literacy practices appears to us to be a critical factor in academic performance.

7. English language learners' literacy orientation in their first language is often a good indicator of an orientation to schooling. Learners who are highly literacy oriented in their first language(s), even if they are temporary struggling with learning English, are strong candidates for academic success. Non-literacy-oriented students struggle academically, regardless of their proficiency in oral English. See Bailey & Pransky (2005); Pransky (2008, 2009).

8. Kozulin (2011); Ben-Hur (1994).

9. Feuerstein's term (2006) (translated from Hebrew) is "culturally deprived." This term, not surprisingly, causes a very negative reaction in many people, as traditionally the term has been a value judgment made about some cultures because they are not like Western culture or middle class culture; but in Feuerstein's sense of the term, it only means being deprived of the systematic transmission of their own culture because of disruptive circumstances. We have adopted the term "culturally disrupted" to better convey to our readers our understanding of Feuerstein's concept.

10. Feuerstein et al. (2006); Kozulin (2011).

11. Feuerstein et al. (2010).

12. Mediation is a concept that is central to sociocultural perspectives on learning; people use culturally created symbol systems, like math or language, to understand and transform the environment and human social life (Lantolf & Thorne, 2006). However, Feuerstein's MLE is more narrowly conceived and refers to the direct interposition of a person, often an adult, in another's learning. This mediator may select, organize, or frame information that a student is trying to learn. In all cases, the three universal characteristics of mediation must be present, either implicitly or explicitly, in the interaction.

13. See Bailey & Pranksy (2010) for an analysis of these three forms of mediation in classroom interaction with culturally disrupted learners.

14. We use the term "alignment" instead of "intentionality/reciprocity." It conveys the same idea and is less cumbersome to use.

15. Here we mean that well-mediated learners a) understand themselves as part of a cohesive bigger picture; b) fit into a broader cultural identity and historical sense of time; c) are agents who act on the environment as well as being acted on by the environment.

WORKING MEMORY:
THE DOORWAY TO LEARNING

A 9th grade science class is in the second day of learning about the moon as part of a unit on astronomy. Students appear busy listening to the teacher's presentation and looking at a diagram in a text of the moon phases, with the goal to understand the changing configurations of Earth, sun, and moon through the monthly cycle. They also learn about lunar eclipses and hear about how the tides are affected by the moon. Toward the end of the class, the teacher hands out a fill-in-the-blank worksheet about the information they have been studying. To the teacher's surprise, some of the students leave much of it blank. Only about a third of the students remember all of the new technical terms and the moon phases they describe. The teacher wonders why so few students were able to take everything in and retain it, especially since they had seemed to be paying attention.

Introduction

Our study of human memory begins with a memory system that is central to everyday life and classroom learning: working memory (WM). While an amazing part of our brain's information-processing abilities, it is also our most fragile memory system and the one most prone to misfiring: *We are introduced to someone new and instantly forget her name. We get a telephone number and rehearse it a couple of times—but forget it before we can put it to use. We attempt to mentally calculate the cost of a few items in a store but quickly lose track of the figures, even though adding is easy for us. We're reading something and suddenly realize we have no idea what we just read.* In this chapter, we will learn how and why this happens, how it plays out in the classroom, and ways we can teach with WM in mind. Because WM is so important to learning yet so fragile, it behooves us, as learning specialists, to understand how it works. Many of our classroom's "best-laid plans" fail because of WM constraints.

WM allows us to hold and manipulate information in the mind over short periods of time. It's like a mental workspace or note pad where we manipulate important information in the course of our everyday lives.[1] But it is very limited in two fundamental ways:

1. the length of time that it can hold new information;
2. the amount of information it can juggle at any one time.

In fact, *one of the most salient features of working memory is its time and space limitations.*

WM is our memory system's front door for processing information rushing in through our senses, and the cognitive space we need for combining or developing ideas. For example, WM allows us to comprehend this sentence by remembering its beginning in order to make sense of the rest.[2] When someone asks us a question, WM allows us to hold the question steady in our mind and allows us to consciously search our long-term memory for the answer. It is in working memory that reading comprehension takes place, where we process mental math, develop and implement goals, and learn new language(s).[3]

WM as Router

We connect to the incredibly vast, virtual world through a small portal: the router. It channels information to the systems we desire, like the computer for surfing and email, Blu-Ray for movies. It can only handle so much information at one time. The router is not changed by the types of information that travel through it. Finally, it is not responsible for deciding what information will be processed or how that information will be used—it just takes it all in.

WM is like the router in each respect!

Before we describe the various elements of WM, we need to note that the term "working memory" itself can be confusing. We will be using the terms "working memory" and "short-term working memory" in ways that are used by many psychologists. But many of us use or have heard those terms used in ways that do not exactly match how we will be using them in this book. We ask you to keep this in mind as you read.

The second issue is that this field uses the term "working memory" in two highly interconnected yet distinct senses: the specific unconscious structure and processes of WM and the executive functions of WM. Executive functions are an array of cognitive skills we use in WM to do things like solve problems, set goals, and plan. They are extremely important to learning, and Chapter 5 is entirely devoted to them. In the meantime, we will do our best to be clear about which sense we are using for the term "working memory."

Basic WM Structure and Processing

WM is composed of a number of information-processing systems, and they all play vital roles in classroom learning.

Short-term WM

Short-term WM is where we process new information flowing in from our five senses—like the router's connection to the Internet. We are bombarded by the richness of our environment, and all that verbal and visual information is filtered through very small cognitive portals.[4] These systems are sometimes called "slave" systems because they are designed to process information automatically and operate below our conscious attention. New information is held just for a blink of the eye, and then either short-term WM does something with it, or it is lost. And for a lot of our struggling learners, much is lost!

We are constantly sorting what our senses take in, what tiny bit to keep while discarding the rest. Think of it as drinking from a fire hose: most of the water will never make it down our throats because the volume coming out of the hose is too great. Likewise, there is simply too much information for WM to handle at any given moment. It is in short-term WM that we filter out most of this torrent of information, letting just a small amount trickle further into our memory system for processing and possible storage.[5] Figure 4.1 illustrates how sensory information (e.g., listening to someone speak, watching a video, or reading) can be processed in WM and connected to long-term memory.[6] WM consists of short-term working memory, which is responsible for the initial processing of sensory

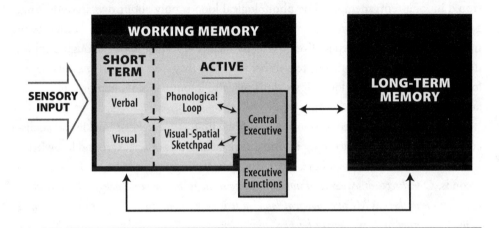

Figure 4.1 | **Working Memory**

information, and active working memory, where this information can be briefly stored and manipulated. The details of this process will become clear in this and subsequent chapters.

Short-term WM poses another challenge as well. New information has to have meaning for us, or we are very restricted in how much we can hold onto. Novel information devoid of meaning is very difficult to process and very prone to being forgotten.

In the 1950s, George Miller, a psychologist, discovered that human short-term memory could only identify and briefly store approximately seven units of information,[7] such as a string of letters, numbers, and words. If you are watching a computer screen, and a random number sequence flashes on the screen, say, 698 375 429 601, you will probably be able to remember just Five to Seven items long enough to write them down. Miller demonstrated that this constraint was biological, and no amount of training could overcome it. He could not even find individuals who had super memories who could get beyond this constraint. For any given moment of our lives, we are limited as to the amount of information we can process and ultimately remember.

Active Working Memory: Visual and Verbal Processors

Alan Baddeley,[8] a British psychologist, has proposed a two-part model of WM that focuses on our ability to process and integrate verbal and visual information.

The Phonological Loop

This function of WM allows us to connect incoming language to the language we've stored in long-term memory. The phonological loop is only about two seconds long. So in order to retain incoming language, we either have to connect it up to long-term memory right away, or keep it alive in WM by silently repeating it long enough until we do something with it. If someone tells us her name, we may have to silently rehearse as we look for a pen to write it down. If we don't rehearse it, our working memory "refreshes" and we forget it.

But that seems outrageous—how do we deal with this as teachers? Luckily, as we discuss in more detail later, incoming information that activates our background knowledge is handled very differently and greatly expands our memory abilities beyond a mere two seconds. *One direct consequence of not connecting students to relevant background is quickly overwhelming their WMs' phonological loop, so it is very important to help students connect new information to their relevant background experience and knowledge.*

Visual-Spatial Sketchpad[9]

This WM function stores images and information about an object's location and movement. The visual-spatial sketchpad also registers information only briefly and refreshes continuously as new visual information comes in. When we remember an image, it really means that we've reconstructed it in working memory. For example, if students are asked what states border South Dakota, they likely need to mentally reconstruct the map, using visual-spatial WM before they can answer the question.[10]

Luckily, the visual-spatial sketchpad and phonological loop do not compete for storage or processing space. They work in conjunction with each other. So when we use a picture in class, it does not make it harder to process the verbal information in WM; in fact, it often enhances the meaning of the verbal input. Because the phonological loop and the visual-spatial sketchpad can be mutually reinforcing, we should use visuals to reinforce our verbal instruction whenever possible.

Teaching Points for Buttressing WM Limitations

WM is often the weak link in learning. Luckily, we can overcome these limitations and tap into the full power of WM by incorporating the following principles into our planning and instruction.

Doing More with Less

While the volume and flow of the curriculum often yank us toward a fire hose approach to instruction, we can resist that pull. We may feel like we're being swept along by the rush of curriculum demands because there's so much to cover. But when we understand WM limitations, we realize how struggling learners often drown in that instructional approach. We can make our classrooms places where our students don't drown, but instead are able to drink deeply. We can help students manage the WM learning load by breaking the curriculum into smaller pieces, making sure students have mastered core concepts and language before moving on to the next piece.

For example, in the astronomy class scenario that begins this chapter, the students may have benefited from a sustained focus just on the moon phases, using the new vocabulary and concepts to more deeply understand how that dynamic system works. A discussion of the role of the moon in tides and lunar eclipses could have been put off until another day. Most of us do this when we see learning hasn't happened as we had planned. However, in light of what we have learned about WM, we recommend being *proactive and intentional* about it in our lesson planning and instruction in order to better manage WM limitations.

By limiting the amount of new information at any one time and creating opportunities for students to more deeply process targeted knowledge, we are truly teaching with memory in mind.

This means it's very helpful when we provide lots and lots of opportunities for students to practice new skills. Practice, whether speaking, writing, listening, or reading, makes for a less stressed WM.

As much as possible, we should try to dictate the pace of curriculum delivery, attuned to our students' learning. But our administrators may not understand why we are "behind" in the curriculum; we can use our understanding of working memory to justify taking the time that students need to learn core subject matter. Grounding such discussions in memory system–related facts makes it hard to refute.

So, for example, in answer to an administrators' question, "Why aren't you where you supposed to be in the curriculum?" we could answer as follows: "I know the district wanted me to be working on _____ by now. But as I've gotten to know this class better, I realize that the students' WMs are being overloaded by way too much new information. I also know that the more kids practice things, the better they get. And my students are learning more now. So I've chosen to give them more time to practice fewer—yet still essential—things so they own the material better and I can build off this in their future learning. What would you like me to do?" If the answer is "Ignore what the kids need—just make sure you're at the 'right place,'" wouldn't that be bizarre? We provide more facts to justify aligning with struggling learners' needs throughout the book.

Backgrounding

In Chapter 2, we highlighted the essential role of background knowledge in learning. We noted how it can be knowledge students have previously learned in school, but that we can't always count on that. Otherwise, there should be a connection to students' lives and experiences outside school, connecting to a major theme of the new learning. But however we do it, activating background knowledge is a primary way to balance WM limitations with learning.

Combining Visual and Verbal

Images can help us make sense of words, and vice versa. We are able to recode what we see in a picture or graph into language. Or we can go the other way and take a concept introduced verbally and create an image for it. Luckily, as we noted earlier, these two systems—the verbal and the visual—do not compete in WM for limited cognitive resources and can be used to reinforce one another.

Francis worked closely with an English language learner from China, Chi Lin. She knew very little English when she arrived and, while literate in Chinese, could read virtually nothing in English. She was in 4th grade and was becoming more and more frustrated with her inability to comprehend English and communicate with people around her. She knew the alphabet and could sound out words, but understood virtually nothing that she decoded.

One day Francis brought a wordless picture book to share with Chi. She could say something about each page, and as they talked (over several days), she described more and more of the images and story. Francis then typed up her words, using sticky paper that could be placed right onto the book pages. Like magic, she could immediately read—and understand—the book even though it was in English. *There is nothing easier to read than your own words.* Chi loved the book and, according to her mom, read it over and over.

The combination of the book's narrative captured in pictures and Chi's own words combined to allow her to read in English for the first time. Francis found a way to use Chi's long-term memory and her verbal and visual processors in WM to juggle the complexities of reading a foreign language.

Overcoming WM Limitations by "Chunking"

Understanding the structures and limitations of WM allows us to design lessons that balance the cognitive demands of academic work with the functioning of our students' WM. We will explore additional ways to work with this delicate balancing act below.

We can process and act upon more than the meager gruel of seven units of information that emerge from short-term WM by efficiently using our long-term memory systems. As we noted earlier, we are very limited in our ability to hold information in WM. However, if we can identify a pattern and make some type of meaning out of incoming information, we can grasp larger chunks of it. For example, if we get a glimpse of the following letter sequence,

V CVEU HUR IUEO LRMYY,

on average we will remember seven of the letters. However, if the identical letters are chunked so as to make sense to us—*I LOVE YOU VERY MUCH*—we quickly grasp and retain the whole sentence, even if exposed to it just for a brief moment. When we can chunk incoming information into meaningful units, then we can dramatically expand capacity within those hardwired WM constraints. We are still limited to seven items or chunks of information, but the more we can chunk together, the more information we can actually process.

A clear example of chunking in classroom learning can be seen as young children learn to read. At first, each letter must be individually processed and with much huffing and puffing combined to form words, phrases, and sentences. WM gets bogged down when a student spends lots of time sounding out the individual letters and laboriously combining them into words. However, as students become more proficient, they are able to process parts of words, such as word families ("cat," "rat"), sight words ("the," "and"), and even phrases ("on top of," "at school") as single units or chunks. And when they get older, there are prefixes, suffixes, and roots.[11] The more they can process letters in chunks, the less the burden on WM to process phonemic information, and so the more they can focus on meaning. From this, we can see why teaching struggling emergent readers to recognize the sound chunks in word families is helpful, as well as automatizing their recognition of common sight words and even entire common phrases.

We can see this play out anytime readers, of any age, run into a totally new word or phrase. The more we have to focus on the individual letters, the more we are likely to lose track of meaning. It's why we see heavy decoders lose track of comprehension as they plod through text.

In other ways, too, chunking helps reading. Meaning is enhanced when we chunk as well—processing *a, piece, of,* and *cake* separately yields quite a different result than processing *a piece of cake.* Finally, guessing a word from context implies guessing the missing piece of a chunk of meaning or grammar. The more readers are focused on chunking for meaning and fluency, the better they read.

In the same way, students can learn multiplication facts as flexible chunks. Ken noted in his book *Beneath the Surface* that math fact sentences such as $6 \times 3 = 18$ will rarely be seen in exactly that form other than on a worksheet. Many students learn the fact but can't apply it if they don't see it in exactly that format. Other students don't even learn the facts well, so their WMs are quickly overloaded by too much unchunked information when they try to solve problems. Instead, if students learn to see 6, 3, and 18 as a chunk of mathematical information, they will know what the missing number will be whether they see the other two numbers in an algebraic sentence, as multiplication or division algorithms, in a word problem, or even as an equivalent fraction (e.g., $1/3 = x/18$). Being able to chunk information into meaningful units is a sign of mastery of new material and connects directly to automaticity, background knowledge, and meaning making.

Central Executive

Baddeley's WM model also includes a *central executive,* which is responsible for all types of mental activities that draw upon long-term memory and require conscious effort.[12] For example, when we are doing mental math or writing an essay, we are using WM's central executive. It is designed to coordinate the retrieval of information from long-term memory, maintain attention on a task, inhibit distractions, recombine new information, and generally marshal the cognitive resources we need to solve a problem or complete a task.

The central executive also plays an important role in making sense of the world around us, including our attempts to interpret a complex reading or lecture. Finally, it is in WM's central executive that input from our five senses and information activated in long-term memory are combined into a single coherent event.[13] The central executive is thought to play a central role in consciousness.[14]

The central executive is just one part of a higher-level system of cognition known as "executive functions." Executive functions are behavioral and cognitive skills that allow us to plan, solve complex problems, and regulate our emotions. They underlie our ability to self-regulate—that is, to use language to regulate mental activity.[15] So, when we are trying to solve a math problem or writing a sentence, the central executive is responsible for weaving together old knowledge and executive function skills such as inhibiting impulses, shifting attention from one thing to another, goal setting, and organizing, to successfully perform the task.[16] The ability to juggle information in WM is also considered an important executive function skill. Chapter 5 is devoted to an in-depth exploration of executive functions.

One of the major differences between the central executive functions of WM and the other components of working memory is that the central executive is involved in conscious processes, while short-term verbal or visual processors, for example, are automatized and operate below the surface of our awareness. Think about a situation where you are reading and taking in information effortlessly. Suddenly, you misread a word or encounter a word that you don't know. The central executive (and relevant executive functions) kicks in and you consciously attend to the written word until you resolve the interruption and return to effortless reading.

The central executive coordinates the functioning of WM and long-term memory. When the term "working memory" is used in the sense of the central executive, the focus shifts from the initial processing of incoming information to the ability to juggle, hold, and manipulate information in WM. This part of WM is the part that incorporates executive functions.

Each and every mental effort we make takes up space in WM. So anytime we have to make a *conscious* effort to retrieve information from long-term memory, WM becomes bogged down. Conversely, when we can recall something with little effort, our WM is freed up to attend to other things. So, a word, date, or concept that we introduced yesterday may be in long-term memory, but still very slow to access or not easy to find. While the learner is trying to call up that information from yesterday, she is not able to pay attention to much else in the "now," including what she is reading or hearing from the teacher.

Related to this is attention. It is clear that attention plays a critical role in learning.[17] Attention is managed in WM by the central executive, and, like so many WM functions, attention is a limited resource. *We can really only pay sustained attention to one thing at a time.* Yes, we can monitor things on the back burner, but only in a superficial way. When you want to learn something new and complex, you have to have the ability to sustain attention on that subject and block out or *inhibit* other distractions. "To put it bluntly, research shows that *we can't multitask*. We are biologically incapable of processing attention-rich inputs simultaneously" (Medina, 2008, p. 85).

Figure 4.2 lists some WM functions connected to the central executive and how they can play out in the classroom.[18]

Figure 4.2 | **WM and Classroom Connections**

WM Central Executive	Classroom Learning Connections
Sending newly learned information to long-term memory	Students are expected to remember new information in classroom lessons, such as new vocabulary or science concepts
Meaning is formed in WM as the result of active processing of new information with information previously stored in long-term memory	Students work on academic tasks that require comprehension of new information of various types: language, images, symbols.
Attention and Inhibition	Students learn what to pay attention to. The ability of students to pay attention to new information requires them to focus and block out all other distractions.
Transforming information	Students recode a written math formula into English or recode visual information on a graph into words.
Engaging multistep problem-solving	Students solve a complex math or science problem involving computation.
Engaging in a conscious and directed search for information stored in long-term memory	Students needs to remember a needed word, name, date, symbol, formula, etc. when doing a classroom task.
Categorizing similar items into a common group	Students learn new ways to categorize and label the world.
Connecting meaningful new information with associated long-term memory knowledge representations	Students build new learning upon old, which requires learners to use WM to connect the new information just being learned to existing knowledge.

WM Central Executive and Classroom Learning

A student in 7th grade is writing a social studies report about colonial America. When the teacher bends down to begin conferencing with him, she notices two things. First, he has mostly understood the main ideas from the thematic unit they have been working on that week. But second, the page he was working on is one long paragraph, composed of a number of run-on sentences and just a couple of periods. The teacher sighs. This student has been learning about punctuation since 1st grade; he can tell you when to use periods and can even do passably well on a worksheet to practice where to put them. Yet when he writes? He hardly ever uses them.

When we can access previous knowledge, and when we're invested in a new learning situation or solving a problem, our WM central executive can help us do amazing things! But our students don't always have their WM ducks in a row, can't access background information, or aren't always invested in classroom learning.

WM Central Executive Limitations

There are three reasons connected to the "hardwiring" of WM that tell us why it is so prone to misfiring. We have already explored two of them: our limited capacity to process new information, and the short amount of time that we can store this information in WM. The third issue is one of *limited central executive capacity.*

Writing is a good lens through which to understand the limitations of WM's central executive, as academic writing is one of the most intellectually challenging tasks that schools ask students to perform. Writers have to juggle many variables: the topic, audience, word choice, organization, style, spelling, grammar, and punctuation. In the above scenario, the student's WM easily got overloaded. As a result, all thoughts of punctuation and formatting disappeared! How many times do we see this happen? We may think that the student is just careless, or not trying, or think, "Why does he still not get periods—he's 13 years old!" *But the "fault" does not only lie with that learner; it also lies in the nature of the task and the burden it imposes on the learner's WM.*

We might tell students, "Don't forget to be clear and persuasive. Remember your audience. Also, make sure your voice comes through. And don't forget to edit for spelling and punctuation." Yikes! Even if we have a rubric for each component we want students to attend to, academic writing taxes all students' working memory capacities, and remembering the rubric takes up lots of WM space as well. It's no wonder so many students struggle to write well.

So, for all the wonders of the human mind, we are not good at multitasking (no matter what teenagers tell you!) and have very limited abilities to manipulate more than a couple of ideas at the same time, especially if the concepts are complex.[19] For example, most of us can't do large multiplication problems in our heads, such as 486×785, not because the problem itself is hard if we know how to multiply, but because we just can't keep track of all the subcomponents of our computation to be accurate. We lose track of the results of our mental math before we complete our calculations. In trying to solve this problem, most of us would opt to write it down (if we didn't have a calculator). Writing it down is like tapping into an external memory storage tank, which has been created by societies to help us overcome WM limitations.

Students have to learn the entire curriculum within the limitations of their quirky WM systems, and many just can't do it on their own. If this sounds a lot like some of your students in your classroom…it is! And now you know why.

Teaching Points: Counteracting Central Executive Limitations

WM limitations pose a serious challenge for all learners. Grounding students in relevant background helps with this. The following are additional ways that classroom teachers can balance heavy curriculum tasks with our learners' fragile WMs.

Write It Down, Put It Up

Using the "external hard drive" metaphor, we can support students' fragile WMs by "holding" information through environmental print. As we teach, we can create temporary external "hard drives" with mind maps, semantic maps, word splashes, notes, drawings, and graphic organizers that capture the main points of what we're teaching. If they go up on chart paper, then we can always roll them back out at some other point when we want students to review. Then they can be used as a springboard for students' academic talk as a means to process new information periodically during a lesson, for journal writing, and so forth.

The idea is that students need us to hold things for them in the short term as well as the long term for their WMs to operate optimally. We revisit charts, organizers, and word walls with specific suggestions in future chapters.

Make It Meaningful

Ultimately, in order to really own our knowledge, we have to find meaning and purpose in it. As teachers, we have to help our students find meaning in academic tasks. For example, we can connect editing—which almost no one likes to do, and most students don't do well—to the concepts of self-presentation. We could show students a series of contrastive pictures, such as a messy room contrasted with a cleaned-up one, or a poorly wrapped gift contrasted with a beautifully wrapped gift, with a bow on top. We could talk with the class about which is more attractive, and why, and also when "looking good" matters. Then we show them a poorly edited paragraph contrasted with a well-edited one. We can segue back to our discussion about the pictures to talk about why editing is important—even if it can feel incredibly boring. Engaging the central executive is a conscious process that takes effort. By connecting writing mechanics (or anything at school) to students' own lives and goals, we mediate meaning by helping them see a value in putting in the effort required to attend to it. (We will have more to say about this principle in Chapter 6's discussion of semantic memory.)

Make It Memorable

Learning is more likely to happen when we are fully engaged. Our central executive plays a major role in this process because it's where attention is handled. By designing multiple sensory experiences and involve learners in surprising, emotionally engaging events, we can maximize the possibility of attention being roused, interest stimulated, and memory systems engaged.

Educator and neuroscientist Judy Willis (2006) described how she learned to engage her students in science learning. "My investigation of brain-based learning research led me to use novelty and excitement through strategies of surprise, unexpected classroom events, dressing in costumes, playing music, showing dynamic videos, putting comic strips or optical illusions on the overhead, and even telling corny jokes, all in the interest of capturing and holding my students' attention" (p. 38).

These kinds of event memories are memorable because they stimulate the limbic system, trigger emotional responses, and provide multiple sources of sensory activation. It is in WM that these multiple sources are bound together to create a holistic and integrated experience.[20] (Finally, something that WM actually does really well!) In subsequent chapters on long-term memory, we will flesh out this concept and its relation to the teaching/learning process in more detail.

Working Memory and Classroom Learning

Despite its limitations, WM takes center stage in the classroom. When students listen to a teacher's lecture, read a challenging passage in a course text, memorize new vocabulary, or write a report, the efficient functioning of WM is essential. When we ask students to write an essay, do mental math, recall an historical date, or interpret a reading passage, we are really saying, "Engage your working memory."

WM Variation Among Learners

Susan Gathercole and Tracy Alloway (2010) are leading theorists in how WM plays out in the classroom. Their research confirms one thing that anyone who teaches in early elementary grades instinctively knows: young children have particularly limited WM abilities. This research-based confirmation of what we already "know" to be true can help guide us as we try and fight off the increasing move toward "rigor" even in lower grades. Children's WM capacities grow as they grow up, and by the time students are teens, their WMs are similar to adults'.

Gathercole and Alloway also have found that there likely is variation in the WM function of students within a given classroom, so that a 12-year-old in 6th grade may have a WM capacity of a 3rd grader, say, and conversely, there may be a 3rd grader with the WM capacity of an average 12-year-old. We should expect variation in WM capacity within our students and so try to accommodate this variation by differentiated instruction. Students with more limited working memory capacity will benefit from just the kinds of scaffolding and interventions proposed in this chapter.

Research has also revealed other variations in WM capacity. Second-language learners appear to have a smaller working memory capacity in their second language than their first language.[21] This means that even very academically proficient students will be more prone to cognitive overload if they are learning new subject matter through a second language. This is probably the result of a slower processing speed for the second language. One implication for us is that when we are teaching English learners, they may exhibit learning challenges, as if they have some type of learning disability. This is most often not the case. English learners greatly benefit from the types of teacher interventions that we are exploring in this chapter.

Extensive testing of WM in elementary-age students reveals that 10 percent of children struggle with poor WM, and this has long-term effects on their academic achievement.[22] Students with weak WM functioning in kindergarten test (on average) lower on literacy skills in 3rd grade.[23] WM capacity is an important predictor of academic performance. While there are no generally accepted methods for actually improving many of the core functions of WM—verbal and visual short-term memory functions and the capacity of attention—many things we can do to support students who have limited or overloaded WMs, as we have explored in this chapter.[24] However, the executive functions of WM can be strengthened, as we discussed in Chapter 5.

Cognitive Load

Cognitive load theory[25] is based on the research of Australian psychologists and educators. They affirm two basic issues concerning WM that we have been preaching in this chapter:

- WM is quite limited.
- Many learners are at risk of information overload during classroom instruction.

In response, cognitive load researchers have explored ways to design and implement lessons that scaffold WM functions. They argue that if we don't carefully manage the complexity of our instructional delivery and materials, the result will be cognitive overload and a disruption in learning.[26] How can we do this?

Teaching Points: Minimizing Cognitive Load

1. Practice, Practice, Practice

The goal for learning many academic skills, such as math facts and spelling conventions, is automatic retrieval from long-term memory so that WM can call it up quickly and use it with virtually no burden on WM while it goes about the task of problem solving or learning new information. Automatization usually requires a lot of repetitive practice. Remember myelin! So we need to plan for opportunities for skills to be practiced until they become automatized.

But there's a lot more to practice than that. Not all information stored in long-term memory is just discrete "skills." It's also concepts, strategies, and networks of knowledge. This takes a different kind of practice than repetition. New information encountered in yesterday's class may have been learned and stored in long-term memory, but it may take a lot of effort to retrieve.[27] Practice makes for effortless retrieval from long-term memory, which supports WM! Chapter 10 is devoted to both repetitive practice for automaticity as well as practice that helps deepen conceptual knowledge and make it easier to recall.

2. Avoiding Nonsense[28]

Nothing overloads WM like nonsense. Trying to remember new information that doesn't have any real meaning makes it much more difficult to process. This is a root cause of WM overload. When students are trying to memorize names, dates, or formulas and don't really understand how they connect to anything else, they will struggle to remember them. Starting in the 1950s, it was discovered that college-age students were only able to retain short nonsense words for a few seconds.[29] You try it—look at the following list of words for 15 seconds, look away, and write down how many you can remember: zaxon, munderly, chud, tuncler, jombly, tekkin, rondis, ploz, inquistical. (Probably not many!)

This research reveals how terribly limited WM capacity is if we can't connect somehow to our "known." Anything that does not connect to background by definition is nonsense—and for many struggling learners, academic learning is nonsense! We can help them avoid this "nonsense" by (1) helping them connect to background knowledge, (2) supplying the background that is needed that some students may not have,[30] and (3) intentionally connecting today's lessons to previous learnings. Key idea: we need to build "anti-nonsense" fail-safes into every lesson.

3. Helping Students Connect Whole to Part

Human beings are better at remembering the gist of an experience than the details.[31] While the details fade away rather quickly, the central ideas and emotional responses tend to last much longer. When students are confused about the classroom topic or the goal of an activity, they either zone out completely or frantically search for a way to make connections to what they already know. This takes precious WM processing space. Understanding how the parts—the words, the dates, the people, the numbers—connect to the overarching lesson theme or topic helps them make sense of what they're learning.

We can help our students manage the limitations of WM by making sure that they are connecting new information to a broader overarching theme through the use of time lines, flow charts, and graphic organizers. Just like writing acts as a temporary external memory hard drive to help us solve complex math problems, these kinds of visuals aid in subject learning function the same way when there's a lot to take in (which in the classroom is almost all the time). The goal is to get facts to hang together as part of some larger knowledge structure or concept until students have understood the concepts and internalized the facts.

Assessing Cognitive Load

One thing we can do is assess the *intrinsic load* of a lesson. This refers to the WM challenge that students face based on *the complexity of the academic task*.[32] For example, when the learning requires students to integrate and manipulate multiple sources of information, the intrinsic cognitive load is going to be high. *Just about all learning in school has an intrinsically high cognitive load!* The WM central executive will, by definition, be heavily taxed. If a student is solving a multistep math problem and must juggle words, the numbers, use the appropriate operation, keep track of key vocabulary, and read the problem, that's a big load! Or if a student is reading a history text and needs to keep track of names, dates, themes, lots of vocabulary, and diagrams or maps, it's a heavy load! An even greater load would be writing a well-constructed, grammatically accurate, stylistically sound, as well as factually accurate and complete essay about it. Unfortunately, we can't undo the complexity of the content other than by the way we teach. So we now turn our attention to another kind of load, which thankfully is more in our control.

Sweller and his associates (1998) label as "extraneous cognitive load" the instructional techniques and procedures we use in our classrooms that go against what we now know about how WM works. If we can spot students who are reaching cognitive overload, we can, among other things,

- go slower;
- revisit the learning objective;
- change the pace and have students get up for a quick physical activity, or turn and talk with a partner about what they're learning;
- start to use visuals or graphics if we haven't yet done so;
- modify our instructional language so it's simpler and avoids sophisticated vocabulary;
- make sure we've connected to background knowledge, or revisit it.

It's also important that we can read students' signals of distress appropriately. The signs of learner cognitive overload are described in Figure 4.3.[33]

Figure 4.3 | **Indicators of Cognitive Overload**

Learner Behavior	Classroom Connections
Confusion on the steps needed to complete an academic task	The learner may be unable to start task independently and require a lot of support from teacher or peers to begin, maintain, and complete academic tasks.
Task avoidance or abandonment	The learner may be so overwhelmed that she avoids doing the task or abandons it before completion.
Expressions of frustrations with task	The learner may complain that the task is too hard, confusing, or boring.
Failure to connect today's learning with previous lesson(s)	The learner may struggle to link current academic work with previous study.
Distracted	The learner's attention is easily pulled off-task.
Fails to use knowledge and skills, already mastered	The learner makes errors on materials that they have already shown mastery in, such as spelling and punctuation or simple math operations.

When we see students struggle in these ways, our thinking should ideally be "Uh-oh, that student is advertising his/her difficulty with cognitive load in my lesson and task. My bad. It's not that he/she is lazy or just doesn't want to do the work. Let me see if I can help the student pinpoint where his/her difficulty lies, or let me see if I can scaffold some of the steps, and see how it goes then."

Cognitive load researchers have found that learners are the best assessors of the state of their WM.[34] *We need to routinely seek out their feedback on the challenges they are facing in our classrooms.* A quick check-in or more formal written feedback about how they're doing, whether they're keeping up, and even what we can do differently as teachers to help them is a way to accomplish this. It is important that we tap into what they are experiencing. Working effectively with WM means not only that we are aware of how WM functions and what it looks like when it is breaking down, but also that we ask students about their learning challenges.

Teaching Points: Managing Cognitive Load

Eighth grade students in an English language arts class are asked to write a report on a story they read. The teacher tells them that they need to use 10 of the descriptive adjectives they've recently been working with. She also tells them to use the six Write Traits™ (voice, connections, fluency, organization, idea development, and word choice) and to remember to self-assess each with the class rubric. Students struggle to complete the assignment, with over half of the class forgetting to do some or most of what they were asked to incorporate and do.

The following are a set of teaching techniques and strategies that can help teachers avoid cognitive overload.

Split Attention

Cognitive load researchers have discovered something known as the "split attention effect."[35] They found that it is a challenge for learners' WM to integrate disparate sources of information, in which the learner has to move her attention back and forth between multiple sources of information. So, let's say our biology students are learning about the structure of plants. It can be helpful if there's a picture, but even more helpful if the picture and text are integrated into one unified whole (e.g., with the plant parts labeled) rather than the picture on one page and information about the picture on another. This avoids the learners having to spend mental energy switching their focus back and forth between image and written text. Anytime students have to shift attention, this takes effort and uses up precious WM resources. (We have more to say about shifting in Chapter 5.)

Psychologists researching WM in the classroom have found that for many students, it is difficult to copy from the board or make good use of charts and posters in the learning environment.[36] It has to do with working memory capacity: the act of looking up, finding and focusing on what is needed from the chart trying to retain it, looking back down to the task at hand, and finally trying to remember what was on the chart creates cognitive overload.

If we find this is the case in our classroom, creating personal or table-size charts can overcome this problem. Another suggestion is to give students enough practice using memory aids in the classroom environment so that it becomes a less onerous cognitive load; in this case, we would advise practicing within content that students know, so that working memory space is not needed as much for processing the information itself and more can be given to the "memory aid" practice. The chart information in audio form for students with special needs could also be used.

Recently, Ken was coaching a 1st grade teacher and the class was copying something from the board. One student (whom the teacher had identified as a very difficult student) started being very disruptive and shouted at a girl in front of him, "I can't see! I can't see!" He could just have moved his head a few inches and seen fine, so Ken thought it might have something to do with the task. The teacher spoke with the boy about his behavior and told him he couldn't join the group until he copied the sentence, as the rest of the class was done and moving to the circle to hear a story. Now the boy became even more agitated. So the teacher asked her para to sit with him. The boy kept on not cooperating, now with the para, who appeared frustrated and at a loss. On a hunch, Ken wrote the sentence from the board on a piece of paper and put it next to the boy, who looked at him in surprise and said, "Thanks!" He proceeded to copy the sentence from the paper and was able to join his class within a couple of minutes.

Simplifying Tasks

Because the intrinsic cognitive load is almost always high in classroom learners, we help struggling learners by breaking down learning into smaller chunks. For example, in the scenario that kicks off this section, we saw the challenges that a writing task posed for many of the 8th grade students. Writing, by its very nature, is always going to be a WM challenge, and we make it even more problematic for students if we try to get them to build Rome in a day. For instance, we should teach, and students should focus on, just one trait of writing at a time. Another way to help is to limit what students look for in editing and revising—any other issues than those, we let it go![37] The rule is, the more students have to pay attention to, the less likely it is that they pay careful attention to any of the things.

Using Simple Examples

When we introduce new concepts, it is helpful to initially build learning on simple examples. We know a 6th grade math teacher who creates all her concept-building math lessons by initially using numbers that are easy to compute. For example, she'll use 5 and 10. While the concept may be complex, at least the computations are simple and do not strain WM capacity, so more cognitive space is available to understand the concept. Similarly, many teachers use a coin toss with its simple 50/50 probability as they enter into the math topic of probability.

Clarifying and Checking Comprehension

A classroom climate that encourages meaning making is designed around dialogue, questions, and active participation. Strategies for meaning making include explicitly drawing students' attention to connections between new and old knowledge—for example, reviewing an idea introduced in a previous lesson to prepare students for a related topic. When we help students fill in missing background information—the significance of a name or date, the definition of a word, the connection of a concept to a broader theory—we are providing an assist to WM as it attempts to weave together new understandings and make sense of it all.

A key element of meaning making is frequently checking all students' comprehension. This can be done informally, several times a lesson. For example, we can ask students to respond to a question by using "thumbs up" to means "true" or "I agree," while thumbs down means "false" or "I disagree." A thumb to the side means "I don't know." We should vary how we do this, so it doesn't become a boring routine. Whatever the method, the goal is to really know whether students are making meaning of the new content, long before a formal exam.

Train Students in Processes and Routines

Classroom learning processes, whether complex, such as cooperative learning or Internet research, or relatively simple, like a buddy system for academic help or even just how to listen and take notes during a teacher's lecture, all add to cognitive load. However, once the process has been routinized, it can ease the cognitive demand. In addition, many students who we think "should know" how to work in groups or listen appropriately, for example, really don't (even in high school)! So practicing routines and procedures also allows students who need to learn them better the opportunity to do so, in addition to reducing the cognitive load.[38]

When we do introduce a new learning process or procedure to the class, it is also helpful to initially work with topics that students are familiar with to reduce cognitive load. For example, if we want to train our class to work in cooperative groups, it makes sense to initially practice with familiar topics and information, so students can learn how to learn in a small group without the distraction of unfamiliar information. Once the new routine has been established, then we can segue to using group work with the regular academic content.

Within groups, also, students need to be trained in how to use "accountable talk" (which is how the Common Core refers to on-task academic conversation) in learning. They need practice in (1) how to engage in on-task academic discussion (both listening and speaking), (2) the ways we engage in academic talk (elaboration, giving examples, synthesizing, summarizing, etc.), and (3) the language we use to structure academic talk (sentence starters, transition words, etc.).[39] By practicing in these three areas within their "known," students develop expertise that they can then transfer to discussions of academic subjects. With charts that illustrate the appropriate language, students can always have a certain time block to "talk like the teacher," where everyone needs to speak like their teachers. This is another fun way that students can intentionally practice academic language.

Working Memory and Struggling Learners

By not being aware of cognitive load and the general weakness of the WM system, we routinely, if inadvertently, overload our students' working memory systems. And it's the most vulnerable of our learners who are most susceptible to WM overload. Non-literacy-oriented students and culturally disrupted learners are particularly prone to cognitive overload, in part because they are learning twice the normal curriculum. They must learn not only the new subject matter content but also the particular learning skills and practices routinely used in our classrooms that literacy-oriented students had developed in home and community.

For instance, culturally and linguistically diverse students may be learning standard English dialect and mainstream social norms and values on top of the academic curriculum. English learners are learning a new language, how to participate in U.S. schooling, and a wide variety of cultural content (which mainstream kids already know), as well as academic content. The amount of novel information that these students have to process and learn puts their fragile WM systems at risk. This also makes these students appear to be "slow," but, in fact, they are faced with a truly formidable (and unappreciated) learning load to master. *Struggling students really need us to understand how to design and implement lessons that avoid cognitive overload.*

Teacher Intervention

In the final section of this chapter, we observe Ken working with a group of 1st graders as he scaffolds their cognitive load while learning to read. Ken is working with a group of 1st grade emergent readers on a predictable book about trucks.[40] They are working on predicting words based on initial consonant sounds. At one point, they begin to discuss the picture of a dump truck above the text: *Trucks carry dirt.* In response to a question, one student guesses that the truck is carrying sand. Ken then directs their attention to the written text to confirm that prediction.

1: Group: Trucks carry sand.
2: Ken: But look at my finger. It's pointing to the last word, isn't it? Let's see if
3: that word is "sssand." What letter is it under?
4: Savun: Sand. The truck is carrying sand.
5: Ken: What was my question? Listen. What letter is my finger under?
6: Savun: Sand? (looking very confused)
7: Ken: Remember letters? (Sings) ABCD (children join in).
8: Now think. I've got my finger under a letter. What letter is it under?
9: Jose: It's a "d"!

10: Ken: Good for you Jose. It's a "d." What sound does "d" have?

11: Jose: *d d d*

12: Ken: Right! And does "ssssssssand" start with a "d"?

13: Jose: (scrunches up face and looks at Ken) No?

...

14: Ken: Does "ssssand" start with *d-d-*"d"?

15: Jose: Mmmm, no.

16: Ken: All right, Jose. "Sand" does not start with "d." But the word in this book does.

17:        Hmmmm. What is something that is like sand but starts with *d d* "d"?

18: Savun: Oh, I know—"dirt!"

So, Savun knew how to predict accurately from initial consonant sounds all along! Then why did he struggle with this task?

A lesson, even an apparently simple one like this, can pose great WM challenges for students. Even a "simple" lesson requires the learner to juggle multiple types of information in WM. The delicate balancing act required to learn new academic material needs teachers who are sensitive to the constraints of working memory and skillful in helping learners manage the complex mental (and social) processes involved in classroom instruction.

This reading lesson required the students to keep track of a number of literacy concepts: *sound, letter,* and *word,* in addition to the sound/symbol correspondences for "d" and "s." These literacy concepts had been thoroughly studied and practiced by these young students but were not yet automatic. They also had to keep in mind the image of the truck, provided as visual support for the written text. They also participated in the instructional dialogue of a teacher-directed reading lesson: comprehending and responding to the teacher's questions, directions, and comments; singing the alphabet song; and listening to peers. These are the conditions for WM overload.

Ken used a range of techniques to mediate his students' learning and avoid overloading their working memory. He knew that this reading task was within their competence but would strain their abilities to integrate meaning and written language to "read" the word "dirt." One of things that is interesting about this example is that the students do all the actual work of reading the text. They know how to decode the letter "d," and they know the word "dirt" and that it starts with the letter "d." They also know that trucks carry dirt. All of this information is stored in long-term memory. The WM challenge is to put all of this information together and read the word "dirt." In the classroom excerpt, we see Ken mediating his students' learning through three instructional scaffolds:

Guiding attention: Ken guides his students' attention to the key elements of the instructional materials: a picture of the truck and the first letter of the word "dirt." This allows his students to focus on the key elements of the reading task: word identification and meaning making.

Activating long-term memory: As many early elementary educators do, Ken asks his students to look at the picture of the truck and predict what it could be carrying. In doing so, the students' long-term memory systems for trucks are activated, and he is able to use this knowledge to help them read the word "dirt." He also activated their knowledge of letters by singing the alphabet song with them.

Questioning: Ken asks his students a question: "What is something that is like sand but starts with *d-d-'d'?"* His question draws on his students' knowledge of things that trucks carry and directly focuses them on the initial sound of the word "dirt." His efforts pay off when Savun reads the word correctly.

Conclusion

As we have seen, working memory is a crucial player in classroom learning, and often it is the weak link in learning. By trying to understand the impact of WM capacity on classroom learning, we enact our role as *learning specialists.* The more skilled we become in assessing the cognitive load that our lessons pose for our students, and the more sensitive to the signs that our students are getting overloaded, the more successful our lessons will be, and the more successfully our students will learn. It will also help us design—and therefore teach—lessons in ways that support our most vulnerable students.

Teachers work in very difficult circumstances: we are expected to cover a vast amount of content *and,* at the same time, support the learning needs of our academically struggling students. We realize that this is a profound teaching dilemma, because struggling learners benefit from a deeper engagement with less information.

However, we can often effect positive change—even if to small degrees—if we can justify decisions we make (or would like to make) in data and current theories of learning. Our advocacy of *teacher as learning specialist* is grounded in the need for us to have information we can use to justify our decisions for supporting struggling learners, including how memory systems operate—in real neurological, physiological, and biological ways—in the process of learning.

It's a huge dilemma for all of us when memory research supports the importance of teachers having control of the pace of instruction with input from our students, yet our districts and states increasingly predetermine the pace of curriculum flow. So often it feels like our field is nuts as we are sent scrambling around in ways we feel in our bones are counterproductive to supporting struggling learners—all in the name of supporting struggling learners! But no one is in a better position than we are to monitor, up close and personal, the moment-by-moment unfolding of our lessons. Frankly, we see little hope of improving the academic lives of underperforming students without being able to teach according to their real learning needs. The more we can justify our pedagogical decisions in language that administrators and fellow educators respect, the more likely they will be to support our classroom decisions. And as we accumulate the data that prove the direct payoff we claim students will get, we become real, positive change agents in our schools.

1. Gathercole & Alloway (2010).
2. Levine (2002).
3. All of these tasks require multiple brain regions, including additional memory systems. However, WM is central to them all.
4. Called short-term verbal WM and short-term visio-spatial WM.
5. Note that we are using the concept of short-term memory in a way that is different from how many people use it on the street. For our purposes, short-term WM processes verbal and visual information, and its processing time is limited to seconds. Anything retained for over a couple of seconds is in the domain of long-term memory.
6. This model of WM has been adapted from Dehn's (2008) "Integrated Model of Working Memory."
7. Miller (1956).
8. Baddeley (2007).
9. Dehn (2008).
10. Gathercole & Alloway (2010).
11. Rasinski (2010).
12. Baddeley (2007).
13. Baddeley's WM model (2007) conceptualizes this function as a distinct component, called the "episodic buffer." We have chosen to simplify this description of WM, by keeping the episodic buffer as part of the central executive.

14. Baddeley (2007).
15. Lantolf & Thorne (2006).
16. Chapter 5 is devoted to an array of executive functions in addition to the executive function called "working memory."
17. Attentional focus increases the likelihood of learning something. However, we can learn things we are not attending to, but this seems to have limited value in the classroom setting See Ortega's (2009) discussion of incidental and implicit learning.
18. The list of WM functions has been adapted from Dehn (2008) .
19. Medina (2008).
20. Baddeley (2007).
21. Harrington & Sawyer (1992).
22. Alloway, Gathercole, Kirkwood, & Elliot (2009).
23. Gathercole & Alloway (2010).
24. See Melby-Lervag & Hulme (2012) for a meta-analytic review of the effectiveness of WM training programs. However, also see Alloway (2011) for a discussion of a promising new program for WM enhancement.
25. Sweller et al. (1998); Plass et al. (2010).
26. Sweller et al. (1998).
27. Remember that it may take days, weeks, even months for new learning to be fully consolidated and become a permanent fixture in long-term memory.
28. Smith (1985).
29. Schacter (2001).
30. Rose (2005).
31. Medina (2008).
32. Clark et al. (2006).
33. See Gathercole & Alloway (2010) and Alloway (2011) for helpful discussions of classroom signs of WM overload.
34. Sweller et al. (1998).
35. Clark et al. (2006).
36. Gathercole & Alloway (2010).
37. John Collins (1997) has a writing program that is very WM-friendly. Among the things he advocates is "FCAs"—focus correction areas. Three focal areas of correction are chosen, named before the writing starts, and scored on a scale of 1–10. For example, in an opinion piece, crafting a good lead could be 3 points, having 3 reasons for your opinion is 6 points, and putting in periods could be 1 point.
38. Wong-Fillmore (1985).
39. Zwiers & Crawford (2011).
40. Pransky & Bailey (2003).

EXECUTIVE FUNCTIONS

Ken was coaching in a 9th grade science class (mostly repeaters). At the start of the class, the teacher had posted a "Do Now." The assignment was to draw conclusions about population growth from a line graph that was related to the previous day's lesson. The teacher told them they could get their notebooks (pointing to where they were) if they got stuck. During the 15 minutes allotted for this activity, Ken ticked off 43 times that he heard students call out, "Missy! Missy!" (the way students at that school commonly addressed their female teachers). The students simply waited for her to come over to help, and until she did, they just chatted with neighbors. Even then, they only did the one thing that she helped with, and they immediately called out "Missy!" again when they finished. Only 1 of the 11 students in the room actually got up and got his notebook and completed the "Do Now" without the teacher's support.

The primary challenge that these students face is directly connected to the functioning of working memory and a bundle of cognitive abilities known as executive functions (EFs). In Chapter 4, you read that working memory is a part of the EF system, and that EFs are behavioral and cognitive skills that allow us to regulate our emotions, plan, and solve complex problems. "Self-regulation" is when we can bring the appropriate EFs to bear to act successfully in a given situation. They enable us to consider the future and hypothetical situations entirely through our thoughts and imaginings, and they allow us to be aware of ourselves as we think and do—like you are doing now reading this text and thinking about what we mean.

The following are just some of the (endless) ways that EFs are needed in classroom learning:

- Sustaining attention
- Picking out relevant data in problem solving
- Knowing what the goal of a task is
- Sticking to the goal, even if the task is hard or something else looks more fun
- Organizing ourselves to begin a classroom task
- Tolerating ambiguity
- Applying learned information and patterns of thought to new situations
- Revising our writing[1]

When we look at this list, we can really empathize with just how much students with less developed EF skills struggle in our classrooms. In their important book *Executive Skills in Children and Adolescents* (2010), Dawson and Guare say the following: "When teachers use direct instruction to teach students how to get through . . . common classroom activities, they are helping them develop habits of mind that are as important as any content curriculum" (p. 75).[2] In fact, the more research that is done in this area, the more researchers are concluding that the cognitive control of behavior is more strongly associated with school readiness than IQ, prereading skills, or math skills.[3] EFs continue to affect academic performance in powerful ways. We have to *intentionally* teach EFs.

It might seem as though students learn EF skills automatically through their experiences in school. After all, as teachers, we act out appropriate EF skills all day, every day, and classroom tasks require them of students. But this is just wishful thinking. EFs will typically strengthen a bit as students get older. And while some who come to school with lower levels of EF skill may develop EFs strongly through schooling, most students in that situation don't.

Ask any group of high school teachers whether all their students can learn without support, and whether they all have similar (and sufficient) levels of problem-solving, organizational, and other EF skills, and the teachers will say, "Not by a long shot!" But how could that be, if all of their students were in classrooms learning EF skills, year after year, kindergarten through high school? Our experience has been that it's usually the students with more well-developed EF skills entering kindergarten who have stronger EF skills in high school, while those who lack well-developed EF skills entering kindergarten continue to lack them in high school. We have to intentionally intervene with struggling learners to avoid replicating the achievement disparities that are the result of EF skill differences.

High Skill Juggling: Literacy, Numeracy, and Executive Functions

Think of the extraordinary amount of information that needs to be juggled in working memory when we read a story in English: We process written phonemic symbols, sequence their sounds, activate vocabulary meanings, pull in grammar knowledge, figure out how sentences are linked together, and pull all that together to create meaning.[4] We also have to keep track of what is happening at that point in the story, remember what characters did earlier that is pertinent now, monitor our understanding, and apply strategies to figure out unknown words. Beyond that, we need to remain aware of the function of the particular text in our own lives, like where we are reading it (e.g., in a 3rd grade classroom, or on the beach), and why (e.g., for pleasure, or to answer a teacher's questions). And it's all happening in our fragile, limited WM space. It's amazing that we don't freeze up or have smoke pour out of our ears! EF skills are *essential* to successful reading![5]

In math, it's the same story.[6] There are numbers, facts, procedures, concepts, and all that math vocabulary. If we are solving a word problem, many of those EF issues connected to literacy arise as well.[7] There's no denying that students need very high levels of EF skill to juggle all that is thrown at them at school—but some students can just juggle one ball. Some students find themselves swamped by the sheer volume of information and complexity of tasks. This undermines motivation and interest, spurs some students to develop poor self-esteem, and makes school insufferable.

We mustn't forget that all cognitive applications take up precious working memory space. The more automatic these cognitive applications are, the less space they take; the more effortful they are, the more working memory space they take. When EFs are automatic, they "oil" the cognitive workspace of working memory and allow us to manipulate information in a variety of ways, and therefore maximize the capabilities of working memory. However, when students are focused on applying EFs, then precious working memory space is being diverted away from the problem-solving task at hand. Teaching reading, writing, and math instruction should intentionally and directly include EF skill instruction for students who struggle.

Special Needs in Executive Functions Versus Cultural Difference

In large part, EFs are developmental. The ability of a 3-month-old, a 3-year-old, and a 13-year-old to sustain attention, for example, are markedly different. There are certain expectations we have for EF development in children by the time they come to school in kindergarten, and school curricula are created with these developmental expectations in mind. For the most part, we are aware of what our students typically can and can't do in the grades we teach—it's a prerequisite for being a teacher of any grade.

Some students have particular neurological or biological dysfunctions that limit EF capacity in certain ways, such as students with ADHD. The question is whether students with special education plans (IEPs) are the *only* students in our classrooms with EF needs, and if not, whether they need special education plans, too. The answers is, *many* students struggle with EF issues, and no, they don't all need special education plans! They *do* need direct, focused instruction to promote EF development.

If one has some suspicions that a student has EF challenges and wants to have him tested (either informally or formally as part of a referral process), it is important to be aware that EF issues may show up in the context of actual classroom tasks that do not show up on discrete, psychological test tasks that evaluate specific EF needs separately.[8] Because classroom tasks involve a number of EF skills as students juggle multiple items, such as vocabulary, concepts, and number facts, the reality of student performance in the classroom can be a better perspective on a student's EF abilities than discrete testing may show. Our observations of students in action—whether informally or using checklists and record-keeping forms[9]—yield excellent information.

Research is now suggesting that different cultural contexts influence EF development, as social interaction norms, expectations, and tasks within different cultural environments are likely to require different degrees and clusters of EF skills at different ages.[10] So in diverse classrooms, we should be aware that not all our students will have the same EF skills, developed to a similar degree—and most of us teach in diverse settings.

You may notice differences in EF skills with culturally and linguistically diverse learners as compared with learners from the dominant culture, even though those children do not—and should not—have IEPs. Difference does not mean disability!

For example, Ken found that many of his Cambodian American students were less able to independently organize and set goals for tackling open-ended tasks than the expected norm at his elementary school (in a small university town in western Massachusetts serving an overall very highly educated community). The school's math curriculum was heavily oriented to building math concepts through exploratory learning tasks. Most of the Cambodian students found this very challenging. In their culture, they were trained to do what they were told at the explicit direction of adults.[11] They were not expected to develop the equivalent EF skills of organization and planning at young ages as compared to their peers from the U.S. mainstream cultures. That's not wrong, just different!

U.S. mainstream cultures are oriented to young children thinking for themselves and developing independence at young ages.[12] The majority of students at Ken's school were not so troubled by the kinds of tasks that required more independence and self-direction. However, other learners required sustained support to succeed within the same types of learning experiences, if they succeeded at all. *It was often not the math that was the challenge, but the nature of the task and the students' ability to juggle complex ideas.*

Alexandra was a Cambodian 4th grader chosen to be filmed for a digital portfolio project about her thinking in math. She had been enthusiastically participating in small-group activities where students used a pair of dice to move around a 100s chart through which she, like the other students, would develop an understanding of equal size groups as a key multiplication concept. For example, if you rolled 5 × 3, it was three jumps of 5 or five jumps of 3 on the chart.

When it was her turn to be filmed, she very proudly showed how eight jumps of 7 landed you on 56. The teacher then asked, "So, Alexandra, what's 8 × 7?" Scrunching up her face in a very serious way, she stroked her chin, thought a second, and answered, "Oh, I think about 100!" We will return to Alexandra a little later on, when we analyze this scenario in relation to goal setting and planning.

Literacy Orientation and Executive Functions

A crucial intersection of culture and memory is seen in the development of EF skills. One of the great advantages literacy-oriented children have in our schools is that their families prepare them to successfully perform in school. An integral piece of this preparation is developing a higher level of EF skills. EF skill development helps us understand the huge achievement gap between literacy-oriented and non-literacy-oriented students—it is *not* an intelligence gap.

An interesting study by Brazilian researchers clarifies this dichotomy. In 1984, researchers studied adult-child interactions in two very different communities.[13] They analyzed adults interacting with 5- to 6- year-olds over puzzles in two communities: teachers (all female) in the city of São Paolo[14] and mothers in a small Amazon village.

The teachers interacted with the children in ways that seem very familiar to us. Overall, they acted as "coaches," while the children did most of the puzzle. When the children made mistakes or got stuck and appealed for help, the teachers' response was to guide them verbally (e.g., "Maybe we should look at the shape"). In the end, the children did the puzzle task with the "distanced" guidance of their teachers.

In contrast, the village mothers acted as "directors." They told the children exactly where to put the pieces so there were no mistakes. The author says (p. 10), "In a sense, the rural mothers used their children as tools . . . [to construct the puzzle themselves]."

The researchers connected these distinctly different kinds of parent-child interactions to differences in the two cultural and economic contexts. In the city, schooling was important, so the adults' goal was for the children to become better independent problem solvers. Mistakes served the development of independent learning (i.e., EF) skills. In the village, because people relied on farming and the sale of crafts, mistakes cost precious time, energy, and money. So, the mothers' goal for their children there was to model and ensure *error-free* performance.

Based on those puzzle-making scenarios, who would probably be a "better learner" at your school, all things being equal: a child from the São Paolo group or from that subsistence village? Recently, other research is beginning to identify these kinds of differences in EF skill development based on socioeconomic status, maternal education level, and parenting style.[15] So another major difference in EF skill development in our classrooms is literacy-oriented versus non-literacy-oriented students, specifically those EF skills that one needs to be a self-directed, independent learner in the formal learning environment of a classroom.

Cultural Disruption and Executive Functions

In Chapter 3, we saw that mediated learning experiences (MLEs) are the primary way that culture, including ways of learning, is transmitted to children. It is through mediated learning experiences with more capable adults (or peers) that we develop in culturally appropriate ways the innate EF capacities all humans possess.

However, cultural disruption is the unfortunate reality for many learners. *Children who have grown up in sustained disruptive conditions, like significant poverty, violence, and stress, often have acute EF needs.*[16] These students require mediated learning experiences to develop EF skills as part of their school education. This chapter is devoted to exploring ways to explicitly teach EF skills that most affect non-literacy-oriented, and/or culturally disrupted learners: internalizing scripts, inhibition control, attention control, organization, planning, shifting, and metacognition.[17]

EFs Take Time to Develop

We're sure many of you will relate to the following scenario at whatever grade or subject you teach: You're a 1st grade teacher, and you are sitting at a table with struggling emergent readers and you don't say a word. The students are doing OK. You spend some time listening and get up quietly to go sit with another group. The students are bent over the table, reading intently. But each step you take away from the table, it's like the kids are connected to you by some invisible string. As you move a step away, their bodies straighten up a bit, until you're at a certain distance from the table and they're sitting bolt upright and nervously call out, "I need help, I need help!"

Why? You didn't say anything when you were at the table, and they were doing just fine! But you were a living, breathing reminder of how to use EFs in the process of reading, and as you move away, the implicit reminders move farther away. Because the students don't yet own these EF skills, they still need (external) reminders.

Rosa, a 6th grade student from a culturally disrupted background, was experiencing particular difficulty in math. She started receiving math specialist support, and it just so happened that the other student in the same small group was her stepsister, a student on an IEP with clear cognitive challenges. After several classes, the math specialist reported to Ken that not only was Rosa not doing well but that "her sister is even doing better than her! I think Rosa definitely needs special ed services for math." Ken was surprised by this and asked if he could come and see for himself.

Later that day, Ken went to the class and sat down next to Rosa, who looked up in surprise and asked, half with suspicion, "What are you doing here, Ken?" He replied that he knew she was a good math student and he wasn't really a good math learner, and so he asked her teacher if he could come down to watch, because he had a bit of free time. Rosa asked, "Really?" Ken assured her that was the case. During the class, Rosa demonstrated no struggle at all with the math and worked well beyond the capability of her sister. The math specialist later said, "I've never seen her work like that before!"

A couple of things were occurring in this scenario. Ken attempted to raise Rosa's very shaky confidence by praising her math ability. But the more significant factor was the fact that Ken had been working intensively with Rosa on a number of EF issues;[18] clearly, she still had not yet internalized them. Her improved performance appeared due to Ken's mere presence, which reminded her of what to think about when doing schoolwork. This allowed her to work at a much higher level than she had been doing without him, like the emergent readers in the first scenario. This interaction taught Ken that he needed to make more frequent and explicit connections to math in his work with Rosa, even though he was not her math teacher.

We need to work with struggling students to develop EFs through a process of mediation, focusing on learning and thinking skills, and explicit teaching. When our focus is the school curriculum, we will need to scaffold struggling learners' use of EFs so they can perform academic tasks. But because they can only focus on one thing at a time, their attention will be less on the EFs and more on the content. So we have to find other times to mediate the development of EF skills explicitly. Mediating for transcendence—that is, connecting today's learning to the past, and also future learning situations—is key, especially when helping students develop EF skills. It's a long process—Rome wasn't built in a day, and neither are executive functions!

Whenever we can, we should work with EF development when there is less cognitive load (i.e., familiar topics and class routines and less demanding academic tasks) so students can use a greater amount of working memory space to focus on the EFs. This combination of scaffolding during academic tasks, and suggestions for helping students with an EF focus during less demanding tasks, is the backdrop for the many teaching points in this chapter.

Teaching Point: Using Charts

In order to support the development of EF skills, students need to internalize language that can help them manage the complexities of academic tasks. We suggest co-constructing charts with students that lay out the steps in doing an academic task or solving a problem. For example, we can make a chart[19] with the steps students need to solve a math problem, or what good readers think about when reading nonfiction. These can be helpful for anything that includes multiple steps and multiple things to think about. *This also takes some of the pressure off WM and allows learners to focus on new concepts and procedures.*

And when there is a breakdown or students get stuck, it allows us just to point the chart out and have the students do the work of self-assessing where their breakdown or "stuckness" might be. The more they actively think about it and make decisions about it, the better they'll get. Our telling usually goes in one ear and out the other, and kids get stuck at the same spot on another day. So we should try to identify EF challenges and scaffold their development until students own (i.e., internalize) them.

As one example, anchor charts are probably familiar to many of you. Anchor charts are posters with the steps for successfully engaging in an academic task. An anchor chart for reading lists the steps that students should employ to read independently and how to problem solve when they encounter a reading challenge. Figure 5.1 is an example of an anchor chart for reading nonfiction.

While creating anchor charts is a very good thing, we also need to mediate our students' ability to internalize and use these steps in the future. This is how we support long-term independent development of EF skills. Whenever possible, students need to take a more active role in their learning and internalize the anchor chart information. We can ask questions and scaffold students' ability to remember rather than just didactically telling them the same information again and again.

| Figure 5.1 | **Anchor Chart** |

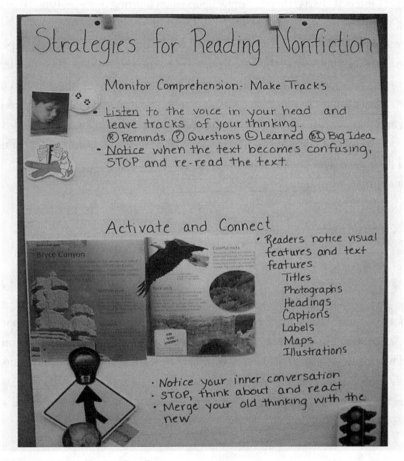

Source: Anchor chart created by Jane Costello

In the end, our goal must be for them to not need the chart because they own the information and are no longer reliant on external reminders. When they sit down to work in classes that don't have these charts up, they need to be able to work successfully anyway. When they sit down for standardized tests and those helpful charts have to be taken down because of test protocols, many students panic and feel helpless because they have been relying on the charts to help them work, but not really *learning* what the charts illustrated. In order to be good problem solvers in—or out of—the classroom, students must own a rich set of "internal charts" they can draw upon when figuring out a challenge that school (or life) throws at them.

Reminding can take the form of nonverbal representations, such as icons or pictures, which the class chooses for a word or concept. It can also be a process where all the words of a sentence are reduced over time to just the key term, and then ultimately to a picture or icon. Students have to remember and start supplying the missing words, then by the end, when they see just the picture or icon, they think, "Oh, right, the key—I have to look carefully for the key words in the problem to see how the numbers are connected. Then I'll know what operation to use."

For example, from the above chart:

1. Start with full sentences or phrases on a chart: "Look for the key words."
2. Cover up some words over time:
    Look—key words
    key words
3. Change the concept to an image or symbol: —◁

Or we can just work with the class to agree on a picture or icon for a classroom academic script, without ever using written sentences. Whichever way we do it, our goal should be for students to do the heavy lifting of their learning, which for some students is not only learning the external school curriculum but also internalizing the language that engages the EFs needed in classroom learning. This connects to the first EF skill we will explore: internalizing scripts.

EF Skill #1: Internalizing Scripts

One of the most important EF skills that humans have is the internalizing of adult speech as the child's own internal *scripts*. This is one of the ways that culture is passed down from one generation to another. Through interactions with parents and caretakers (especially mediated learning experiences), we appropriate the speech we hear them use, little by little, for culturally meaningful activities and make it our own.[20] Scripts of all kinds are stored in long-term memory (see Chapter 6). They are models for all manner of cultural activities and routines.[21] Embedded within scripts are goals, roles, props, actions, and, importantly, *language use*. Verbal scripts launch other EFs that enable us to solve problems and direct our minds to set and reach our goals.

An example of an EF-related script is when we mentally run through a list of resources to get together before we start a new project. Another is the Brazilian teachers' suggestion to their young charges during the puzzle-making task, "Why don't we look at the shape?" As the child appropriates that and other similar generalized language prompts for her own internalized script, they become available for her aid in future similar tasks when no adult is present to help.

In contrast, the child in the subsistence village setting hears the adult script "Put this here!" That is a context-specific command that cannot be generalized to aid the child in future similar situations without an adult to direct the interaction.[22] The charts suggested in the previous teaching point are a great way to teach appropriate EF-related classroom scripts.

To sum up: Adult-child interactions in a culture with a heavy literacy orientation provide children with the kind of EF scripts they can use to engage confidently in school tasks. Non-literacy-oriented children may have different kinds of EF scripts and have different developmental levels of EFs. Culturally disrupted learners often lack sufficient culturally appropriate EF scripts. *The reality of our classrooms is that most of us will have all three kinds of students in front of us and therefore should intentionally teach EF-related scripts.* At the close of each EF section, there will be *suggested* scripts to model for students. They are intended as examples of dialogue in an MLE with a particular student, but these kinds of intentional interactions could be turned into a "think-aloud" for the whole class. Modeling academic scripts and helping students internalize them is a key teacher strategy, the benefits of which are huge for EF development.

Teaching Point: Slogans and Aphorisms

Using this idea of scripts, Ken had success with struggling learners by creating slogans for younger students and aphorisms for older students about successful learning and academic behaviors in the classroom. They arose out of classroom interactions where students demonstrated some level of misunderstanding about how proficient learners act in the process of classroom learning. Having students recite a slogan or reflect on an aphorism helped them cue into the concept the script symbolized, and so remind themselves about it.

For 1st grade students, Ken created the slogan "No listening, no learning."[23] He found that many of his struggling learners understood "listen" as mainly a behavioral command, because in their home, that's how it was used. For example, "You listen when I'm talking to you!" is more a follow-up to some sort of disobedience that requires the child to show remorse than a request for him to engage his brain for learning. Ken also found that they were not so aware of listening as an active process, quite distinct from "hearing." In fact, many thought that eyes and bodies (even more than ears) were what we listen with because their teachers had often coupled "listen" with "eyes on me" and "turn your bodies to me."

After clarifying with students how "listen" is really "pay attention with your brain to what I am saying because you have to think about it to learn," Ken summarized it in the slogan "No listening, no learning." When students weren't listening, he might say, "Uh-oh, no listening…" and the students would chorally reply, "…no learning!" Or before he started a lesson segment that involved a longer stretch of teacher talk, he might ask, "I'm about to tell you something. So what should you be thinking now?" A couple of other slogans he used with younger children were "Trying hard is being smart" and, copying from Aesop, "Slow and steady wins the race."[24]

In the case of older students, Ken created more philosophical aphorisms, which always grew out of discussions about learning with students at some point of breakdown. He would then post them on the wall as sentence strips. "Having a plan is better than hoping for luck!" "Being organized is better than being random!" "Think before you jump!" and "In things that are similar, there can be many differences; in things that are different, many things can be similar!" are examples of these sayings. When a student started a task impulsively or started in on a problem before he really thought about how to attack it, Ken might ask, "Hmmm. Which saying do you think I'm going to ask you to think about right now?" If lines from movies the kids watch or song lyrics by popular musicians fit the bill for this, it's a great way to connect!

EF Skill #2: Inhibition

A bedrock EF skill is the *ability to restrain ourselves* from doing the easy, automatic, or habitual thing, as well as knowing when it's in our best interests to do so. This behavioral EF allows us to (1) delay or prevent a response leading to an immediate consequence, (2) stop ongoing behaviors when unsuccessful, and (3) manage distractions and interruptions that may interfere with learning.[25] One definition of inhibition is "the executive control of desires, beliefs, thoughts, and goals" (Sodian & Firth, 2008, p. 111).

Students with ADHD have particular issues with inhibition. But we have heard many teachers comment on the increasing numbers of students, and not just those with a diagnosed need, who seem to struggle with this. Feuerstein et al. (2010) identifies the inability to restrain impulsivity as one of the main consequences of cultural disruption. Impulsivity is particularly debilitating academically because it undermines many other EF skills and leads to poor performance.[26] For students struggling with impulsivity, learning at school is like trying to build a house on quicksand.

In a 1st grade classroom, Ken was working with a group of three students who were struggling to learn to read. He had a shoebox full of objects that start with a "b" sound, such as a bear, doll boots, a belt, a plastic bananas, and so on. He wanted to see if the students could guess objects using the clue of the initial consonant sound before they applied the same skill to the more subtle and challenging task of guessing words from pictures based on initial consonant sounds in early-leveled readers.

Ken opened the lid of the box and peeked in. The plastic bananas caught his eye. The conversation went something like this:

Ken: OK everyone, this is the "B" box. What's the sound everything will start with?

Students: b-b-b!

Ken: Right! So will we guess "d-d-dog" for something in this box?

Students: Nooo!

Ken: How about "b-b-balloon"?

3 kids: Yes!

Ken: Why?

Student A: "Balloon" starts with "b."

Ken (to Student B): Is he right?

Student B: Yes!

Ken: OK, so here we go. Oooo, I see something I like to eat. It's a fruit…

Before the word "fruit" was fully out of Ken's mouth, a student from Cape Verde we'll call Luana, called out, "Apple! Apple!"

Ken: Luana, what's the first sound for everything in this box?

Luana: b-b-b!

Ken: Does "apple" start with "b"?

Luana: Nooooo…

Ken: So should we say "apple" anyway if it doesn't start with a "b," even if we *really* know a lot about apples?

Luana: Noooo…

Ken: OK, let's try again. I'm thinking of a fruit, it's yellow…

Before the word "yellow" was fully out of Ken's mouth, Luana called out, "Mango!" Here, Ken could have decided Luana needed a lot more work on the "b" sound—twice she guessed words that did not start with "b." But Ken suspected impulsivity was the issue because of the way she often blurted out her answers and her overall excitement with this guessing game.

"Luana, close your eyes for a sec, and feel yourself breathing." She was practically hyperventilating from the excitement of the game. He waited until her breathing had slowed and said, "OK, Luana, I'm gonna say the clues again, but you're gonna keep your eyes closed, and you can't say anything until I say to open your eyes. OK?" She nodded. "I'm thinking of a fruit. It's yellow." Ken silently counted to 3. "OK, open your eyes. What is it?" Clear as a bell and with an even voice, Luana said, "Banana."

Luana, a student from culturally disrupted circumstances, struggled with impulsivity throughout the school day, and it constantly undermined her considerable energy, enthusiasm, and talent for learning. In this scenario, several interrelated EF issues affected Luana's thinking. One was the ability to juggle multiple sources of information and keep what was most important steady in working memory as new data were encountered. Apples (the fruit she'd heard the most about in Massachusetts) and mangoes (the fruit she liked the most) overwhelmed the much more subtle phoneme "b" in her mind. She could not shift her mind from the more emphatic, egocentric "I love mangoes!" or "I hear about apples all the time!" to the more subtle object of the lesson, which had nothing directly to do with her at all.

Though Luana proved that she did have sufficient knowledge of English phonics to make a skillful guess, once her impulsivity was controlled, she lacked the *independent* ability to restrain it, which led to an impaired ability to shift her thinking, manipulate the information in working memory, and orient herself to the task instead of trying to orient the task to herself. Ken often found that impulsivity masqueraded as a lack of phonemic skill in young learners, like Luana and the boy Savun in the "trucks carry sand" anecdote in Chapter 4. While our instinct may be to focus on the content ("Luana can't make guesses accurately with the 'b' sound, so she needs more 'b' practice"), it's quite often the student's ability to marshal appropriate levels of EF skill and juggle information in working memory that is the *real* issue.

To mediate Luana's limited ability to inhibit her impulsivity, Ken spoke with her about her own perceptions of her learning: when did she feel she was learning her best in the classroom, and when did she feel least successful? This mediated "meaning" because it was about her, her own performance in the classroom, and her own ability to be successful. By connecting her to her past performance, he mediated transcendence. He asked her about when she played similar games in the future, how would she try to think, which also mediated transcendence.

Intentionality and reciprocity were embedded in the nature of the conversation (e.g., it was about her own behavior, so there was value for her, and it was based in her EF need at that moment), and the goal of Ken's interaction was for Luana to become a better thinker. He was also helping her develop metacognitive awareness of her own behavior. It's important to emphasize that no one MLE interaction can change behavior; it is the systematic accumulation of MLE interactions that leads to learner development and change.

In a famous landmark behavioral study at Stanford University conducted in 1972,[27] children between the ages of 4 and 6 were put in a small room at a table with a marshmallow. The researcher told them that he was going to leave the room and they could eat the marshmallow, but if they could resist eating it until he returned to the room, they'd be given two. They were left alone in a room with the marshmallow for a couple of minutes. Some couldn't resist and immediately gobbled it up, most resisted for a while but eventually ate it before the researcher returned, and about a third resisted long enough to get the second marshmallow. A follow-up study in 1990 with the same subjects showed that the ability to restrain impulsivity at 4 correlated with higher SAT scores, as well as their parents reporting higher levels of teenage competence. Being able to inhibit impulses and knowing when it's in our best interests to do so, regardless of how we feel otherwise, results in much higher levels of learning and performance.

Teaching Point: Working with Impulsivity

It is important to recognize how certain behaviors signal EF challenges. If we can accurately label student behaviors in this way, we can more directly meet our students' needs. Some student behaviors that signal the inability to skillfully inhibit are as follows:

- Habitual calling out
- Starting-erasing-starting-erasing (in writing)
- Answering before they've really thought about something
- Difficulty waiting for a turn
- Not being able to stay still for long

Here are some classroom strategies dealing with the issue of impulsivity:

- Clear class expectations and rules, co-constructed with the class and periodically revisited
- Periodic time built into lessons for movement[28]
- Arranging your classroom with an unobstructed view of whole class, and positioning yourself to see the whole class when working with individual students or small groups so students know you can always see them

Here are some individual strategies to mediate learners for impulse control:[29]

- Students encouraged to center themselves—for example by closing their eyes and focusing on breathing for a few seconds
- Naming and praising impulsive students' positive behaviors
- Talking with the student about when he/she works more carefully in life outside school, and how/why that is (e.g., playing a video game, making something the student really wants to make, doing a hobby) and bridging that back to working more successfully in the classroom
- Establishing a secret signal with a student for "slow down"

Here are some sample strategy scripts:

- For younger children: "Remember how your body feels when you want to just call out an answer?" Or if it's after the fact, "Ooo, what did we forget to think about our body just now?
- "When I feel like I want to blurt out something, I touch my lips instead."
- Before an activity, asking, "Now Sam, what slogan should we think about before we start this activity?" (e.g., "Think before you jump!")

EF Skill #3: No Attention, No Learning!

We think everyone would agree that attention is critical for learning.[30] Classroom learning is intentional learning, which takes effort. In Chapter 4, we saw that attention is what we are focused on in active working memory, whether it's new information emerging through short-term working memory or information activated from long-term memory. *And, due to working memory constraints, we can only really pay sustained attention to one thing at a time.* If a student is hungry all the time, bullied on the bus, having problems at home, or feeling disconnected in the classroom, he is paying attention mostly to that, not the teacher's instruction. If a student is having a great time hangin' with her buds in the back of the class, she will not be attending to the biology lesson. It is easy to understand how attention is central to learning.

In Chapter 3, we provided a mediated learning lesson plan structure. One of the recommended lesson segments was tied to alignment: *the importance of starting a lesson in a rousing or interesting way to gather attention.* The goal is for the teacher to help struggling students get centered in the moment, so they can marshal their attention and focus. If we don't help them jump-start their fragile working memory system, they may tune out entirely when the academic language starts pouring in.

In a 10th grade history class in a vocational school whose population was mostly academically struggling, disenfranchised Latino students, a teacher was beginning a lesson on the settling of the American West in the 1800s. It was Monday morning, first period. He gave the students a handout and kicked off his lesson talking about some of the major themes they'd be studying. The presentation was all verbal, supported by the handout.

Apparently, 19th century American history was not on these kids' radar screens, especially not at 8:15 on a Monday morning. After about 10 minutes, they began to chat with one another quite loudly. The teacher then brought out an iconic picture of the Old West of a buffalo hunter posing atop a small mountain of buffalo skulls (Figure 5.2).

As he passed around copies of the picture, the kids suddenly were transfixed. "Wow, he shot all those?!" "How'd he do that?" "That guy, how many buffaloes he kill, anyway?!" These kinds of comments flew around the room, and there was no trouble with the kids' attention at all! But after a short time, the teacher returned to his lecture . . . and the kids to their disinterest.

Figure 5.2 | **Buffalo Skulls**

If the teacher had started the lesson with a hook like that picture, he would have helped align his goals with the students' motivation, which would have stimulated their attention. If he had developed a lesson that connected them personally to that period of history, he could have helped the students direct their attention. If he had then designed the lesson for the kids to make periodic shifts, such as a standing activity after sitting, or a Think-Pair-Share after listening, it would have been easier for the students to sustain attention (discussed later). If the students' attention had eventually begun to flag, as often happens in spite of our best-laid plans, he could have talked the kids through their need to persevere over tough spots, building on the kids' previous buy-in and engagement.

Meanwhile, in the history class next door, the 9th graders were given a letter on school letterhead and signed by the principal to give to their parents. In it, they read that their parents were going to have to be taxed for all the paper in the school, and that a new policy had been created by the principal that their teachers would be able to spend the night in the students' homes if they wanted, since some of the teachers had long drives home and they might be tired.

The kids were incensed! How dare the school do that kind of thing! The talk was fast and furious for a while. The teacher then explained that it was a joke, but that those were the same things that got the American colonists so angry at the British and led to the Revolutionary War. And so how do they think the colonists felt? At the end of the class, the students decided to play a joke on their parents and take the letters home. Anyway—no attention problems in that early morning history class!

Teaching Point: Attention Span Rule of Thumb

Although everyone agrees that our capacity for sustained attention is limited, there is no real agreement between experts as to the length of our students' attention spans.[31] Estimates vary quite a bit. Some calculate "age + 2 minutes." Others say 3–5 minutes per each year of a student's age. Yet others say adults have a 20-minute attention span before some refresher or break is needed. Moreover, increased time interacting with visual media may be diminishing the length of time many children can attend without a break. Culture also may affect attention span.[32]

But in spite of this wide range of possibilities, having some rule of thumb would be helpful, and in our experience teaching and coaching, the "age + 2 minutes" is a convenient starting point. If the students are 6 to 7 years old, that's 8 to 9 minutes. If students are 15, that's 17 minutes. *Of course, if students are poorly motivated, the attention span could be zero!* Conversely, if your students are *really* into a lesson, they can go longer. This rule of thumb is meant to be a baseline—we each need to gauge what our particular class can manage.

When Ken is coaching, he often notes that when teachers approach (let alone pass) the attention span limits, more and more students begin to fall off task, and the teachers must shift to behavior management. By understanding attention span as a concrete physiological limit, we can avoid blaming kids when we exceed it. We use their off-task behavior as a signal to ourselves—"Uh-oh, I must have been going on for too long. (check clock) Yup—time to change the energy flow!"

We are not talking about students' self-directed, self-motivated attention. Attention spans are much longer when we're doing what we really want to do. The "attention span limit" applies to activities that students have to do, for which there may not be a great deal of intrinsic motivation—in other words, a lot of schooling! What this means is that when we sense wiggliness or growing distraction, we need to make one or more of the following changes of energy flow:

1. Movement—if students were sitting, have them do a quick activity standing or moving around.

2. Language domain—if students were listening, have them talk in a quick pair-share or a more organized small-group discussion; or if they were reading, do a quick write about what they've learned from the text so far.

3. Subject—briefly change the topic to something the students find more interesting—for example, tell a compelling or entertaining story (personal or drawn from the subject area) and relate it directly to the topic being studied.

Any change of this type resets the attention timer so students are more ready to learn again. We can go back to our lesson for another appropriate-sized lesson chunk. When we plan, we can divide the time we have by the attention span limit of our class. In first grade, if we have 45 minutes for math, say, that means roughly four to five lesson chunks. That means as we plan, we can intentionally plan three to four "energy changes" in our lesson. If it's a sophomore history class in high school with a 90-minute block, that's about five changes. This also fits nicely with taking care with cognitive load: any transition points we build in are also opportunities for students to process the newly taught information and thus reduce the stress on working memory.

Another approach to the issue of timing is from John Medina.[33] He notes that the brain periodically needs a break from the relentless flow of classroom facts and figures and advocates that teachers use "hooks" every 10 minutes to help students reground and recenter themselves in the learning. The hooks should trigger emotion, be relevant to the class content, and serve as bridges at transition points in a lesson. A hook can be a story that personalizes the subject matter, a powerful image that will captivate students, or simply the use of humor to change the dynamics of the classroom. Intentionally planning for energy switches is much healthier for our students—and ourselves—than exceeding their attention span limit and having to switch to disciplining students for off-task behavior!

One suggestion for energy switches is *index card checks*.[34] Index card checks are a way to check students' comprehension, degree of understanding, or belief before, during, or at the close of a lesson, as we noted in Chapter 4. We get much more, and more accurate, information that way about our students than asking, "Do you understand?" For example, on a 6×8 index card, students write "True" on one side, "False" on the other. Or, *A* written at the top of one side, *B* written at the bottom, and *C/D* on the other side, which can be used for multiple choice,[35] degree of agreement (e.g., A = I agree 100 percent, B = I mostly agree, etc.), level of understanding (A = I know I understand, B = I think I understand, etc.), or degree of belief (A = I'm sure it's true, B = I'm pretty sure it's true, etc.).

Of course, separate cards with those possibilities written out, rather than A, B, C, D, is another option. Either way, we can say, "OK everyone, take out your True-False cards. I've just been talking about the water cycle. So is this true or false?: The water cycle ends when rainwater seeps into the ground." Or, "OK, get out your *how much do you believe it?* cards. Ready? What do you think about this statement: When rainwater seeps into the ground, that water cycle is over, and a new one starts." Not only do these quick index card games help us manage attention span limitations in a snappy, fun way, but they are also an opportunity for student reflection on their learning, as well as a valuable informal assessment for us. It helps students recycle the information that they need to store new information securely into long-term memory.

In his helpful book *How the Brain Learns,* David Sousa (2011) describes what is known as the "primacy-recency" effect. In brief, research shows that we retain a lot of what we hear and do at the start of a learning episode and at the end, but we often experience a downtime in the middle. The longer the learning episode, the greater the downtime. So, similar to the attention span rule of thumb, another way to structure lessons would be no longer than 15- to 20-minute input chunks (i.e., our instruction) before there was practice or processing. This lessens the downtime (given that the 20 minutes are engaging and well spent) to 10 percent+/− of the total chunk, as opposed to a 30-minute chunk, say, which would be about 25 percent (10 or so minutes) of brain downtime.

Teaching Point: Helping Students Focus

Some student behaviors that signal the inability to sustain attention are as follows:
- Failing to complete tasks on time
- Stopping before work is done
- Switching activities frequently
- Getting distracted easily
- Having a hard time listening to read-alouds

Some classroom strategies dealing with attention:
- Seating students who struggle with EF skills strategically—not near windows or doors and not in the back with friends
- Having a class discussion about what distractions there are for students when they work and suggestions for dealing with them
- Discussing what "paying attention" and "listening" mean and look like, and why they're important
- Being very intentional about the attention span rule of thumb
- Making tasks shorter or creating more discrete steps

Some individual strategies to mediate student learning:
- Establishing a signal when the student realizes his or her attention is flagging
- Developing a checklist or plan with students that they can use to self-monitor
- Talking with a student about when he or she is able to focus for longer periods in life outside school (e.g., playing video games, playing with friends, watching TV) and relate this back to classroom learning
- Establishing a signal to the student for the teacher to use when he/she suspects the student's attention is flagging

Some sample strategy scripts:
- "Am I right in thinking that it's hard for you to finish work at home? What do you think you can do to help you do better sticking with your homework?" Then the next day, follow up with "How did it go? What worked/didn't work?"
- "I've noticed that you give up quickly a lot of the time. It could be because things are hard and you're frustrated. It could be because it's hard for you to keep going. It could be because you get bored and want to do something else. I guess it could

even be something else, too. Can you help me understand what makes you want to stop working so much?" Depending on what the student says, talk about how the student can signal a need for help when she feels like stopping work, and follow up with, "So tomorrow, what can I expect to see when . . . ?"

- "José, before you start this work today, tell me what you're going to do when you feel you might be wanting to stop and do something else?"

EF Skills #4 and #5: Planning and Setting Goals

Planning and goal setting are central to academic learning. Planning allows us to better organize ourselves to reach our goals. Conversely, unless we have a specific goal, there's not much to plan for. In combination, these EFs help us marshal the energy and resources required for completing tasks and solving problems. (Of course, then we need to organize ourselves, the focus of the next section.)

In many different classroom tasks, some students struggle to independently get started and therefore can't complete the task without a lot of our help. Many of these students have a lot of difficulty with planning, and some with goal setting, and some with both. This creates a great challenge, especially as students move up through the grades, and work gets more complex and abstract.

Teaching Point: Clear Learning Objectives

It is very important to be sure struggling learners understand the main point of a lesson —what is it we want stuck to the students' brains? From a mediated learning point of view, setting clear learning objectives is one way we communicate our alignment with our students about their learning.

Many of us use learning objectives, but we may not know or remember to incorporate all the characteristics of quality objectives into our lessons. The following are important elements of any learning objectives:

- We need to communicate them to students in language *they* understand.
- In conjunction with that, we recommend phrasing them as "We will . . ." or "You will . . . ," as opposed to the common "Students will . . ." When we use the

latter phrase, we tend to be talking more to ourselves, and the language level rises beyond the very students who most need clear, comprehensible objectives from us.

- There shouldn't be more than one or two learning objectives per lesson.
- Ideally, the learning objectives are measurable in some way; that is, they should be specific and concrete, not general and abstract.
- Each objective should be its own sentence, rather than in a compound sentence with "and."
- They should be written and posted.
- We should bookend our lesson with objectives: making sure that students know where the lesson is headed at the start, and when the lesson is over, reflecting on what they learned through learning logs, paired talk, written reflection, or index card flashes (discussed earlier); midcourse checks can also be very helpful.

Learning objectives are not activities. They are what students are expected to learn as they do the activity. Remember Alexandra and the 100s chart? Well, the major issue for her was lack of a clear learning goal. So she happily participated and "did the activity," but she did not learn what the teacher (and math program) expected. She needed explicit guidance to connect to a specific learning goal before, during, and after the lesson. Otherwise, it was just a fun thing to do.

The following objectives are not very good, because they break one or more of the above "rules." Can you decide why? (Our answers are at the end of this chapter.)

- Grade 2: "Students will discover the relationship between counting on and subtraction."
- Grade 6: "You will work with a partner and compare the two main characters."
- Grade 9: "You will learn the three basic ways that mountains form and also about tectonic plates."

There is no universal agreement on the format of learning goals. From the struggling learner's point of view, though, it really doesn't matter what form they take as long as we (1) create objectives for them, (2) "follow the rules" about objectives, and (3) communicate our goals for the lesson to our students and try to assure their aligned response.

Another very helpful use of objectives is to sit down with students and ask them to talk about what their objectives are for themselves for the year (in general or for a specific subject), how they plan to reach those objectives, and what help they'll need. Periodically have "review" conferences where you and the students evaluate how they're doing. At the end of the school year, have students read their objectives to see if they have been met: if so, what did they do to make it so, and if not, what could they have done differently? Students can also look forward to next year and set new objectives. Certainly, as teachers, we can contribute a goal or two to the students' list (although too many goals defeat the purpose). Students can also set goals around EFs, and this can be particularly helpful when we've pinned down what areas of EF a student struggles with most.

Teaching Point: Helping Students Set Goals

Here are some student behaviors that signal the inability to set goals and plan:
- Consistently late work
- Going off track easily, losing the thread of the learning

Some classroom strategies aside from posting objectives that address this issue:
- Goals: close off open-ended tasks for some struggling students—in other words, tell them what they need to find out or learn.
- Planning: post the steps in multistep problem solving, or the steps in directions.
- Planning: give struggling students just one or two steps at a time (this also helps students with working memory issues).
- Planning: break down the steps in long-term projects, with clear due dates and expectations, plus a list of resources and supplies they'll need.

Some sample strategy scripts:
- "Johnny, why are we studying this topic?"
- "What is the learning goal for today's lesson?"
- "Maria, before you get started here, can you let me know your plan?"
- "How many of the steps in the directions can you remember at one time?'

EF Skill #6: Organization

This chapter opened with an anecdote in which 9th grade students needed their teacher for support in every step of a fairly simple academic task tied to the previous day's lesson. Even though the teacher had pointed out what resource they could use to help them, students still made little independent progress. Why is this?

In large part, they lacked appropriate organizational scripts. "What do I have to do? How do I know if I'm doing it right? Aahh—I need help!" might be their script. Maybe they have a goal, and possibly even a general plan; what they lack is the skill of marshaling their resources to put it into practice. And we always need to keep in mind that students are using their fragile working memories trying to pull all of this together. Obviously, students with this EF weakness will struggle in any activity that is not highly scaffolded and monitored.

Organization is a part of goal setting and planning (the two EFs we just discussed). It is hard to imagine organizing oneself to start a task without a specific goal for that activity, and a plan to reach that goal, so usually all three issues are present. But organization itself could be a weak EF skill.

Organizational skill takes a long time to own. In culturally disrupted circumstances, where there is very little predictability from one day to the next and life is a day-to-day struggle, it follows that the development of organizational skills would be one of many EFs that are negatively impacted. Some of us grow up with organizational challenges and have perfectly productive adult lives. However, at school, disorganization, coupled with other EF issues such as a lack of school-matched language, becomes a serious issue for some students. Writing is particularly susceptible to challenges with organization, as are solving multistep problems or completing complex projects. These are all linked to working memory limitations.

Teaching Point: Helping Students Organize

Some student behaviors that signal the inability to organize:
- Failing to complete tasks on time
- Losing things, especially homework
- Inability to get started on tasks

Some classroom strategies dealing with this issue:
- Do a lot of classroom organizing/clean-up, with discussions about why it's important.
- Teach through graphic organizers.
- Periodically do a class "clean and organize" of desks, notebooks, and backpacks.

- Periodically do lessons on ways to organizing ideas after a brainstorm; use "think-alouds" to talk about what *you* might do, and have students talk about how they might do it (also see Chapter 6).

Some individual strategies to mediate:
- The above strategies, one-on-one with individual students.
- Help students figure out when they are successfully organized in their life outside school, and how/why that happens (e.g., video gaming, having a party, parts of their room; segue back to the classroom).
- Teach routine little by little, with periodic practice opportunities.
- Praise when students are successful and reflect on what made that possible.
- Have students write a list of "what makes some kids' desks really neat looking."

Some sample strategy scripts:
- "Uh-oh, Don, no homework again? Forget you had it? Let's talk about what you could do to remember, and how we might help you get better—then I want you to pick something to try, starting with tonight's homework. We'll talk about how it went tomorrow."
- "I've noticed that you have trouble finding things in class. What do you think the problem is? How do you think we can make it easier for you to find things? So, tomorrow when I pass back your work, what are you going to do with it?"

EF Skill #7: Shifting

Shifting is the cognitive skill we use to change focus, direction, or tactics. Shifting is directly tied to inhibition. If we inhibit a habitual way of acting, we will likely need to shift to another set of behaviors. Sometimes students struggle with both impulsivity and shifting. At other times, just the shifting is problematic for students. Cognitive shifting is really all about flexibility.

It's like walking on a path and seeing a large stone in the way. Successful students look for a way around the stone, but some students stand in front of the stone (some even cry that it's blocking their way) and stop moving. Others see the stone, turn around, and go back the way they came. In academic tasks, we're sunk if we only have one way of dealing with problems and that way doesn't work!

Many students also struggle when shifting from one activity to another. For example, in writing, this may manifest as a lack of punctuation during the process of writing a first draft. Getting the ideas down and remembering to use mechanics correctly are two separate tasks. In switching from one to another, learners have to be able to shift cognitive processes, and that takes both time and effort.[36] So mistakes in this area could be related to cognitive load (see Chapter 4) but could specifically be connected with trouble shifting. In other words, the student is literally not cognitively flexible enough to move in any other direction than the one he is presently going, or to see the need for it.

Ken was coaching a teacher in a 9th grade science class. One day when he arrived, the students were doing an experiment about permeable membranes, following a previous class in which they learned about permeability. The teacher had created little tubes of plastic wrap filled with syrup. The students weighed a tube, put it in a beaker of cold tap water for 30 seconds, and then took it out and reweighed it. They repeated this process several times and noted that the weight slightly increased each time. They may have also noticed that over time, the syrup got lighter and more transparent. They were supposed to draw the conclusion that the membrane of the plastic was permeable as the tubes absorbed more and more water.

Ken went up to a pair of students and asked them how it was going. They were enjoying the experiment. Ken asked what they were finding out, and one of them said that the syrup tube was getting heavier. Ken asked why. "'Cause it's getting colder." When Ken asked if she could explain her thinking a bit more to him, she said, "You know, like when you put water in the freezer, it gets heavier. The syrup is going into the cold water, and so it's getting heavier."

So much is going on in this interesting exchange, including the student's faulty schema (retrieved from long-term memory) about the attributes of physical objects. But from an EF perspective, the student is also demonstrating an inability to shift. The experiment was clearly connected to the previous lesson on permeability—that was the whole context of the experiment, and the teacher had told the students the day before during the lesson on permeability that they were going to do an experiment about it. There was nothing about temperature at all in this experiment or in the permeability lesson. That student, however, was unable to shift her thinking away from her previously held expectation to be able to think, "This is an experiment about permeability, and temperature doesn't have anything to do with it. Hmmm . . . . The syrup is getting heavier each time. So some of the water must be getting inside the plastic! There's no hole in the plastic, and the ends are tied, so it must be getting in through the plastic itself."

She did employ cause-effect reasoning to her data collecting as she was supposed to do, but because of her difficulty shifting, she hijacked the experiment to conform to a previously held (erroneous) belief that had nothing to do with the experiment.

In a fine example of how to skillfully work with shifting, a talented special education teacher colleague of Ken's trained her students to do a "threshold check" before they went back into their classroom after being with her in a small-group room. Some of the students could not reenter their classroom appropriately—they made noise, or they loudly interrupted the teacher to ask what was going on, or they got panicked because they didn't know what was going on. So she got them to stop in the doorway threshold, before actually going into the class, to think through what they should do when they walked in: wait to ask the teacher until she was finished talking, or quietly put their books away and get out the text the class was using, and so on. She had great success in helping students more appropriately and smoothly shift with this EF-friendly threshold check.

Teaching Point: Fostering Cognitive Flexibility

Here are some student behaviors that signal the inability to shift:
- Distractibility
- Inflexibility
- Problems with transitions
- Perseverating

Some classroom strategies dealing with the issue of shifting:
- Carefully organize the classroom environment so there is not a lot of distracting stimulation and so that information is clear to students.
- Practice new routines so that students are able to easily shift from one routine to another.
- In math, model multiple ways to solve problems, but be sure all students are competent and feel confident with at least one way first.
- Use visual schedules and checklists.

Some individual mediation strategies:

- Give a visual signal (or auditory signal, such as a chime) or verbal cue before transitioning, such as pointing to the clock before you announce to the class that one activity is finishing up and another will be starting; you could also have sticky notes with an icon (say, an arrow) symbolizing "transition," and you stick it on a student's desk before you announce the transition to the class.
- Limit choices.
- Praise flexibility and staying on task.
- Set and post clear learning goals that are discussed at the start of a lesson, revisited during the lesson, and reflected on at the close of the lesson.

Some scripts for learners to use to mediate the ability to shift:
- "What are two or three things we've talked about doing if you start the math problem and realize you can't remember how to do it well?"
- "Carla, when I start feeling that what I'm doing isn't working very well, I close my eyes and try to relax before thinking what I should do next."
- "Pedro, you play video games, right? When you're playing well, do you just do one thing the same way all the time, or do you switch strategies? Tell me how you decide what to do."

Conclusion

In a profound way, executive functions define us as human beings. The ability to set goals and plan for them, solve complex problems, get others to assist us in getting our personal needs met, be flexible, inhibit impulses, and use internalized language to direct ourselves set us apart from other animals. They *certainly* define what it takes to be a successful classroom learner! So many students who struggle to learn and retain information and concepts in the school curriculum actually struggle with the process of learning (i.e., having culturally appropriate EF skills for classroom learning tasks), not with the material itself. The more we focus mainly on "teaching the curriculum," the more those students continue to struggle.

And we *all* work with students with different levels of EF skills. This could be because the student has a specific EF-related disability, or because of cultural differences, or because of a nonliteracy orientation, or cultural disruption. But whatever the reason, recognizing this reality requires us to integrate work with EF skill development into our classroom instruction, which will greatly support the learning of non-literacy-oriented and culturally disrupted learners. It also requires us to mediate EF skill development with particular children.

This chapter was not intended to be an exhaustive treatment of EFs and schooling. There are excellent books available on EFs and classroom learning,[37] even if they do not address EF issues related to culture and cultural disruption. In the space of one chapter, the topic is much too big for a comprehensive treatment. Our goals were to

- clarify what EFs are and how they are crucial to the functioning of working memory;
- sensitize us all to the range of students who experience EF challenges;
- describe some of the more impactful EF challenges students experience in a classroom setting, so we can recognize and label EF issues when they manifest in our classroom;
- lay out the framework of a strategy system to enable us to move forward and begin helping individual students, and/or the whole class, with EF challenges.

So although there are more EFs than just those explored in this chapter, and more strategies for helping students through their EF challenges, we hope this chapter has provided you with solid ground for practice and further exploration of this fascinating and very important topic.

Next, we move from working memory to the part of our memory system where all new learning goes—our long-term memory storehouses.

Our Answers for "Writing Effective Objectives"

- Grade 2: "Students will discover the relationship between counting and addition." Problems: (1) It is phrased "students will . . ." (2) As expected, it then uses sophisticated language struggling students could not understand. (3) It is not measurable.

Suggested rephrasing: "You will be able to show me or tell me how counting on and subtraction get the same answer."

- Grade 6: "You will work with a partner and compare the two main characters."
  Problems: (1) The first part is an activity. (2) It is unclear. (3) It is not measurable.

Suggested rephrasing: "You will be able to describe at least three ways that the two main characters are similar and two ways they are different."

- Grade 9: "You will learn the three basic ways that mountains form and also about tectonic plates." Problems: (1) One part is not measurable or clear. (2) Two separate goals are written as one sentence.

Suggested rephrasing:

1. You will be able to explain the three basic ways that mountains form.
2. You will be able to define *tectonic plates*.

---

1. De La Paz et al. (1998) describe a study that showed how executive function support from teachers during students' process of revisions resulted in a significantly greater number of revisions by those students than by students who revised without this support.
2. See also Best et al. (2011); Marcovitch et al. (2008); Sasser & Bierman (2012).
3. Blair & Razza (2007); Molfese et al. (2010); St. Clair-Thompson (2011).
4. Children who are deaf will not activate sounds while reading.
5. Blair & Razza (2007); Booth et al. (2010); Booth & Boyle (2009); Cartwright (2012); Cutting et al. (2009); Jerman et al. (2012) Swanson (1999).
6. Blair & Razza (2007); Jerman et al. (2012); Kostopoulos & Lee (2012); Toll et al. (2011)
7. "Math skill" per se is often not the issue when students have difficulty solving math word problems, because of the added EF and working memory load added onto the math by the act of reading. When literacy skills haven't been automatized, the working memory space needed for the math may get diverted to dealing with the process of reading.
8. Barkley (2012); Kaufman (2010).
9. Dawson & Guare (2010); Kaufman (2010).
10. Lewis et al. (2009); Lan et al. (2011).
11. Pransky & Bailey (2003); Pransky (2008).
12. Rogoff (2003); Delpit (1996).
13. Lantoff (2000).
14. Although the adults in the city were teachers and not the children's parents, the implication is that the teachers would interact similarly with their own children.
15. Fernald et al. (2011); Bibok et al. (2009); Hughes & Ensor (2009).
16. Bibok et al. (2009); Blair et al. (2011); Buckner & Kim (2012); Fernald et al. (2011); Herbers et al. (2011); Hughes & Ensor (2009).
17. Two other important EF skills we will not be taking up are emotional control & time management.
18. Ken was using the Feuerstein Instrumental Enrichment cognitive education program with "Rosa's" group in his ESL room. See Bailey & Pransky (2010).
19. Instead of a wall chart, it could be a handout, book mark, or placemat.
20. Vygotsky (1978).

21. Shank & Abelson (1977).
22. Of course, children in that setting will develop other internalized scripts that are appropriate for the needs and expectations for that cultural context.
23. Pransky & Bailey (2003)
24. In fact, folktales and fables often have morals that are quite applicable to classroom learning (e.g., slow and steady wins the race). It's a great segue from a class read-aloud of a fable to a discussion of the moral and then finish up with a discussion of how it applies in the classroom.
25. Dawson & Guare (2010).
26. Blair & Razza (2007); Booth & Boyle (2009).
27. See http://en.wikipedia.org/wiki/Stanford_marshmallow_experiment.
28. Medina (2008).
29. One strategy for any EF is creating or using premade self-assessment forms with students, geared to their particular EF struggle. Meltzer (2010) and Dawson & Guare (2010) are two excellent resources not only for these kinds of forms, but on EF issues in general.
30. Schacter (2001).
31. See http://www.clarksvilleonline.com/2009/09/21attention-span-can-lead-to-success-or-failure-in-school/.
32. Interestingly, Korean students seem to develop more ability at younger ages to sustain attention in large groups (Lewis et al., 2009).
33. Medina (2008).
34. Himmele & Himmele (2011).
35. This can be used as a "pretest" as well. By putting up some questions with multiple-choice answers on a whiteboard or using an ELMO, we can see which students already know the lesson, and who doesn't yet. That can help with how to differentiate. Then as a quick "posttest," we can use the same questions and see whose previously incorrect answers have changed to correct answers.
36. Medina (2008).
37. Dawson & Guare (2010); Kaufman (2010); Meltzer (2010).

6

SEMANTIC MEMORY:
FOUNDATION OF ACADEMIC LEARNING

In a 1st grade classroom, Ken read a Japanese folktale aloud to his students in preparation for a writing task. Ken, there as an ESL inclusion teacher, then led a discussion about settings in stories along with the classroom teacher. After that, he met with a small group of academically struggling English-speaking students and academically struggling English language learners. The students were going to be writing stories of their choosing. Ken wanted to brainstorm possible settings with the group before they started, so that they would name a setting in their story. He asked, "So, what are some settings we could have in a story?" One of the students said, "Japan," the setting of the story Ken had just read to the class. Ken wrote "Japan" on a piece of chart paper and said, "Very good, Japan—like in the story we just read. What's another setting, or place, we could have in a story?"

The students looked at him blankly. Ken asked the question in a couple of different ways, eliciting no response other than shrugs. Then he asked, "Like if I go to a restaurant, that's a place, isn't it, so it could be a setting for a story. So . . ."

One of the students broke in, calling out, "McDonald's!" And that was followed by KFC, Burger King, and Taco Bells, all of which Ken wrote on large chart paper. Then silence again. Ken began a similar pattern of dialogue about their school, which elicited places in that school: lunchroom, K-1, K-2, and K-3 (the names of the three kindergarten classrooms the kids had been in the previous year), computer room, and so forth. This pattern was repeated a couple of more times.

After the lesson, Ken reflected on how the students did not engage with the general concept of settings or places—schools, houses, countries, playgrounds . . . any place at all—but could only name specific places, and only once that category had been cracked open for them. This was in contrast to the more academically proficient students who had had no difficulty in the whole-class discussion talking about "settings." That is, they could talk about places in general (houses, schools, forests, palaces) as well as quickly generate a variety of specific examples of each. Ken further reflected on the number of struggling students in grades 5 and 6 who continued to experience this same difficulty of accessing abstract conceptual categories as required by more advanced school work. Why would this be?

Semantic memory[1] is our memory storehouse; it's like a giant hard drive. If you know your phone number and recognize H^2O as the symbol for water, you have a functioning semantic memory. And that is a very good thing, as just about everything we know about the world gets stored in our semantic memory. While we all have memories of personal events in our lives, such as the day we got married or the class where the teacher got extremely angry, semantic memory is where we store the facts of our lives, and much of this knowledge is abstract.

Semantic memory consists of a vast network of highly integrated information. Spreading activation is a model[2] of the way that semantic or verbal concepts are activated within long-term memory. Think of it like the concentric circles that radiate from a stone thrown into a pond, expanding out in all directions from a central point. Once a concept is activated in semantic memory, the activation radiates out to related (even distantly related) concepts. For example, if you read the word "fireman," related words and concepts are instantly activated: fire truck, smoke, water, danger, bravery. Because semantic memory is an interconnected network of concepts, we are primed to quickly recall related information. This is why so many of us do "warm-up" activities with our students to get them ready for a lesson.

It is also important to understand that the concepts stored in semantic memory are not only interconnected but also stored to represent *relationships* among concepts. These can be cause-effect (a virus can cause a cold, but cold symptoms never create a virus); if-then (if we heat water to 212 degrees Fahrenheit, then it will boil); whole-to-part (a finger is a part of a hand), probability (the noun phrase that follows the verb "commit" is likely to be something bad, like "robbery" or "murder"), among others.

This system of semantic memory lies at the heart of human thought and learning. In this chapter and the next, we explore its function and structure and ways that we can support students as they go about the challenging task of expanding and enriching their semantic memory systems in service to literacy and academic development.

Schemas

Schema[3] was introduced in Chapter 2 as synonymous with "knowledge representations." Schemas can incorporate

- Concepts: themes in literature or the distributive property
- Propositions: Democracy is the best form of government.
- Symbols: ABC, $, π
- Facts: $3\times4=12$; Mt. Everest is 29,028 feet high.
- Frames:[4]   A rectangle has four square angles, two sets of parallel lines, and opposite sides of equal length.
- Scripts:[5]   visit to the dentist, solving a two-step math problem, inferring the meaning of a word from context

Semantic memory also houses words and their meanings. If we want to know how to spell or pronounce a word, we rely on semantic memory. When we hear or read a sentence, we draw on our ability to recall the meanings of individual words and phrases from long-term semantic memory. *We can connect semantic memory with any meaning making we do or communication we have about the world around us, our experience in it, and our relationship to it.*

Learning Schemas at School

As teachers, we are responsible for ensuring that our students learn and store the astonishing amount of official curriculum about science, history, literature, and so on in their semantic memory and be able to manipulate that information as the need arises. And when we test our students, we are usually assessing their recall of subject-specific information from semantic memory.

Children form "everyday concepts" in their lives through direct experience, and they use them to deal with common situations: boiling water can burn, so watch out around a stove; dogs can bite, so avoid growling ones; flowers smell good, so they're nice to pick and give Mom. However, the goal of schooling is to help learners create what Vygotsky (1986) called "scientific concepts." Scientific concepts are abstract, consciously constructed, always tied to language, interconnected in hierarchical relationships, and have formal definitions.[6] These are found not only in science but also in the humanities and social sciences. When students are studying writing, they learn a set of interconnected concepts, such as word, phrase, sentence, paragraph, and genre. In history, they encounter a system of linked concepts on the causes of societal change, including economic, political, and cultural factors. Once students begin to get more comfortable with scientific concepts, it changes the way they think about and relate to the world. Increasingly, it allows us to manipulate ideas about the world, in the abstract.

The highly interconnected nature of our semantic memory system allows us to compare people, things, events, and places that seem to have no direct real-life connection at all.[7] If we wanted, we could compare Oreo cookies and beach balls, because they are man-made, round, and kids like them; and we could compare Genghis Khan and his Mongol armies with Plains Indians, though thousands of miles, a whole different language and culture, and a very different history separate them. This kind of abstract thinking and manipulation of schemas takes place mostly at school.

Think back to Chapter 4 where we highlighted the importance of "chunking" information. By processing larger units of information, our short-term working memory system is better able to rapidly identify information and send it to long-term memory for storage. Semantic memory plays a central role in this process because the chunks of information held in working memory are primarily drawn from semantic memory, such as the formula for finding perimeter, or the fact that "-ly" is an adverb ending.

When we teach, we are basically helping students structure knowledge into a new schema and integrate the new schema into existing schemas. It is then available as background information for new learning. As we will explore here, knowledge structures play a vital role in classroom learning.

Building Schemas

As we learn, we take schemas we've stored in semantic memory and use them to create more complex schemas. We can combine our schemas for electricity and motors and embed them into our schema for cars to create a new category, *electric cars*.[8] This ability to use and creatively combine schemas lies at the heart of human intelligence.

In school, we use our everyday concepts to construct scientific concepts. For example, we use our experience that things always seem to fall to the ground to inform the scientific schema for gravitational force. Then as we understand that better, we can learn how our moon stays in orbit and doesn't smash into Earth. Eventually, we come to understand how gravity holds entire galaxies together.

We also build schemas by making associations among events and objects within a time sequence, such as turning a car key and the motor starting, or hearing a bell and lining up after recess. We also make associations into categories. One kind of category schema is things related to a common topic, such as desserts we like to eat, or all the technical words that go with poetry. Another category might be among objects that have similar perceptual attributes, such as a tabletop and the geographic feature mesa. Finally, we can build a function category schema, such as a pencil, pen, and marker belonging together because they are all writing tools.

Expert Versus Novice

One challenge we face in the classroom is the difference between our schema knowledge about the subjects we teach, as compared to that of our students. The integration and extent of schema knowledge defines the difference between *experts* and *novices*. Students are novices and may have formed schemas about school subjects that have few, if any, connections to other schemas in their background knowledge. For example, they may remember the fact that whales are really mammals, not just big fish; but their mammal schema is not well developed, so they don't go a step further and automatically conclude that this must mean whales give birth to live babies, are warm blooded, and so on, unless they are told or read about it directly.

In contrast, as experts, classroom teachers have (or at least, should have) an interrelated network of rich and complex schemas on topics we teach. This allows us to retrieve and use information more efficiently and effectively. The question is, can our novice students keep up with the way we "experts" do it? We have all experienced, whether in the classroom to kids or outside the classroom to other adults, trying to explain something we know a lot about to someone who says, "Wait a second, you're going too fast."

Inside the classroom, it often "goes too fast" for struggling students. There are two key reasons why novice students get overwhelmed in the classroom. The first is that they are unaware of possible "substeps" that exist in concept building or problem solving, while we experts forget they're even there. The second is that the students have interconnected partially formed (or even erroneous) schemas, which separate them not only from the knowledge structures of their expert teachers, but even from more advanced students.

Noticing substeps is often connected to having scripts to help us with the steps of solving a task or problem. For example, word problems in math often seem incredibly mysterious to some students. Experts eyeball the following 4th grade problem and instantly know what operation it entails because of the language signals we pick up on, and the subsequent "substep" thinking we do. We conclude, "That's got to be a multiplication problem":

> *Mrs. Smith bought a number of reward gifts for her 2nd grade class for their hard work during the year. She made small gift bags for each of the 25 students. Each bag had a shiny pencil, a big eraser, some stickers, and a tangerine-colored highlighter. She spent $4.75 per bag. How much did she spend on her class?*

So how do we know so quickly what to do, while novices aren't so sure, even if they can multiply accurately? One big issue is linguistic. The word problem–solving schema includes the language schema and the subsequent language-related script that is processed really fast in the mind, below the conscious level. Experts notice the key words "each" and "per." We know those words signify either multiplicative reasoning or division. Then we notice where this key vocabulary falls: if it's in the body of the problem, it will almost always be a multiplication problem; if we see it in the question, it's usually the opposite operation. We also decide the flavor of the problem as early as possible—in this case, Mrs. Smith bought things for her class, which doesn't yet show us the direction of the problem, but as soon as we read a bit further and see that she's making bags for her students, we conclude it's most likely multiplication (especially due to the *"each"* signal here). So by the time an expert is ready to do the math, the language part of the word problem schema has done its job.

Another substep a novice may overlook is inhibiting any "distractor" numbers that may be present but are not needed for the calculation—in the above problem, maybe it also reads that Mrs. Smith spent three hours shopping, or that she bought an ice cream for herself for $3.50 because it was a hot day. Many struggling learners just grab any and all of the numbers they see in a problem.

We experts can help our struggling learners (the most novice of novices) by trying to deconstruct the substeps of concept building or problem solving to become more aligned with their needs. Teaching different substeps may require *explicit practice, without solving the whole problem.* Cognitive load researchers recommend that we provide students with lots of examples of problems with all the steps worked out.[9] In these ways, we can help students harness their attention to practice the substeps without the brain getting hijacked toward an answer search, overloading working memory and diverting attention away from a focus on learning the substeps. The best teachers understand how they got to be experts and remain empathetic to the novice perspective.

For younger children, a lot of math skill is based on the number sense schema—what the number is right before or after a number. Experts may not even think of that anymore and lose sight of the fact that the ability to do mental math in subtraction is based on the number sense schema and the ability to mentally "look backward" on a number line. And as students get older, math involves an increasing amount of language schema and substep problem-solving scripts.

The second expert/novice issue is illustrated by this situation: A class is learning about life that can be found in freshwater ponds, with a culminating activity of a class visit to a local pond. They will be taking water samples and looking at the kinds of invertebrates they find in order to evaluate the health of the pond water. They learn what an invertebrate is and the names of a few invertebrates that can be found in pond water, and how different types of invertebrates can be indicators of the relative health of pond water. Most students can participate in further conversations and readings that expand this experiment to other environments, but other students—even those who successfully did the experiment—can't keep up.

More expert students can take the knowledge they got from the classroom activity and field trip one step further into the abstract and connect schemas without prompting—that the health of *any* pond water can be determined by the invertebrate population, not only the pond they will be taking the trip to, and that health of other environments may also be evaluated by the type of organisms present there. Then the new conversations and readings are filtered through a rich conceptual web. But struggling (novice) students often do not create a schema for this beyond the class activities and field trip, so they continue to struggle.

Teaching Point: Helping Students Build Schemas

There are a number of things we can do related to schema formation and closing the expert/novice gap.

Mapping

In *How Learning Works* (2010), the authors[10] suggest a number of research-based teaching ideas for helping students organize knowledge in ways that are connected, meaningful, and flexible. One of their suggestions is to map out our own knowledge structure for a particular subject area so that we can be better aware of our knowledge organization. Creating a visual representation of our knowledge of a subject can highlight key concepts and relationships that are fundamental to a unit of study. These representations can be created as we teach a unit, ideally coconstructed, with the class helping decide how information is connected.

This mapping can be extended to periodically helping students see how all parts of the unit fit together, how the activity they do Wednesday is related to that thing they did Monday and what they'll be doing Thursday morning. As the authors note, "Do not assume that your students, especially those who are new to the content area, will see the logical organization of the materials you are presenting" (Ambrose et al., 2010, p. 60). Helping students see these connections can be done visually with maps, or verbally, as in the following strategy.

Essential Questions and Sharing Unit Goals

Another suggestion is to sensitize students at the start of a unit to what's coming —telling students what the overarching unit goals are and where the unit is going. Essential questions[11] at the start of a unit can also help students build schemas about the new content by helping them connect to broader themes they already have some knowledge about and experience with things they are somewhat experts in already, in contrast to the novice role most will have as they start learning new content. For example, in the unit on life in a freshwater pond, we could start out by asking, "Does pollution affect you and your life?

If so, how?" Most students will probably know something about pollution, and the effects they name are likely applicable to pond water, so students can connect *pollution—water health—invertebrates* more easily (through spreading activation).[12]

Emphasize Comparisons

Brain and learning guru David Sousa (2011) has created a helpful aphorism: *we store by similarities; we retrieve by differences.* In other words, our brain automatically connects schemas by similar categories, but when we go to retrieve that information, we have to sort through differences among them in order to select just the right knowledge representation. Harnessing this aphorism in our teaching can help in schema building.

For instance, when we learn the word "considerate," we store it in the "nice to people" category, along with similar words like "kind," "helpful," and "sensitive." But when we want to use a word that means "nice to people," we have to choose just the right word for the situation, and this requires that we focus on the differences among the category's words.

Arecelis is writing about a time her best friend, Marta, offered to give her a ride to gymnastics class because she knew Arecelis's mom was sick. Arceelis decides that "considerate" is the best word to describe her friend's actions, as it means *helpful when you're not necessarily expected to be helpful.* She chooses it over "kind" (helpful in a gentle, almost loving way), "helpful" (you help someone when they have a problem), or "sensitive" (in tune with the feelings of another person), given the context. But they're all so close in meaning!

When we teach the word "considerate," we need to help students move it into the "nice to people" category, where they already store "helpful," "kind," and "sensitive." But we also should emphasize how being considerate is being nice when you don't have to be, or being proactively helpful, which is a meaning that "helpful," "sensitive," and "kind" do not really carry, because they will be retrieving the word based on contrasting shades of meaning. By intentionally helping students understand the differences among similar words (or concepts, symbols, frames—really any element of a schema), we facilitate their future retrieval from semantic memory.

Figure 6.1 is an example of how graphic elements can be used to clarify shades of meaning. It is from Ken's 2012 book, *My Fantastic Words Book,* a young student's thesaurus. These kinds of graphic displays can be turned into a word wall or vocabulary learning practice activities, in addition to being a word resource.

Figure 6.1 | Thesaurus Page

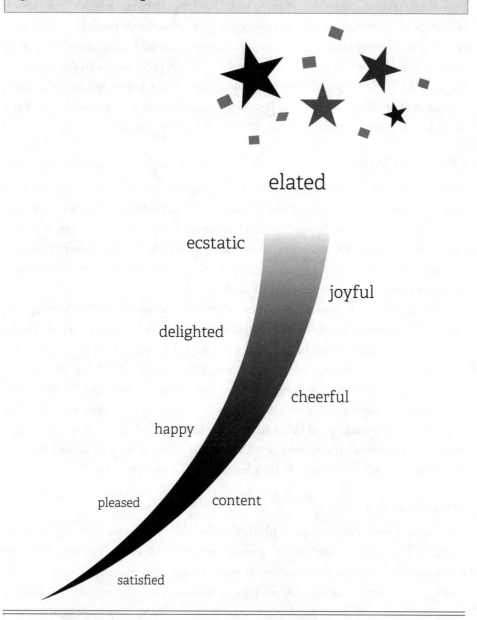

elated

ecstatic

joyful

delighted

cheerful

happy

pleased   content

satisfied

Source: From *My Fantastic Words Book* (page 29) by K. Pranksy, Northampten, MA: Collaborative for Educational Services. Copyright 2012 by Collaborative for Educational Services. Artwork by 4Eyes Design.

Reinforce Connections

Periodically revisiting our concept maps with the class to take stock of where we're at is helpful. Students can also make their own concept maps as the unit unfolds, which helps deepen their schema building. The same goes for objectives and essential questions. Asking students to make their own connections among concepts positions the students as active learners: "How is this case different (or similar) to the discussion we had last week about the causes of the Civil War? Turn to your neighbor, and come to some conclusion about this. I'll pick a name out of the can to call on in about two minutes."

Sorting Activities

Asking students to sort cases, theories, or concepts into categories helps deepen their understanding,[13] which is another way of saying that it helps them to make semantic connections among schemas. In class, we can have students do all different types of sorting tasks from simple to complex. In the pond water unit described earlier, students could sort the invertebrates more simply by appearance, or in a more sophisticated way according to the water pollution level they would be found in.

Sorting tasks can help us quickly assess where our students are in their learning. For example, in a science class on the ocean, students could sort sea animals such as fish, sharks, porpoises, turtles, and so on, in any number of ways. By asking them to categorize the animals however they want, we start to see how they are thinking. Then if we ask them to figure out another way, we can see how far their understanding goes. Students who mainly categorize by superficial features—that is, by appearance—are showing us that they have not yet really understood the main scientific features of what they are learning (e.g., biological categories such as warm vs. cold blooded, or the level of the ocean they inhabit). We see that our teaching job—and their learning job—is not yet done.

Multiple Pathways

In Chapter 2, one of our core principles is that the brain seeks to learn through multiple channels. This certainly informs how semantic memory stores information best. The more connections it can make, the more retention there will be. As teachers, we should always avoid presenting information (or requiring that students learn) through just one learning channel. The more different kinds of experiences that students can engage in, the deeper the learning will go.

Teaching Point: Metaphorical Thinking

Unlike other animals, we can learn about historical events we never witnessed and famous people we've never met. We can debate passionately about democratic ideals. We can learn about things not in front of us now, such as how volcanoes erupt, without having to take our students to see one. Sometimes, though, we are left scratching our head as to how to get abstract concepts across in our teaching. As students get older, what they need to learn will increasingly be abstract ideas they read about in heavy, dense texts and hear about via equally heavy verbal explanations. What can we do when our students don't understand those terms through text and academic explanations?

So often, we need to come up with alternative ways to help students understand complex academic concepts. If we are stuck having only one perspective on how to teach, it can be very hard to help students understand a new concept if they don't get it the first time around. Doing it the same way yet another time usually doesn't help much. We need to become skilled at helping students build rich, diverse, and *meaningful* connections among concepts stored in long-term memory.

Metaphors and Similes

One way to do help students make connections is to use metaphors and similes to link knowledge schemas together, which can help reveal new and unexpected insights. For example, nearly 400 years ago, our understanding of the human body was propelled forward when an English doctor, William Harvey, first got the idea to think of the human heart as a hydraulic pump.[14] For young students who are stuck in adding by ones, we can say that learning to skip count is like a cheetah compared to a turtle. To help students understand the structure of a cell, we can explain that the cell with its various organelles is like the school—the nucleus is the principal's office, the cell walls are the walls of the school, and so forth.

Personification

Students can ground their understanding of new complex concepts in familiar real-world images and concepts. For example, photosynthesis is like eating; division is like sharing cookies among friends; civil wars are like fighting with siblings. As we have learned, connecting to prior knowledge is essential in learning. Personification is a way to connect the subject being learned to students' personal lives.

We do need to be aware that in diverse settings, any images we choose are likely to be affected by culture and student backgrounds. In one of Ken's classes, a 4th grade pull-out ESL group, he used a hiking trip to the mountains to represent the structure of chapter books. The beginning is often the least interesting part of the book, but it's like driving to the mountains, because unless we drive there, we can never climb. Then the middle sections are like the climb up to the top; the plot tension and excitement tend to increase as we get closer to the climax (the peak). Finally, just as the mountain trip ends with us coming down the mountain, the end of a chapter book also ends with a "coming down" feel. Ken drew this out on a piece of cardboard.

As he discussed this with the class, he got the feeling that it wasn't working. The kids weren't seeing this metaphor as a means to understanding story structure. Finally, Ken asked, "Have any of you gone hiking or climbed a mountain before?" No. Then he asked, "Well, do you think getting to the top of the mountain would be the best part of the trip?" No. The students talked about how hard it would be, that it might be boring walking all that way, and so on. Finally, Ken asked, "So what do you think would be the most fun, exciting, best part of a trip like that?" Every student said running down the mountain at the end! So in their mind, Ken was using a metaphor that described the final chapter of a chapter book as being the most exciting one—which, of course, was the opposite intent of his metaphor!

Can you think of metaphors, similes, or personifications for the following concepts that fit the grade and subject you teach and would make sense to your students: *solving the Pythagorean theorem; cell structure; what makes the seasons; subtraction; monarchy?* (Our suggestions are at the end of the chapter.)

Learning and Forgetting in the Classroom

One question many of us ask ourselves is, why do so many students seem to forget things so quickly? They seem to understand it one day, and by the next day, poof. Gone! For instance, why do some students seem to learn the rules for solving a math problem or punctuating a sentence yet not apply the very same rules when actually solving a math problem or writing a sentence?

Short-term Versus Long-term Development

There is an important difference between short-term learning and long-term development. It's possible for students to temporarily store knowledge in long-term memory for hours, or days, or even weeks without permanently filing it away.[15] All new learning must be connected to prior knowledge, but the fewer connections there are, the less the new learning will stick. Isolated bits of information are more difficult to locate and use productively because there are fewer neural pathways leading to them. That is another reason why it is important to teach new concepts through multiple pathways. If something has been taught verbally, then also deepen the connections with a visual example. If students have been writing about a topic, also have them try to verbalize the information in a class discussion, debate, or role play.

Information that has little meaning for students, such as empty formulas, word forms with no meaning attached, or jumbled concepts, is not deeply integrated into the neural system and will often be quickly forgotten. Meaning is in these neural networks, and to understand classroom content is to activate the relevant neural connections. Knowledge that is connected to rich webs of schemas sticks better and enables students to think more and more like experts. It facilitates the transfer of knowledge or, using Feuerstein's term, *transcendence.*

We should not be satisfied with teaching for short-term learning to make it through the tsunami of curriculum, because much of that information is forgotten within a relatively short period of time. And even if some of that information stays in for a longer period of time, it is not integrated well enough to be of much use. Being aware of the following four things can help us make sense of why learning often seems to just drop away over time.

1. Consolidation

After we initially learn a new word or concept, it may take hours, days, even months before it becomes fully integrated into semantic memory. This period of consolidation[16] is aided by repeated exposure to the new ideas and opportunities to use it. When assessing learning, the real test is not whether students can recall the information at the end of that class, but whether they can remember it the next day or after several days. Students need time and repeated practice to internalize learning in a permanent form.

2. Prior Knowledge

We have beaten the "background" drum many times in this book. New information and concepts that can be connected to preexisting schemas are more likely to stick.

3. Practice

The goal of practice is to repeatedly activate the new information and stimulate and strengthen new neural connections (making goop). It may help to think of this process as tightening a screw. Just a turn or two will fix the screw to a wall, but over time it will become wobbly and fall out. The screw needs multiple turns so that it is flush with the wall and stable. Productive practice (speaking and writing) are stronger turns of the screw than receptive practice (reading and listening). Chapter 10 is devoted to an exploration of practice.

When learning is grounded in background, has had enough practice, and has been revisited enough to keep it from dropping away, voilà—it sticks and becomes not just short-term learning but long-term development, available for future problem solving and making sense of the world.

4. Multiple Connections

As discussed in Chapter 2, successful teachers are able to help learners build new networks linking words, images, and attributes through classroom lessons that afford students multiple pathways and multiple exposures to learning. This process connects back to background grounding. If we can help students connect to a preexisting network of vocabulary or experience, we facilitate the integration of the new learning into semantic memory. And then when we teach, if we plan on more than one sensory input in our lessons as appropriate—such as hearing and seeing, touching and hearing, smelling and seeing—we intentionally allow students to make connections through multiple pathways.

How Information Is Stored in Semantic Memory

Learning about semantic memory can help us make sense of many situations we have all experienced with students, when they left us with the vague feeling that they were showing us something about the way they think, but we just couldn't quite put our finger on it. We need to better understand two basic ideas about semantic memory to understand our students better. First, there are different ways to organize information stored in semantic memory, and this has direct implications for teaching and learning. Second, the development of semantic memory has a cultural foundation: as children develop, their cognitive systems are shaped, to a significant degree, by the language, cultural interactions, and experiences that surround them. We explore these ideas in the next sections of this chapter and in Chapter 7.

Semantic Knowledge Drawers

One way to conceptualize semantic knowledge is to think of a vast system of mental file cabinets with an unbounded number of drawers (Figure 6.2). Each drawer has a specific label, and when we open a drawer, we have access to all kinds of information about that topic.

Figure 6.2 | **Semantic Memory Drawers**

Suppose Francis and Ken are reading a news story about basketball. When they open their mental basketball drawer, they find all kinds of words, images, and concepts stored there: *ball, net, basket, backboard, center, referee, power forward, NBA, rules, fouls, uniforms, behavioral norms, dunks, three pointers,* and so on. And, while much of the information is in words, some of it is stored in images of basketball courts and famous players. Episodic memory also contributes: they have mental videos of spectacular shots and famous games they saw, and games they've played themselves. Any given drawer in our semantic memory cabinet can be stuffed full of information or be fairly empty. But while Ken and Francis's basketball drawer is pretty full, there's not much rolling around in their nuclear physics drawer.

Information stored in a semantic memory drawer is organized, and this allows us to readily retrieve old information and store away new information about a topic. Within each drawer, we could have all we know organized alphabetically, say, or color-coded. There are different ways knowledge networks can be organized, and that informs how we can most easily find information in semantic memory. The next section of this chapter describes the organization most common to many of us, and certainly that matches the organization of the school curriculum and our instruction: hierarchical networks.

Hierarchical Networks

Humans have the ability to store immense amounts of information in systems of hierarchically organized networks. These networks connect closely related information into superordinate (larger, more inclusive, and overarching) and subordinate (smaller, more specific, and detailed) categories. A subordinate category contains all the features of its higher superordinate category, plus one (or more) distinguishing trait.[17] *The higher up the category chain we go, the broader the concept; the lower we go, the more discrete the details and examples.*

Any information can be stored in these types of hierarchical relationships. Hierarchical relationships are also referred to as *taxonomic,* and that is the term we will mostly use. They allow for quick and accurate access to information, as required in real-time interactions. The complexity of these networks of information in semantic memory is demonstrated in Figure 6.3 (from Gluck et al., 2008, p. 100).

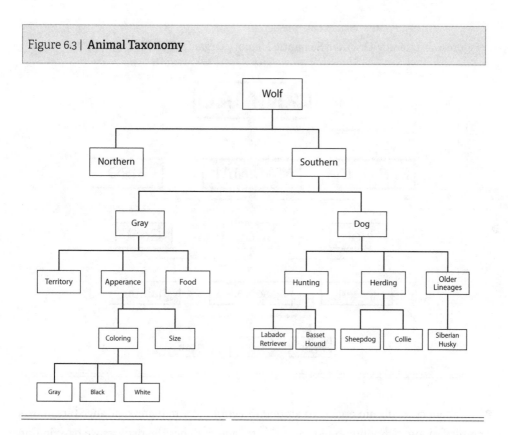

Figure 6.3 | **Animal Taxonomy**

This sort of categorical thinking undergirds much of a literacy culture's approach to understanding of the world, first generated in the home and then refined and developed in the formal learning environment of school.[18] Proficiency in classroom learning is nearly inseparable from facility with this type of semantic memory structure and access.

What might this look like in the classroom? For example, it would be quite common for a teacher to ask her class to think about dogs as a segue to a lesson about mammals. Literacy-oriented students in our schools are likely to be oriented through taxonomic semantic memory to this task, and when they open their "dog" drawer, they would access an information chain such as Figure 6.4.

Figure 6.4 | **Literacy-Oriented Semantic Memory Organization for *Dog***

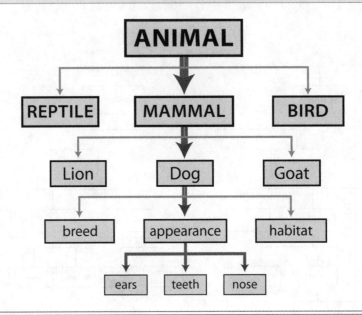

School curricula are organized around categories (content areas) arranged in a taxonomic fashion. Schooling builds on, adds to, and enriches the drawers we have in our information cabinet. Academic subject areas such as science, mathematics, and history are typically introduced to students as topics with multiple categories. In science, there are differences between physical and social sciences. And within physical science, there is biology, physics, and chemistry (among many others), and each of these have many subcategories. A principal organizing feature of the sciences is its taxonomic structure—that is, information flows from broader categories to more specific subcategories to individual examples of those categories, and the farther down the information tree one goes, the more discrete the details that differentiate one subgroup from another. The taxonomic aspect of semantic memory is the one that most separates literacy-oriented students from non-literacy-oriented and culturally disrupted learners in a school setting.

In the anecdote that opened this chapter, the students in Ken's group could access neither the subordinate categories for *setting*, such as "school," "restaurant," "house," "forest," nor even specific examples of subordinate categories lower down the tree, such as "McDonald's," without prompting with a question with a taxonomic structure: "So, what are some settings we could have in a story?" For the children in that class who were comfortably in sync with a taxonomic organization of semantic memory, the following "tree" of knowledge might have become activated (see Figure 6.5).

Figure 6.5 | **One Possible Settings "Branch"**

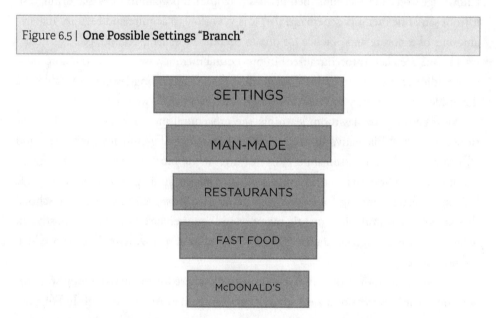

A discussion with these students about "settings" would proceed as we'd assume it would, as indeed it did with some students in that 1st grade classroom, because the flow of the students' semantic memory access and retrieval matches the top-down flow of the discussion.

However, this structure might look quite differently for students who struggled with this activity. We continue to explore this issue and its implications for the teaching-learning process in Chapter 7 as we turn to the social shaping of semantic memory.

Procedural Memory

Before we close this chapter on semantic memory, we need to mention another long-term memory system where learning is stored: procedural memory.[19] Procedural memory stores a different kind of knowledge than semantic memory, which stores knowledge that we can consciously access. Procedural memory holds implicit knowledge, which can't be accessed consciously and can't be verbalized, such as the memory required for muscle movements. Knowledge stored in procedural memory has two other important features that distinguish it from semantic memory schemas. First, it is very slow to acquire and requires massive amounts of exposure and practice for one to become proficient. Second, once its neural tracks have been laid (proceduralized) in procedural memory, we can access it automatically, without conscious thought. The upside is that it's quite long-lasting and stable; the downside is that it is very resistant to change, if we ever decide we need to.

Most germane to classroom learning, the procedural memory system is where we store grammar. While native speakers use their knowledge of grammar to accurately and effortlessly produce an astonishing range of utterances, most people cannot say much about how their grammar actually works. If we explicitly study grammar, such as while learning a second language or learning the basic parts of speech in elementary school, that knowledge is stored in semantic memory and can then be accessed consciously. But when we start speaking, our brain switches over to the grammar we have in our procedural memory system.

Procedural memory's downside comes into play here for many struggling students who are English learners or dialect speakers of nonstandard American English. For English learners, it will take a long time and a lot of repetition to establish stable, appropriate grammatical systems in procedural memory. We can't rush it even if the Common Core wants students to deeply analyze text, because part of that analysis is deconstructing the grammatical organization and flow of English. It takes years to develop grammatical skills in another language, and while that process is occurring, students will continually make mistakes.

For nonstandard English dialect speakers, it's a bit different. They already have a stable, established grammatical system in procedural memory in English. The problem is that different dialects differ in some or many respects from what is called the standard dialect. The resistance to change built into procedural memory makes it extremely challenging to develop a parallel grammatical system in that same language. We may think different dialect speakers of English are making "mistakes," but that is an issue with our value judgment, not the objective reality. Language differences are not language pathologies, communication disorders, laziness, or resistance. It's the procedural memory system moving like a sloth.

They say that a child's language is her "language of love." So rejecting a child's language use by labeling elements of it "mistakes," or "not good enough," is dissing the child's family, home, and community. Yet, students do have to eventually master standard dialect (formal register English) to be able to "do school" well.[20]

Teaching Point: Working with Procedural Memory

The following teaching suggestions are for students struggling with the formal, academic English of schooling and are compatible with the way the procedural memory works.

1. Provide "Comprehensible Input"

Human beings require massive exposure to a new language they are trying to learn to lay down grammar tracks in procedural memory. For the process to work, this language input must be comprehensible.[21] If we sat in a university lecture in China every day for a year, it's likely we would have barely learned any Chinese, because none of it would have been comprehensible to us. So in our classrooms, we have to strive to make our language and instruction as comprehensible as possible. Among other things, this could entail

- lots of visuals,
- pausing between phrase breaks and sentences,
- frequent rephrasing and repetition,
- using our voice intentionally to emphasize stress or rhythm,
- some slowing down of our speech for beginning English learners,
- paring sophisticated vocabulary away from around the words we want to stand out,
- providing time and space for students to ask clarification questions, and
- continually checking our students' comprehension, to serve as a formative assessment as to whether the level of our comprehensible input is appropriate or not.

Just because students nod when we ask if they understand doesn't mean they actually understand. We have to go out of our way to build comprehension checks into our everyday routines. Once we start doing this, we'll be amazed what our students are *not* understanding in our lessons.

Most of these strategies are just as useful with non-literacy-oriented and culturally disrupted learners who do not own formal register, Standard American English dialect as they are for English language learners.

2. Provide for Lots of Practice Time

In the same way that students need lots of comprehensible input, they need lots of opportunities to meaningfully and actively use the new language, orally and in writing. They need a chance to try out new vocabulary and grammar and get feedback on both the language form and meaning. Too many English language learners sit quietly in our classrooms, too fearful and shy to speak up. When we encourage their active participation—within a safe classroom environment that honors the limbic system—we build not only their confidence but also their language skills.

For different dialect speakers, this can be accomplished through a kind of contrastive linguistics activity. Periodically, have a class take something from their text and translate it into their dialect (e.g., how they'd say it to their buds when they're not in school). Conversely, they could take song lyrics or something friends would say and turn it into a "how the teacher would say it" text. Students at all ages have a great time with this, and trying to "say it like my teacher" is excellent practice for academic English.

3. Provide Language Supports

Because we tend to learn what we pay attention to, students need opportunities to really focus on language development, even in content classes. For example, they need to combine grammar stored in procedural memory with words (and their meanings) stored in semantic memory. All school subjects require students to develop their linguistic repertoire, and struggling learners can benefit from focused attention on (and practice of) these new forms. For example, students can benefit from the study of models of good writing and examples of the kind of language we are expecting in an essay or science report.

Providing students with sentence starters models specific language they can use in oral or written reports (e.g., "This essay discusses . . ."; "This issue is important because . . .";

"To conclude, . . ."). Jeff Zwiers, the academic conversation guru, suggests using "discussion cards" to structure language use in small-group work.[22] The group has several cards in an envelope. A student picks a card and has to start his sentence with a particular phrase. He has another envelope with instructions to do something with what another group member just said. Maybe the card says, "Add something to . . ." ("Add something to what was just said"), and that student has to add something to what the first student said. Or maybe it says, "Give the opposing point of view about . . ." This works well for 5th grade and higher for small-group work, but we can also use it as a whole-class activity even with kindergarten-ers during classroom discussions. Figure 6.6 gives some examples of the two kinds of cards.

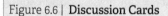

Figure 6.6 | **Discussion Cards**

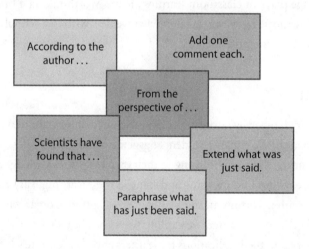

Words and phrases that show up in a state's standardized testing (e.g., "According to the selection…" in ELA) can be used to great effect on discussion cards. If we weave these into sentence frames, discussion cards, and our instructional language throughout the year, when students come up against those same words and phrases on the test, it will be a con-fidence booster ("Hey, I know that!") rather than a confidence sapper ("God, something else I can't understand!"). The various elements of vocabulary or grammar can be used as language objectives in the same way that content objectives are helpful in sharpening the learning goal for struggling learners. Here's a very short list of some language features that could be used as language objectives with select students or even the whole class:

- Connecting words ("in contrast," "however," "although," etc., instead of "but")
- Creating compound and complex sentences
- General academic vocabulary that is not specific to a subject, and so is not usually explicitly taught, and which many students may not really understand well (e.g., "explain," "describe," "structure," "process")
- Verbs and expressions of belief (*"could," "might," "probably," "almost certain,"* etc.)

Whole books have been written about academic language and the classroom.[23] This has been a quick survey of some of the many moves that we can make around explicit language teaching, connected to how procedural memory functions. Because of the pivotal role language plays in classroom learning, it was worth taking a brief detour away from semantic memory. However, most of what we deal with in a school setting involves knowledge stored in semantic memory.

Conclusion

Semantic memory is where we store information, connect information together, and organize that information. We enhance student engagement and learning if we help ensure that students can connect classroom learning to their own real-life knowledge and experience, ensure that students can find meaning and value in their learning, vary the ways we help students engage with new content, and highlight the taxonomic organization of classroom information. In the next chapter, we explore ways that our social environment shapes semantic memory and the implications for learners and classroom teaching practices.

METAPHOR/SIMILE/PERSONIFICATION IDEAS

- Solving the Pythagorean Theorem: "We often like to find shortcuts."
- Cell structure: the organization of the school building, how different rooms have different functions, messages go back and forth
- What makes the seasons: "When we tilt our faces toward the sun, we feel warmer."

- Subtraction: when a big brother or sister takes something of yours
- Monarchy: in a home, the parent or grandparent may be the "absolute ruler"

1. Tulving & Donaldson (1972); Grossman & Koenig (2002).
2. Collins & Loftus (1975).
3. Baddeley et al. (2009); Bower (2000).
4. We are following Baddeley et al. (2009) in this use of the term "frame" as "information about objects and their properties" (p. 128). Note that this is not what "frame" means in cultural studies of the mind when they refer to the human ability to impose a set of conditions or beliefs when interpreting some phenomena or solving a problem (Frawley, 1997).
5. Grossman & Koenig (2002).
6. Swain et al. (2010).
7. See Kahneman (2011) for his discussion of "system 1."
8. Bower (2000).
9. Renkle & Atkinson (2010).
10. Ambrose et al. (2010).
11. Wiggins & McTighe (2005).
12. If they don't know much about pollution, the essential question could shift to something like, "Would you rather eat clean food or dirty food? Why?"
13. Ambrose et al. (2010).
14. Harvey (1628/1941).
15. Gluck et al. (2008).
16. Ibid.
17. Taylor (1995).
18. Willis (2006).
19. Gluck et al. (2008); Schumann, et al. (2004).
20. Delpit (1996).
21. Echevarria, Vogt, & Short (2008).
22. Zwiers (2007); Zwiers & Crawford (2011).
23. Schleppegrell (2004); also see Zacarian (2013) for a discussion of ways to promote academic development among English language learners.

SEMANTIC MEMORY:
A SOCIOCULTURAL PERSPECTIVE

7

Children's home and community environments play an important role in shaping their memory systems. This is particularly true of semantic memory. Semantic memory stores the system of symbols and meanings that comprise much of culture,[1] while culture helps select and shape much of the information stored in semantic memory. According to Russian psychologist and Vygotsky scholar Yuriy Karpov, school is the main place that school-age children in a literacy-oriented culture develop their conceptual schemas.[2] U.S. public schools are cultural institutions and are run by society's dominant classes. They reflect the values, beliefs, and thinking skills of a culture oriented toward literacy practices. Schools provide access to many of the culturally appropriate schemas that animate a society, which includes cognitive tools, symbols, and scripts. In this chapter, we explore ways that semantic memory is shaped by social interaction and how that affects academic learning.[3]

Vygotsky (1986) argues that the development of "higher mental functions"—that is, cognitive skills that enable us to use logic, do math, engage in abstract reasoning, and think metaphorically—originates in social life. It develops as children interact within meaningful activities with more experienced adults and peers. A growing body of cross-cultural cognitive research supports the notion that cognitive skills such as perception and memory are shaped by one's social environment.[4] Michael Cole and Sylvia Scribner (1974), leading researchers in the cultural roots of cognitive development, succinctly stated the core insight of this field more than 35 years ago:

> But just as it is fanciful to conceive of man existing outside of social life, we cannot imagine any intellectual function that does not have a sociocultural character. Perception, memory, and thinking all develop as part of the general socialization of a child and are inseparably bound up with the patterns of activity, communication, and social relations into which he enters. (p. 8)

This perspective has two implications for us. First, cultural diversity reflects cognitive diversity.[5] Learners from communities that are different from our own are more likely to engage in ways of thinking that are different from what we expect or are used to. Second, the way we think in our culture is not universal—it is the product of a set of historical-cultural processes.[6] Students who have not experienced the same types of cultural mediation that U.S. schooling is built on need support as they struggle to internalize a new cultural system. And this difference will be reflected in diverse ways to store and integrate information in semantic memory. It's not easy for learners or their teachers in diverse settings. Yet, what alternative do we—and our students—have but to try to make sense of the diversity of our classrooms and make it work for everyone equitably? We explore ways to address these issues in this chapter.

Memory and Social Practices

Given the symbiotic relationship between literacy-oriented communities and schooling, it's not surprising that children raised in middle-class or affluent, literacy-oriented homes consistently achieve at higher levels than their economically and culturally diverse peers.[7] The lower academic achievement of many culturally and linguistically diverse learners is rooted in mismatches between the demands of school learning and the way they have been trained to learn in their home and community,[8] which includes semantic memory organization.[9] If we do not explicitly help non-literacy-oriented and culturally disrupted students learn the skills that literacy-oriented students own, the achievement gap will continue to remain as large as it has always been.

In saying this, we recognize that the capacity to store knowledge about the world in webs of semantic memory networks is universally available to people of all cultures and backgrounds. Semantic memory networks develop through everyday life experiences as well as schooled learning events. However, the orientation toward the use of particular organizational schemas in semantic memory differs across cultures, communities, and individual learners, and it is this orientation that helps sort students so consistently into higher and lower achievers.[10] One of these orientations is how information is organized in semantic memory. Literacy-oriented students who seem to do so well in school are not smarter—they are luckier, because their home and school worlds are seamlessly intertwined.

Cognitive Tools

We noted earlier that artifacts, symbols, tools, and ways of thinking and believing in a culture mold and channel the human mind and connect our present to our cultural past. In sociocultural learning theory, this is called the "mediated mind."[11] Just as physical tools extend the abilities of the human body, cognitive tools extend the abilities of the human mind to help us to attend, remember, and problem solve. When children first encounter a new cognitive tool, they require assistance from an adult or more advanced peer to understand its function and effectively use it. Over time, if properly mediated, a child makes the tool her own; she can use it independently and creatively to solve academic or everyday problems, and skillfully interpret and respond to what she encounters in the world. Schools play a fundamental role in students' further development of these cognitive tools. In culturally diverse settings, there is often a clash between school expectations and the cognitive tools that some children have developed in their own communities during their preschool years.

Barbara Rogoff (2003), an anthropologist who has studied cognitive development in many societies around the world, argues that cognitive tools include language, mathematics, narrative structures, and scientific systems. All of these systems have their origin in the broader society, and they are internalized and stored in semantic memory by children as they interact with adults and peers in home and community.

Two examples of mediating artifacts in math are manipulatives and fingers, both of which can help us count. Arabic numerals and algorithms are math-related symbols we use—though in other parts of the world, math symbols and tools may be different, such as in Iran where their numerals are ١, ٢, ٣, ٤ (1, 2, 3, 4). In much of Europe, it's 1.007,78, not 1,007.78. When we internalize and automatize the use of artifacts, symbols, and tools of a given context in long-term memory, we can much more easily solve problems related to it.

Another example is that the spatial organization of a multiplication problem affects our ability to solve it. Students are taught to set up multiplication problems "properly," using a "math script" stored in semantic memory, which allows them to draw upon their cultural intelligence to solve the problem correctly. To appreciate this point, how hard would it be for you to solve this multiplication problem, with its horizontal format?

$$839 \times 976 = ?^{12}$$

For most of us, it would be a real challenge to keep track of the calculations unless the numbers are arranged vertically. But if we lived in a culture where the abacus is a cultural tool for solving math problems, such as Japan, the arrangement of the problem may not be a barrier at all to solving it. Or how about needing to do long division in France, which looks like this:

$$\overline{493} \,\bigl|\, \underline{5}$$
$$43 \,\bigl|\, 98,6$$
$$30$$

Sociocultural researchers argue that language is the most important cognitive tool that humans have developed. Language is more than just a tool for communication; it plays an essential role in cognitive processing. It is a primary bridge that helps us move cognitive tools encountered through social interactions into our semantic memory system.

> [Language] is one of the processes through which external experience is converted into internal understandings. Language makes thinking more abstract, flexible, and independent from the immediate stimuli. (Bodrova & Leong, 2007, p. 14)

When we internalize cognitive tools, our culture does part of the thinking for us. The more literacy-oriented semantic memory tools we have, the more "effortless" our thinking becomes in school, and the better we do.

Amplifiers

Newman, Griffin, and Cole (1989) use the word "amplifiers" for cognitive tools. They conducted some groundbreaking research about the role of semantic memory in school learning in a diverse 3rd grade classroom in California. The class was studying Native Americans. Their hypothesis was that higher-achieving students achieve more because of what they know about the subject *prior* to instruction. In other words, they believed that higher-achieving students have more relevant background information, largely stored in semantic memory.

The unit was introduced on day 1 and the information written up in chart form: *Food Getting, Government,* and *Homes* were the columns, with descriptors, or concepts, for those categories from various Native tribes as the rows (see Figure 7.1). At the end of the first day, the chart was taken down, and the students were then given a multiple-choice pretest about the information. The unit was then taught over two weeks and, according to the researchers, was engaging, hands-on, and meaningful. At the end of the unit, the pretest was readministered as a posttest. The researchers hypothesized that the higher pretest achievers would score higher on the posttest as well, because they would have known more about the topic from the beginning.

But the researchers found that the group of students who scored highest on the post-test actually scored marginally *lower* on the pretest; their peers who scored lower on the posttest scored marginally *higher* on the pretest! Hypothesis blown! And when they looked more deeply at the test results, they found something even more revealing: the primary difference between the higher- and lower-achieving students was in their *wrong* answers on the pretest. The students who scored higher on the posttest had chosen wrong answers *from within the same category* as the right answers (e.g., choosing "tepee" if the right answer was "wigwam") in the pretest. They were attuned to the organization of the curriculum by taxonomic categories, which was replicated in the chart's organization. In contrast, the students who scored lower on the posttest had been more likely to select wrong pretest answers at random, *from outside the category* of the right answer.

The researchers concluded that the lower achievers had two curricula to learn: (1) the external, information curriculum and (2) the "hidden curriculum"[13] of how it is taught and organized. In other words, their semantic memory systems were not well aligned with the organization of school curriculum. Double the learning to do, with guidance in only half of it!

Remember that in academic learning, students learn what they pay attention to, and they can really only pay attention to one thing at a time. They will be less likely to improve their performance vis-à-vis the higher-achieving students until their attention is intention-ally placed on the following:

Figure 7.1 | **Native Americans Chart**

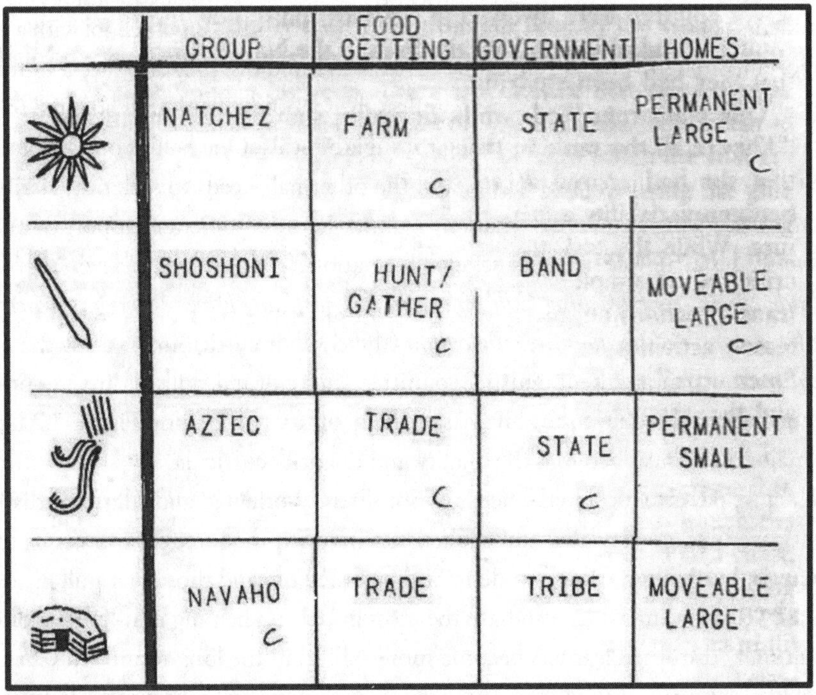

	GROUP	FOOD GETTING	GOVERNMENT	HOMES
☀	NATCHEZ	FARM c	STATE	PERMANENT LARGE c
╲	SHOSHONI	HUNT/ GATHER c	BAND	MOVEABLE LARGE c
〜	AZTEC	TRADE c	STATE c	PERMANENT SMALL
〰	NAVAHO c	TRADE	TRIBE	MOVEABLE LARGE

- the *knowledge organization* of the curriculum itself;
- how to use this *knowledge organization* to their advantage;
- practice in using this *knowledge organization*.

Higher achievers already are aligned with this hidden curriculum. That knowledge, stored largely in semantic memory, enhances their school performance, and in turn, the school curriculum further develops their semantic memory strengths. The researchers termed this mutual resonance "amplification." Literacy-oriented students walk into kindergarten predisposed to school-based organization of semantic memory, which amplifies their academic learning, because the school curriculum, and usually our instruction, flows taxonomically. In turn, learning at school amplifies their skill with taxonomically organized semantic memory, which in turn facilitates school learning even more. The rich get richer!

Conversely, if a student is not predisposed to a taxonomic organization of semantic memory, it adds to the burden of their classroom learning. Remember that while many of our most vulnerable learners—English language learners, students with learning disabilities, students of poverty, students from disrupted backgrounds—enter school with a variety of important strengths that we should always try to build on, they also face a number of significant challenges in a school setting, unless the school curriculum is adapted to *them*.

It's like we need to view our teaching through bifocals. One half of our lens needs to look at the explicit school curriculum, and the other half needs to seek out, clarify, and teach the underlying structure of that curriculum, in order to better support our culturally diverse and/or novice students' schema formation. In Ken's book *Beneath the Surface: the Hidden Realities of Teaching Culturally and Linguistically Diverse Young Learners, K–6* (2008), he calls this the *quantity curriculum* (the content curriculum) versus the *quality curriculum*,[14] which are the linguistic, cognitive, and cultural skills of literacy-oriented students that enable them to readily master the quantity curriculum. Figure 7.2 lays out some major differences between the quality and quantity curricula.

When we pay attention to the needs of non-literacy-oriented and culturally disrupted students, we become very aware of the tension between the forces that push us toward the quantity curriculum, which students will be tested on, and those that pull us towards the quality curriculum, which can have the most impact on helping non-literacy-oriented and culturally disrupted learners become more skillful in the long term.[15] In Chapter 4, we provided some suggestions about how to talk with decision makers and administrators who may be unaware of the fragility of working memory; these tips can be equally applied to professional conversations about the importance of teaching to the quality curriculum when we teach struggling learners. Becoming proficient in the quality curriculum is essential for non-literacy-oriented and culturally disrupted learners to become independently successful in a school setting.

Teaching Point: Making the Taxonomic Organization Amplifier Visible Using Word Walls

In Chapter 6, we offered some suggestions for helping connect students to the organization of a unit or lesson. We can also create word walls for the same purpose. But it won't help to put words up on a wall randomly, alphabetically, or without cues to meaning. For example,

Figure 7.2 | **Quantity Versus Quality Curriculum**

Quantity Curriculum	Quality Curriculum

• Content Curriculum
  — information
  — scope and sequence
  — standards and frameworks
  — content vocabulary
 	
Note: A simple way to understand the quantity curriculum is that it is the subjects that the school day is explicitly organized around (math, Language Arts, science, social studies, health, etc.).
	• Ways of Thinking
	  — cause and effect
	  — comparison/categorization
	  — whole-to-part/part-to-whole
	  — analysis
	
	• Ways of Using Language/Vocabulary
	  — non-content-specific academic words
	  — transition words
	  — rich adjectives and adverbs
	  — discourse skills
	
	• Ways of Organizing Information

Figure 7.3 is a reproduction of the basics of a word wall Ken had created with a 4th grade ESL inclusion class. Geometry terms were very difficult for his struggling learners to keep straight. For example, many students confused "polygon" with "quadrilateral." So in a class with many struggling learners, a word wall was created to become an environmental resource for students to clarify word meaning.

Several graphic features enhance meaning. First, *letter size* corresponds to *concept size*. *POLYGON* is a *bigger* concept than quadrilateral, as it refers to all closed shapes, as opposed to just four-sided shapes; the larger letters help students think, "That's right, polygon is all closed shapes, It's got the biggest letters." *Color* is used consistently, in this case differentiating three- from four-sided shape words. In addition, important prefixes are *underlined*. The spacing of words also helps show the relative "closeness" of their relationship within a category—in this case, shapes that share more attributes are closer together.

As new words were generated, Ken had a conversation with students about what colors and size letters they should have, and where they should go. Periodically, students were asked to reorganize the words in other ways; for example, "equilateral" and "square" could be put together because they are both shapes that have equal-sized lines and equal-sized angles.

Figure 7.3 | **Geometry Term Word Wall**

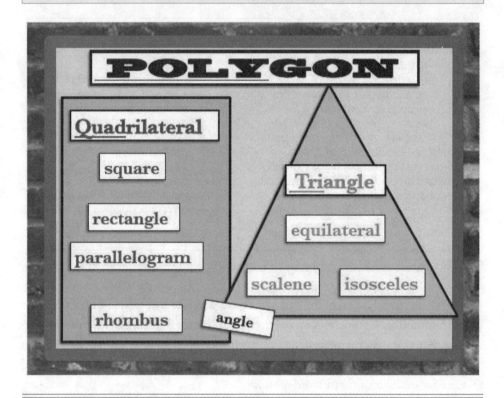

Teaching Point: A Word of Caution, and a Word of Advice, Regarding Graphic Organizers

We should be clear that when using graphic organizers to support the learning of new material, students should not be simultaneously trying to refine the thinking skill illustrated by the organizer, such as cause-effect reasoning or comparison. Remember that because of our fragile working memory systems, there's no texting while driving! If students are filling in a cause-effect organizer about the causes of the Revolutionary War, while the activity will help them see the relationships between the events, they will not necessarily become more skilled in cause-effect reasoning. To develop the thinking skill itself, students should practice filling in graphic organizers about a topic they already know well.

To improve their cause-effect reasoning skill, students might fill in a cause-effect organizer about decisions they make on a basketball court or in a video game, or to illustrate the deteriorating interpersonal relationship between two quarreling friends. To practice taxonomic organization, they could fill in an appropriate organizer about their house, its rooms, and what's in each room, or music, or food they like, or video games.

Most educators are aware of the large number of graphic organizer resources available on the market. They range from simple to quite complex and ornate. Three bits of advice: First, it is common for teachers to use their own organizers. However, we should ideally use the *same* organizers schoolwide as it allows students to become proficient with the same set of cognitive tools. Second, simpler is better. The focus should be on design elements that channel thinking, not distracting elements like curly lines or butterflies flying in the margin that merely have a decorative function. Thinking Maps™ is a strong program that uses a specific set of relatively straightforward organizers across grades.[16] Third, while graphic organizers are great at representing complex ideas visually, many students need practice in expressing these ideas both orally and in writing. The ultimate goal is for students to develop the ability to think and talk about the ways that complex concepts and schemas relate to one another. Graphic organizers can help to establish meaning, but their job isn't done until students can communicate those meanings to others.

Teaching Point: Developing Comparison Skills

Robert Marzano and fellow researchers (2001)[17] evaluated teaching strategies that were linked to higher standardized test performance. They identified nine key strategies and ranked comparison skill instruction as having the highest correlation to learning outcomes. Owning an ever-expanding repertoire of ways to compare objects, events, processes, and states is very important for academic success across grades and content areas. Comparison skills directly connect to semantic memory as this is the place where we store categories of information with their many attributes that are used as the basis for comparisons.

One issue that is quite prevalent in struggling learners is what we call "living at the extremes."[18] That is, they have few categories to compare things. They tend to classify things only at the most basic, obvious level, such as "the same" or "different," or "easy" or "hard," or "I know it" or "I don't know it." This is particularly true for students who have had fewer mediated learning experiences. Once, one of Ken's culturally disrupted learners told him the school assignment was "a little easy, and a little hard." This type of limited verbal skill in basic categorizations of experience (connected to lower levels of vocabulary) is not aligned with the requirements of academic work.

Ken asked a struggling 5th grade student to look at a page of snowflakes and find the two snowflakes that were *exactly* alike. He quickly spotted two that were fairly close and stopped his search, saying, "Well, these two are the same, but probably a little different." His ability to hold more subtle differences steady in his mind was overwhelmed by the more obvious similarities. This was consistent with how he approached all his work at school.

A large variety of attribute categories is essential to compare nearly anything: size, shape, color, number, use, dimensions, material, age, value, and so forth. However, many struggling students have a rather limited range of attributes to draw upon. Feuerstein et al. (2006, 2010) has found that culturally disrupted learners are more likely to latch onto the most obvious sensory input (e.g., bright, shiny, loud) or things that have personal meaning. For example, if they think puppies are cute, and there's a lesson about mammals with a picture of puppies drinking their mother's milk, their attention may get so sidetracked by their liking of cute puppies that they miss the significance of the picture: an illustration of mothers that provide milk for their babies as one characteristic of mammals.

In Ken's experience, when shown two markers that were the same color—say, blue— but not even the same shade of blue and different in nearly every other respect, many struggling elementary-age learners would often quickly say that the two markers were the same, and they would need a lot of support to name any differences such as those related to length, thickness, tip size, shade of blue, kind of cap, writing on the marker, or scent: the notion "they're both blue" was all they could think of unaided—and, more important, all they thought they needed to think of.

Spontaneous Comparisons

Comparisons help bind experiences and objects in the world together. Feuerstein, interestingly, also considers "spontaneous comparative behavior" as an important area of mediation for some struggling learners. In other words, some learners often don't make independent attempts to see how things fit together, how similar things may be different and dissimilar things the same, such as the students just discussed who were quite satisfied to stop thinking past the notion that "the two markers are both blue, so they're the same." This signifies passivity and inflexibility in learning. In contrast, students who do spontaneously compare are actively engaged in interpreting their environment, on the lookout for information, more "masters" of their experience. This is what we want for all of our students.

To model spontaneous comparative behavior for younger children, we suggest shifting gears midlesson and enthusiastically asking the class to help compare two things that are everyday objects or ideas—markers, children, clothes. Then when the teacher summarizes the activity and names (or better yet, writes up) the various attribute categories that were used, it helps to connect that activity to future comparison opportunities. As students engage in this activity, prodding them with "Great job, you found three ways—how about one more?" and "Great, now you found four ways—see if you can get five or six!" keeps students moving forward. Then sharing all the ways the class found further expands students' consciousness around this process. For high school students in need of this kind of mediation, we might say, "OK, hip-hop or rock—which kind of music is better? Why? Justify your thinking!" We also recommend engaging students in a follow-up "meta-thinking" discussion about how it's really helpful in life to be able to quickly compare things in lots of ways. Helping struggling learners take an active, questioning stance on their learning and experience is one of the most important things we can do. One way to help them develop this "habit of mind" is through practice with spontaneous comparison.

In Chapter 6, we noted that we store information by similarities but retrieve by differences. This point clearly connects directly to comparison skills. First, we need to emphasize the important attributes of what we're teaching, helping students to connect to background and create a rich network around that content. But if we also intentionally contrast the information to something else similar during the "storage" phase, we facilitate retrieval.

How Information Is Stored in Semantic Memory

Functional Organization

Non-literacy-oriented students may rely on organizing the world through functional rather than taxonomic categories. That is, they may connect items based on meaningful cultural activity rather than on the more abstract taxonomic schemas favored in literacy-oriented societies.[19] A pen, pencil, and paper may be functionally organized as all are necessary for the activity of writing, but in our literacy-oriented culture, we may be more predisposed to categorize the pen and pencil as writing instruments and paper in a different category. It seems to us quite possible that more people around the world rely on functional relationships than hierarchical taxonomic categories, which are widely used mainly in literacy-oriented communities where schooling is a central tenet of child rearing.

So although functional organization is an equally legitimate and important way to categorize the world, students who are primarily attuned to functional categorization may have less facility with taxonomic categories that are so important in school. In the research project on Native Americans we referenced earlier the researchers concluded, "We found that topics in education are more suited for taxonomic representation . . . what our society considers appropriate for education does not favor a functional-relational organization of domains" (Newman et al., 1989 pp. 128–129).

If a student's primary organizational schema is functional,[20] it puts them out of sync with schooling. Think back to the classroom lesson in the previous chapter, where the teacher asked her students to think of "dog" as a prelude to the study of mammals. Some students may relate to the concept of dog in a more functional way (Figure 7.4). When the teacher segued to a discussion of mammals, these students would be out of sync, look slower, and miss a lot of connections. They are lacking the amplifier of taxonomic semantic memory organization.

Accounting for differences in how our students may store and retrieve information will enable us to better understand them as learners, better respond to differences in apparent learning speed, and better help them learn the quantity curriculum.

"Fuzzy" Categories

All children form categories about the world they have been born into. Categories are essential to thinking and learning because they allow us to reduce the limitless variation found in the world to manageable numbers.[21] By knowing what category something is in, we have instant access to key attributes about it that we had identified. In fact, categorization skills are directly connected to comparison skills, which is why helping struggling learners develop stronger comparison skills is so important. Once we can place something, such as a piece of furniture, in a category, we know something of its function and structure and can readily compare it to other items (if we have strong enough comparison skills).

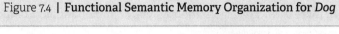

Figure 7.4 | **Functional Semantic Memory Organization for** *Dog*

We may think categories are pretty clear-cut: either something meets all the required conditions for category membership or it doesn't: an animal is either a dog or not; a person is either a U.S. senator or not. In these cases, all members of a category meet all of the necessary and required conditions for that specific category. This is the classical, or Aristotelian, notion of a category;[22] it is the model that is used in academic disciplines and is the focus of school instruction.

However, many categories are actually organized a bit differently. Think of the large and messy categories embodied in a word like "democracy" in which there are a multitude of "democratic" political systems (e.g., parliamentary, federal, representative) around the world. Or consider "family," which currently includes two-parent or single parent families, families headed by a guardian, heterosexual or same-sex families. The human mind seems to be comfortable with both classical and fuzzy category types.[23] However, schools are designed to develop learners' classical categorization system, an important piece of the tool kit that forms a literacy orientation.

Teaching Point: Category Formation

Human development specialist Usha Goswami (2008) proposes that children develop three foundational areas of knowledge based on their direct experiences with the environment: physics, biology, and psychology. For example, kids learn that balls bounce, animals get stinky when they're dead, and a favorite uncle always brings presents when he visits. All children bring categorical information about these domains to their school experience, but many struggle when they encounter a new, formal, academic domain of knowledge at school. There are some helpful things we can do to support the development of categories.

Highlight Differences

While all students will come to school with complex and rich categories of living and non-living things, we may need to help struggling students, in particular, re-form the natural categories into formal subject matter categories, useful for the sciences. For example, many children think that the way something looks accurately reflects its scientific category. So, many children assume that butterflies are pretty much the same as moths—maybe they belong to a "pretty things that aren't birds but fly" category, which is a valid category, just not a scientific category. If we were teaching a lesson on butterflies, we should emphasize the fact that butterflies and moths are not the same and explore how they are different in order to help students create a more scientific category system (even if moths are not the focus of the lesson)—and many of us would do this instinctively. *But we should also focus the class on the fact that categories in science may not be the same as the way they categorize the world, rather than just assume they'll figure it out.* In short, the focus of instruction must include the structure of knowledge, not just the content.

Ken recently observed in a 10th grade science class that was reviewing the characteristics of living things. The students were in small groups sharing their ideas, and then sharing out one idea they all agreed on. The characteristics of living things was something that the students had probably first learned about in kindergarten and certainly at other points in school before 10th grade. But this was a school serving a population of academically struggling, culturally and linguistically diverse learners, so all bets were off. One of the groups shared, "It can smell." Amazingly, these 15-year-olds' category for "things that live" revolved around animals with noses! Clearly, the issue of categorization is not something that only applies to very young children. Think of novice students' schema formation, and consider how out of sync these students will be with their 10th grade biology text!

Don't Just Use the Verbal Channel

A purely verbal definition approach to category learning too often leaves students with a shallow understanding of academic categories, while leaving their older natural categories untouched. A student may dutifully memorize the definition for mammals, say, but be unable to apply that definition to accurately categorizing dolphins, which they are sure are really fish. Some of us can still recite definitions of trigonometry terms from high school yet are unable to solve a trigonometry problem. We even may have memorized a fancy definition for a star, like "A self-luminous celestial body consisting of a mass of gas held together by its own gravity in which the energy generated by nuclear reactions in the interior is balanced by the outflow of energy to the surface." But all we *really* know is that it's round and is made of really hot gas. Vygotsky (1986) calls definitions devoid of real meaning for the learner "empty verbalism." Wouldn't we all rather not engage in "empty verbalism" with our students? So what to do?

Research on concept instruction[24] supports the view that it is most helpful when learning new concepts to have students both work with illustrative visual or graphic examples *and* build verbal definitions.[25] This dovetails with the principle established in Chapter 2 that we should use at least two learning channels when we teach.

Choose Good Exemplars

For our instructional examples, we use what are called "prototypes" or "exemplars," which are culturally familiar examples that clearly exhibit the appropriate attributes. In a lesson on mammals, for instance, we are likely to use a dog or cat; they are culturally familiar and clearly have all the characteristics of mammals. In contrast, we probably would not start off with a water buffalo, which is not culturally familiar here, or a whale, which looks more like a fish and does not obviously have hair.

Whenever we are introducing a new topic to a diverse classroom, we should ask ourselves, "What would a good prototype example be? And will all my students share the background/schema knowledge that the prototype comes out of?" Maybe we need two or three exemplars, to cast a wider net. Our exemplar choices may vary from class to class, depending on its social and cultural diversity. If it's a lesson on the food groups, then typical exemplars for grain would be wheat, and for fruit might be apples, and spinach for vegetable. But if we have some students of, say, Southeast Asian heritage in our class, we might want our exemplars to be wheat *and* rice for grain, apples *and* mangoes for fruit, and spinach *and* long beans for vegetables. And for the lesson on mammals, the water buffalo might be a good example.

This notion of teaching through good examples extends to using models and rubrics in math and writing. The value of presenting a model of written work, for example, and analyzing the qualities of that kind of writing, *and* what makes it a good example, is well understood by teachers to scaffold stronger performance in writing. However, in our experience as teacher trainers having observed teachers in multiple districts and across all ages of instruction, it is still far too common for writing to be taught *without* showing and analyzing good models for students to strive toward. Helping struggling students form a clearer notion of the characteristics of the *extremely* fuzzy category "good writing" is essential.

Figure 7.5 is a sample piece of writing that we might use as a model with a 4th or 5th grade class studying the causes of the Revolutionary War. We know that they need to write an essay explaining what led to the war. Just because they know the information does not mean they can do a good job of turning it into a three-paragraph essay. So we want to provide a model that we can look at, analyze, and have our students try. Our model is about "a fight I had with my brother." They will write one about a fight with a sister, or friend, or parent. After that, they will be assessed with a three-paragraph essay on the causes of the Revolutionary War.

This model could either be distributed readymade to the class and analyzed together (see below), or co-constructed with the class. Dialogues such as this become an instructional dialogue through our "think-alouds"[26] and based on student input. Either way, students' attention is drawn to the proper organization and transitions of a solid piece of writing in that particular genre. We would have every expectation of a stronger assessment piece of writing about the causes leading up to the war after students have had a chance to think about, and produce, a model relevant to their own lives.

Figure 7.5 | **The Causes of My Fight with My Brother**

The Causes of My Fight with My Brother

My brother and I were real close once. However, we ended up having a big fight. It wasn't just a big change in one day. A number of things happened that made me angrier and angrier at him.

The first thing that happened was that he kept coming into my room without asking. But could I go into his room like that? No! I didn't think that was fair. One day, my brother had a bunch of his friends over. It used to be that I could hang with them, but my brother told me to beat it, and his friends laughed. That really ticked me off! Then one day he was in my room and messing around with my favorite toy truck. I asked him to stop, and he said, "What's the matter with you? Chill! Nothing's going to happen." But he broke it by accident, smashing it into a chair leg.

Finally, the last straw was when I sneaked into the kitchen and grabbed some cookies our mom had said *not* to eat yet. My brother saw me. Later, our mom called us and demanded to know who had taken the cookies. My stupid brother pointed at me and said, "Ken did."

Well that did it! I jumped on him and we punched each other and rolled around wrestling until our mom separated us. He went to his room, I went to mine, and I thought, "If I never see him again, that's fine with me!"

Foster Flexibility

Another related issue is that culturally disrupted learners are described by Feuerstein et al. (2006, 2010) as being less flexible (i.e., rule bound; having a narrower range of schemas) in interpreting the world. That makes dealing with fuzzier and relative categories such as "large things" more challenging than we might think. For example, the category "large" is only relative—while we may commonly say "elephants are large and mice are small," we also know that compared to a sequoia tree, elephants are quite small, and compared to a mountain, they are very tiny indeed; conversely, compared to an ant, a mouse is a large animal, and compared to a mite, it is gigantic! Culturally disrupted learners who are inflexible will have a harder time understanding that an elephant is anything but large, because compared to them, it is huge! This is a big challenge for them, because *most of our conception of the world is based in relative concepts.* Mediated learning experiences help get students unstuck from rigid concepts like this.

We suggest asking lots and lots of questions that make students think, take a stand, and question their present worldview. If a student says that a lion is ferocious during a science lesson about the savannah biome, we might stop the science flow for a minute and say, "Well, maybe. But what about compared to a T-Rex? Which is more ferocious? [Most everyone would say the T-Rex.] But then can we say that a lion *isn't* ferocious? Jot down a few ideas about what you're thinking about this, then I'll ask you to share them with your partner. Then we'll talk about it together."

This type of activity will help students build more complex and flexible schemas about the world, and also provide practice opportunities for clearly verbalizing their thinking. This kind of student engagement is more important overall to the students' schema formation than any bit of savannah biome information they might learn.

Background Grounding and Semantic Memory

We want to briefly revisit the notion of backgrounding again. Without being able to relate previous experience and schemas to present circumstances, learning becomes almost impossible. We need to help students connect to their lives outside school and not only refer back to some lesson students had participated in earlier that year or a previous year. The "fight with the brother" essay is an example of this. When working with the students discussed in the opening anecdote about "settings" in Chapter 6, Ken could have asked, "What is one of your favorite places?" and then used their responses to activate and build the (taxonomic) category of setting. Here again, graphic organizers can be helpful to first organize the familiar categories of students' lives and then using the same knowledge structure to organize subject-matter content.

In this chapter, we are hoping to draw attention to the fact that memory structure itself is subject to social organization: an appreciation of the cultural diversity that students bring to the classroom should also account for cognitive diversity. Obviously, children also have so much more to draw from when we help them access similar "real-life" (outside school) background experiences and knowledge.

Teaching Point: Labeling

Feuerstein et al. (2010) argues that verbal labeling plays a decisive role in learning. During the input phase of learning, labeling events or objects help us notice them; during the processing phase, it allows us to develop more precise scripts and define problems better; and at the output phase, it allows us to communicate more clearly. Students who have to rely upon gestures as they describe objects or events that are distant in time and place, or frequently use phrases such as "you know, that thing," need a lot of help with labeling. Many of us may have been trained to recast unskillful student responses in better language for students, especially when working with English language learners.[27] However, this may not be adequate for struggling students, who continue to create blurred or unspecific labels for their learning as they get older.

Below we return to the writing model we discussed earlier, marked up as a way to label the things we want to be sure students apply to their own writing (Figure 7.6). In this figure, we use italics to identify transitions[28] and underline key sentences: the topic sentence, the factual statements of the problems, and the conclusion.

In the appendix of her wonderful book about working with struggling learners, *Getting to "Got It!"* Betty Garner (2007) describes a powerful five-step "Lesson Plan for Cognitive Engagement": (1) explore, (2) describe, (3) explain, (4) demonstrate, and (5) evaluate. The first two steps—exploring and describing—emphasize, and give important time for, noticing the characteristics of what is going to be learned, and labeling them, which the subsequent steps build off. Too often, we just launch into teaching something, assuming our students will focus on the most salient features of the new learning and be able to label them accurately.

Figure 7.6 | The Causes of My Fight with My Brother (Marked Up)

Key sentences

Transition words

The Causes of My Fight with My Brother

My brother and I were real close once. *However*, we ended up having a big fight. It wasn't just a big change in one day. *A number of* things happened that made me angrier and angrier at him.

The first thing that happened was that he kept coming into my room without asking. But could I go into his room like that? No! I didn't think that was fair. *A little after that*, my brother had a bunch of his friends over. It used to be that I could hang with them, but my brother told me to beat it, and his friends laughed. That really ticked me off! *Then* one day he was in my room and messing around with my favorite toy truck. I asked him to stop, and he said, "What's the matter with you? Chill! Nothing's going to happen." But he broke it by accident, smashing it into a chair leg. *Finally*, the last straw was when I sneaked into the kitchen and grabbed some cookies our mom had said *not* to eat yet. My brother saw me. Later, our mom called us and demanded to know who had taken the cookies. My stupid brother pointed at me and said, "Ken did."

Well that did it! I jumped on him and we punched each other and rolled around wrestling until our mom separated us. He went to his room, I went to mine, and I thought, "If I never see him again, that's fine with me!"

Ken was observing a group in a 2nd grade intensive pull-out of struggling learners. The lesson was about sets and fractions of sets. The teacher told Ken that the kids really were struggling with sets. They had been studying it over several classes, both in their regular classroom as well as that extra-help setting. To start the lesson, the teacher asked, "So, what's a set?" One student volunteered, answering, "Things." The teacher's response was, "That's right, a set is a group of things." Ken reflected on how this student's continued use of blurry language (i.e., lack of clear labeling) to describe what a set actually is was symptomatic of a poor understanding of sets. If he had been able to state in some way that sets are "things that are grouped together *for a reason*," he would have approximated an understanding of sets. Indeed, in the subsequent lesson he showed that he really did not grasp what a set was: when pictures and graphics about various sets and fractions of those sets were put up, he continued to get the denominator (the total number of objects or people in the set) wrong.

Another thing that may have been missing initially in this situation was a good exemplar for "set" to kick off the *first* lesson about sets. A set of chess pieces, toy soldiers, doll-house furniture, or trading cards might have helped establish the notion of a set as things that go together in some way. If that had been contrasted with each student's concept of "my stuff," which would include many things that do *not* really form a set when taken together, it would have helped solidify a key element of the meaning of set as "things *that go together for a reason.*"

When students are left to their own devices, such as on standardized tests, they have to rely on their language storehouse to identify, define, and solve problems. If they access their language label for something when they're on their own in a high-stakes standardized test situation, say, and all they can find is just "that thing," it doesn't help them much! It is essential to help students who typically use blurred and very general language for concepts and learning to develop the ability to use language carefully and accurately. In the class in question, the teacher might have asked the students to repeat what she'd said about sets, ask them to find several possible sets of things or people in the classroom and justify how they fit the definition, and then, at the conclusion of the class, give the students a chance to say again what a set is either to the teacher or in a learning log. They could have been asked to think about sets of things they have in their home.

The ability to use clear, descriptive language is a hallmark of a well-mediated, successful school learner. Labeling helps learners identify the salient parts of a problem and therefore be more likely to be able to solve it and recall information and processes, and it is a signal of clearer comprehension. One of our primary jobs should be to help struggling learners develop more skill at labeling.

Conclusion

In diverse classrooms, many students will come from cultural contexts that emphasize different social and language skills; if these children are well mediated into a literacy orientation, they will have a foundational set of cognitive skills that will serve them well in their new school environment as they learn a new language and adjust to the social organization of schooling. However, children raised outside literacy-oriented families may come to school with quite different experiences and capacities with the cognitive tools used in schools; they experience multiple mismatches between home and school and struggle to achieve academically.[29] The neediest group of students are those who have had fewer quality mediated learning experiences and thus have not developed the cognitive tools that are the foundation for learning.

Schools need to identify students who will benefit from systematic work on semantic memory development. Students without a primary semantic orientation need to learn in classrooms in which the semantic organization of language and the curriculum are made explicit. We believe that semantic memory development must also become a focus of *direct, systematic instruction* for students who need it in order for them to optimally profit from the curriculum and instruction of dominant-culture classrooms. This will enable them to accelerate their semantic memory development to match, at a younger age, their dominant-culture peers. This intervention should start in the earliest grades.

But we can never forget the importance of avoiding double-planing! We and our students *cannot* accomplish two learning goals at once. Students need to focus their attention specifically on the development of semantic memory. Helping non-literacy-oriented and culturally disrupted learners develop facility with the taxonomic organization of semantic memory is a matter of social justice. Because semantic memory organization is such a crucial literacy-oriented amplifier connected directly to academic success in school (and beyond), it should be front and center in our minds as we teach. That means intentionally and explicitly doing the following:

- *Teaching and developing comparison skills*: This includes expanding students' ability to use attribute categories and superordinate category labels. This should help students to *independently* make spontaneous comparisons whenever they are reading, solving a problem, or engaging in academic work.
- *Helping students develop school-matched scripts*: This enables them to more skillfully approach problem solving and academic work, as well as to generate metacognitive reflection. (also see Chapter 5)
- *Supporting students in using accurate verbal labels and precise language.*
- *Connecting subject learning to multiple pathways*: This enables concepts to be learned and retained better, especially when supplemented by exemplars, combined with verbal definitions.
- *Helping students make direct, clear connections between the curriculum and their lives outside school.*
- *Highlighting and teaching the taxonomic organization of the school curriculum, in addition to the subject matters*: This enables non-literacy-oriented and culturally disrupted students to develop some of the academic "luck" that literacy-oriented students have, and on which successful school learning is predicated.

---

1. See Geertz's (1973) discussion of culture.
2. Karpov (2003).
3. Gauvain (2001).
4. Rogoff (2003).
5. Nisbett (2003).
6. Ibid.
7. Reardon (2013).
8. Philips (1983); Heath (1983); Scollon & Scollon (1981); Bailey & Pransky (2005); Fu (2003)
9. Newman, Griffin, & Cole (1989).
10. Nisbett (2003).
11. Lantolf (2000).
12. See Rogoff (2003), Chapter 7, for an enlightening discussion of cognitive tools.
13. The hidden curriculum refers to the social beliefs, values, and practices that undergird schooling, but are not part of the formal curriculum. See Giroux (1983). We extend this notion to include learning processes and the structure of knowledge in school settings.

14. The word "quality" absolutely is *not* meant to imply a value judgment of better versus worse. It refers to the qualities of the linguistic, cognitive, and cultural skills that enable one to be more independently successful in academic settings.
15. Pransky & Bailey (2003).
16. Hyerle (2008).
17. Marzano and coauthors (2001) are educational researchers at Mid-continent Research for Education and Learning (McREL).
18. Pransky (2008).
19. Cole et al. (1971); Luria (1976).
20. Cole & Scribner (1977); Rogoff (2003).
21. Taylor (1995).
22. Ibid.
23. Lakoff (1987).
24. Marzano & Pickering (2005).
25. Tennyson & Cocchiarella (1986).
26. Baumann et al. (1993); Davey (1983).
27. Student: *The triangle, it have 3 things.*
    Teacher: *That's right, a triangle has 3 sides.*
28. There would also be lists of transition words of different categories (e.g., contrast, time) on the wall for students to access during their writing.
29. Pransky & Bailey (2003); Pransky (2008).

EPISODIC MEMORY

Ken had a pull-out 4th grade ESL class consisting of two culturally disrupted Cambodian students born in the United States who had strong conversational skills in English but struggled academically, and a literacy-oriented student from Sri Lanka who was an advanced beginner in English. So while the two girls had been in American public schools for more than four years, the Sri Lankan boy had barely been here for one year. The previous day, they'd gone with the rest of their 4th grade class on a field trip. The purpose was to figure out the relative health of the water in a local pond. The day before the trip, they'd had a lesson in how determining the number and type of invertebrates in the water was a way to determine how healthy the pond water was. At the pond, kids took water samples and looked at them under a microscope to identify the invertebrates they found. They also spent some time hanging out at the pond and having a picnic lunch. The students had a lot of fun and were very eager to share their experience with Ken.

It quickly became clear that the three students related to the learning on the field trip in very different ways. The two girls talked about what they had experienced in their answer to the question, "So, what did you learn about the health of the pond water?" They told him it was dirty because "there was trash" in the water—true, but not what they'd gone on the field trip to learn. At another point they said they learned there were frogs in the water. They talked about looking in the microscope in reply to

Ken's question about what they had done at the pond. But they didn't refer to it at all in reply to his question, "So, what did you learn about the health of the pond water?"

In contrast, the Sri Lankan boy immediately connected the invertebrates he saw in the water under the microscope to the more general concept of the health of the pond. The two girls said chorally, "Oh, yeeaaah!" But they still had great difficulty creating their own "I learned that . . ." sentences about their learning. It was striking how much more in tune with typical academic expectations the Sri Lankan boy was, in spite of how much less English he knew and how little time he'd spent in an American public school up to that point.

The next memory system to explore is probably the most familiar part of the memory system for most of us—the place we store our personal memories. When we recall where we were yesterday at 3 p.m., those gorgeous mountains we saw on a trip, or the music we danced to at our wedding, it means we searched for and found that particular memory in what is called *episodic* memory. Endel Tulving (2002) contrasted the "knowing" we do in semantic memory with the "remembering" we do in episodic memory.

Our episodic memories are detailed memories, firmly rooted in a specific place and time, with ourselves at the center.[1] We can remember small things in great detail or entire events. It's like a movie we are starring in, filled with sounds, images, emotions, and physical sensations.

We create endless episodic memories without even trying, and if we just kept on accumulating them without getting rid of any, we'd get overwhelmed. So, over time, unremarkable or infrequently accessed episodic memories fade away and new ones take their place. Our episodic memories are not always reliable; the farther away we get from the original event, the more our memories are open to change. Occasionally we clearly "remember" things that never happened at all! But overall, episodic memory does its job pretty well.

In fact, we'd have a really hard time making sense of life without our episodic memory system. What would we do if we could not remember shared experiences with friends and family? What if we kept making the same mistake over and over, because we couldn't remember what had happened before? What if every trip to the supermarket, or our child's school, or to our doctor, required a map or programming the GPS because we couldn't remember the landmarks along the way?

Semantic memory and episodic memory work hand in hand at hyperspeed, sometimes in a conscious way but often below the level of our conscious mind, and these two types of memory constantly coordinate to help us make sense of our experiences. Research[2] shows that when we draw on semantic memory, we simultaneously draw on related memories in episodic memory. For example, if we are planning a math lesson, we not only call up the relevant knowledge representations of the math concepts, but also draw on related teaching experiences from episodic memory.

Conversely, our interpretation of experience is profoundly shaped by knowledge representations stored in semantic memory. And as we accrue episodic experiences, they inform the development of scripts, schemas, concepts, and so on that we store in semantic memory. The functions of episodic memory that have the most direct relevance to classroom teaching and learning, and the focus of this chapter, is when we consciously draw something from episodic memory into our working memory space, where it becomes the center of our attention and conscious thought.

The following illustrates how episodic memory can be used to help us figure out what semantic memory schema to apply when faced with a novel problem or challenge. John McPhee, a writer for *New Yorker* magazine, recounts a time when he was really stuck on writing an article.[3] His memories of his beloved high school English teacher, Mrs. McKee, and her requirement that all writing assignments had to be turned in with a structural outline, helped him move forward with his writing. "I thought of her and the structure sheets," he writes, and then he describes how these memories prompted him to categorize and organize his notes, which enabled him to write. His episodic and autobiographical memories of that class mediated his own framing of the challenges he was facing in his current writing; those episodic memories led him to a script for writing in semantic memory that he could apply to his present writing task.

Teaching Point: Teaching to Episodic Memory

We can enhance our students' learning experiences by thinking of their episodic memory system, creating multiple sensory experiences, and involving learners in surprising, emotionally engaging events—the kind we easily remember as episodic memories. Educator and neuroscientist Judy Willis described a science class in which her teacher had released hydrogen sulfide (rotten egg smell) into the classroom, as he lectured.

We groaned and laughed, and looked around for the offending source. To an outside observer entering our class at the time, we would have appeared unfocused and off-task. However, this demonstration literally led me by the nose to follow his description of the diffusion of gases though other gases. It is likely during that class I created two or three pathways to the information about gas diffusion that I processed through my senses and ultimately stored in long-tem memory. (Willis, 2006, p. 13)

These kinds of event memories are memorable because they trigger emotional responses and provide multiple sources of sensory activation.

The following are several ways to incorporate the episodic memory system into our classroom instruction:[4]

- Create common classroom experiences that all students can share in and we can use to connect to the curriculum (more on this later).
- Draw upon students' personal experiences outside the classroom to help them connect to academic content.[5]
- Change the room arrangement with each new subject (if elementary) or topic (if a secondary content teacher); later in the year, refer back to a distinct class arrangement: "Remember when the chairs all faced the back of the room?"
- Color-code information and other visual supports.
- Meaningfully integrate strong sense experiences into lessons as appropriate.[6]
- Take a field trip before a unit starts, rather than as a culminating activity, to give students with less familiarity with a subject an episodic experience to build new concepts on.
- In the same vein, watch a relevant movie before the class reads the book or text, or begins the content study, as this provides struggling learners an episodic scaffold for understanding topics that are outside their background experience.

The following three suggestions are related to test taking:

- When we test students, arrange the room in the configuration it was when that topic was studied.
- Wear a certain color when we teach a certain subject (or topic); again, on test day, wear that color.

- Let students who receive services in a subject area take their tests in the room where they did the learning; ideally, the same teacher who teaches the information should also be the one to give the test.

Harnessing the Power of Episodic Memory

One of the core principles described in Chapter 2 was that concrete, engaging experiences that involve multiple senses allow our brain to make deep connections and promote learning. Ideally, we create experiences like this for students in our classroom. Then, when we build new concept learning on these classroom experiences, we can reconnect our students to that experience as needed: "Remember a couple of days ago when we . . . ? What did we say we learned when we did that?" This allows students to reconstruct what they'd previously learned and the conclusions they drew.

Many students benefit from first experiencing a concrete, episodic experience before engaging with the more abstract and purely semantic construction of schemas and knowledge through reading or listening to a teacher's lecture. For example, think of the differences between reading about mitosis versus watching it happen under a microscope, or listening to a lecture on life in colonial America versus going to Plymouth Plantation.

Our episodic memory system encodes engaging learning experiences to promote learning in the following ways:

1. They can be very **motivational.**

As we established in Chapter 2, enjoyable, engaging learning experiences that directly involve students are often much more motivating than typical classroom routines. And they often also can be motivating as we reflect back on them. In our experience, when students come back after many years to visit, what they talk about is usually some interesting or fun experience they had: the famous guest speaker, a field trip the class took, or a memorable class project. By deliberately trying to create memorable experiences, we help students harness the power of the brain through the richness of the lived experience and the creation of powerful episodic memories that can be tapped for future learning.

2. They are multisensory.

In the same way, the more connections the brain can make in the process of new learning, the more likely it is that the information will be deeply processed for meaning and become integrated into semantic memory. And these are also the kinds of experiences we are more likely to retain in rich detail in episodic memory. Even after students have made connections to semantic memory, recall can be strengthened when paired with the episodic memory. Episodic and semantic memories support and reinforce one another.

For example, the field trip to Gold's Pond described earlier provided students with a motivating, exciting experience. It provided a wealth of varied sensory input that was retained in episodic memory. Memories of events like this may last a lifetime. Certainly, the episodic memory system is a powerful form of memory!

Episodic Memory and the Challenges of Academic Learning

Although classroom experiences automatically create episodic memories, they do not automatically improve academic performance. A primary goal of academic learning is to create abstract knowledge that can be generalized to multiple contexts. This is the domain of semantic memory. Episodic memories, organized around the specifics of an event, cannot be used for inferential reasoning or generalizations in the way that semantic memory can.[7] Semantic memory, with its schemas, rules, and formulas, represents the ways that knowledge can be used in service to academic tasks. So just rich classroom experiences are not enough.

Language, which is stored primarily in semantic memory, allows us to capture generalizations that no episodic memory can match. Even if a student remembers yesterday's experience using manipulatives to learn fractions, there's no guarantee that the specific learning of yesterday was stored as a general concept in semantic memory, as we explained earlier. Remember that episodic memory is tied to a specific time and place. However, knowledge stored in long-term memory that is available to apply *any* day, *any* time, *any*where, in *any* applicable new learning context is the elusive goal of education.

If I'm a student creating a series circuit with batteries and a lightbulb in an electricity unit, and drawing a schematic diagram, somehow I need to understand that while I can certainly be happy and get a sense of satisfaction when I first see the lightbulb begin to glow, that is not the *real* goal of the activity. Nor is it the goal to draw an accurate schematic of that particular circuit. The *real* goals are (1) being able to explain what happened using the vocabulary of the field to describe the effect of adding batteries so that the lightbulb filament glowed; (2) being able to look at *any* schematic of a series circuit and understand what it is showing; (3) being able to draw a schematic of any series circuit I see, even if I didn't physically set it up; and (4) hypothesizing what I might need if I had AA and not size C batteries to work with, or I wanted a larger lightbulb filament to glow. I could have successfully done the experiment, and done the drawing, and had fun in the process—and still not have automatically learned the academic goals.

As we noted in Chapter 6, the primary goal of modern education is to develop in students a network of what Vygotsky called "scientific concepts," which are abstract, systematic, and consciously available.[8] Culture has generated a set of these powerful cognitive tools, including language and math systems, which enable us to move beyond the limiting specifics of our episodic experiences. The most important of these tools is language, but the set of tools also includes mathematical systems, scientific systems, knowledge of narrative structures, and many others. In sum, it's important to remember that

- an experience does not automatically transfer into academic learning; and
- we have to help our students make connections between their episodic experiences both in and out of the classroom, and the long-term knowledge representations stored in semantic (and procedural) memory.

Think about that field trip to Gold's Pond. All three children created a set of rich episodic memories, but they did not all automatically transform those into generalized academic knowledge. But these kinds of abstractions, which are linked closely with symbol systems, are a powerful tool of human problem solving and cognition.

Recoding Episodic Memory into Language

Episodic memories and semantic memories have a quality that other kinds of memory do not possess: they can be "recoded" into language or symbol systems, such as mathematics. The process of recoding is an important step toward transforming lived experience into the types of abstract generalizations that are valued in academic learning. Luckily, episodic and semantic memories are highly integrated. That means that representations stored in episodic memory can be transformed into semantic knowledge through language and symbols (Figure 8.1).[9] In fact, it is our ability to verbalize knowledge stored in both episodic and semantic memory that prompt psychologists to categorize them as types of "declarative memory," because both memory systems can be verbalized (i.e., "declared").

Oral and written texts provide rich opportunities for study, dialogue, and long-term learning. While a lot of the rich detail of episodic memory is lost in this process, what is retained goes to the heart of academic learning. Through this recoding of experience, we can share this learning with others, study it further even though the event is over, and make connections to past experiences and future problem solving.

Figure 8.1 | **Recoding**

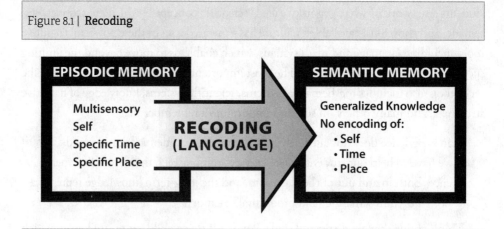

Teaching Point: Planning for Recoding in the Classroom

Recoding is a powerful means for moving out of the specific to the abstract. The following are examples of this process of recoding in the school context:

- **Personal experiences:** Personal experiences can be connected to historical events, as we saw in Chapter 7 in which a story of two argumentative brothers was connected to the core ideas of causes of the U.S. Civil War. A unit on health might require students to keep a diary of their food consumption. Each night before bed, students would draw upon episodic memory in creating a summary of foods eaten that day.

- **Science experiments:** Hands-on experiments are a powerful way to engage students in the active exploration of science. However, the curricular goal of the experiments is not simply to have a fun experience, but to learn about the scientific method and the subject matter at hand—biology, physics, and so on. The write-up of the experiment allows a student to recode personal experience into forms of academic discourse that are central to the interests and perspectives of scientists, which is the long-term goal of academic learning. Long after the episodic memory of the specific science experiment has faded, the more abstract understanding of science is (hopefully) retained and is available for future applications.
- **Math games:** In the same way that science experiments need to be turned into linguistic learning to fully meet the academic requirements of classroom learning, hands-on math activities need to as well. For example, if you recall Alexandra and the 100s chart from Chapter 5, she had a great time rolling dice and moving around the 100s chart, but she made little connection to the content learning. We believe this was in large part because of a weakness with executive function control. However, if the teacher had built a recoding step into the lesson, Alexandra might have processed her episodic memories of the fun activity she did as multiplication algorithms, as well as the linguistic learning that "one meaning of multiplication is equal-sized groups."

Teaching Point: Experiential Learning

There is a long tradition in U.S. education that advocates hands-on experiential learning in (and out of) the classroom that involves what we are terming "recoding." John Dewey (1938) was an early advocate for getting students to actively process and reflect upon their own experiences as an important part of the school-based learning. American educator David Kolb (1984) proposed an approach to education, experiential learning, in which students would actively process their experiences and transform them into academic knowledge that could be applied whenever needed (Figure 8.2). Here are the four steps of experiential learning as proposed by educator Carol Rodgers (2002):

1. **Concrete experience:** Experiential learning begins with a concrete, specific event (or set of related events), such as a science experiment, class project, demonstration, or a field trip. *For example, a guest speaker comes in who takes care of injured raptors (birds of*

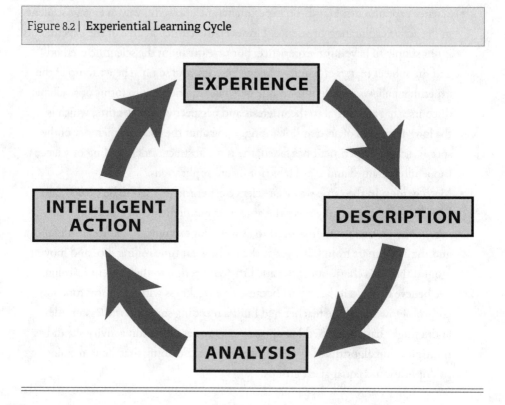

Figure 8.2 | **Experiential Learning Cycle**

prey). He shows the kids a falcon, an eagle, and a hawk. The kids ooh and aah, especially when they see how huge the eagle is.

2. Description of the experience: The purpose at this step is to recode students' episodic memories of the experience into language, creating a written or oral account. This is a reflective process, and once created, the text can be used for sustained reflection and dialogue. *For example, after the birds of prey are shown, the students write down what they remember about each bird. The class then brainstorms all the descriptions, and the teacher writes it all up on chart paper. She types up the list to hand out the next day.*

3. Analysis of the experience: In the third phase of the process, the students and teacher analyze the experience, using the theories, models, concepts, or frames of the field under study. This is a pivotal stage of the process where students create connections among their concrete experience, their abstract, generalized knowledge held in long-term memory, and theories and concepts that apply to the subject of learning. *The day after the birds of prey are shown and the students brainstorm, the teacher presents the characteristics of raptors in a minilesson. Then she hands out the typed-out list of features the class brainstormed the day before, and she asks the students to work in pairs and circle all the features that are specific to raptors and underline the features they think are common to all birds, based on her presentation. The students compare their lists and have to be ready to explain their decisions when asked.*

4. **Intelligent action/experimentation:** The final step of the experiential learning cycle is consolidating the knowledge gained from the experience and putting it to practical use. In the classroom, this would include having students put what they have learned from their analysis of the focal experience into words, and describe how they could use this knowledge to solve problems or interpret experiences in the future. *In the next lesson, students are shown pictures of exotic birds, only some of which are raptors. The students sort the pictures into raptors and not-raptors, and they are told to be ready to justify their decisions using the scientific vocabulary about raptors they had learned. Maybe they also draw and label their own picture of a make-believe "super-raptor," exaggerating the characteristics of raptors in their drawing. Finally, they're given pictures of dinosaurs, some of which are plant eating and some of which are carnivorous. The students are asked to hypothesize about which dinosaurs could be related to raptors and why. Now, the class is also poised to discuss evolution.*

This cycle echoes the way that new skills and applied knowledge are actually acquired in everyday life. We try something out, make a mistake, reflect on what went wrong, come up with a better idea, and try again. It is how we learn to do complex tasks and activities. This model of education draws directly upon the rich understandings of lived experience that is captured in episodic memory, and transforms it into the kind of academic knowledge that is the ultimate goal of schooling.

However, there are two issues that we face in the real world of the classroom. The first is that not all students enjoy this type of learning at school. So there are no guarantees just like there are no guarantees with any one way to approach the teaching-learning process. Some students enjoy the projects but are totally disinterested in the recoding and analysis steps. Others just want to be told what to learn so they do well on the test, because that's what they think school learning is. Experiential learning can be hard work that requires students to be actively engaged in their own learning. At the various points of student resistance that arise in our classes, little by little and over time, we will need to mediate our students' understandings of perseverance, feelings of competence, executive function issues, and other affective or attitudinal issues that hinder learning.

The other challenge in this type of learning is that not all students have the skills to take advantage of active learning opportunities in a school setting. Some students are coming from educational systems where they are expected to just copy the teacher/adult models faithfully. As a result, they may not position themselves as active participants beyond the "doing" of the activity and just passively await the teacher's word about what to make of it. If we think some of our students have this relationship to the concrete, experiential learning opportunities we set up, we need to explicitly teach them the skills required for each step of the experiential learning cycle and mediate their understandings of the importance of this type of academic work. And to avoid cognitive overload, these students may need to initially engage in this process through a familiar, nonacademic topic. For example, have students practice the experiential learning cycle using an everyday experience like making a sandwich, playing a video game, or practicing foul shots.

Whether we plan a strict experiential cycle or not into our lessons, at the least, we help our students' learning if we (1) provide periodic experiences that engage the senses and are motivating, (2) provide some recoding time so students who need a leg up out of episodic engagement into semantic learning get it, and (3) there is time for metacognitive reflection on the learning, or the process of learning.

Teaching Point: Lesson Design for Academic Learning

In the field of English language learning, there is a helpful graphic called "Cummins Quadrants"[10] (Figure 8.3), created by second-language educator Jim Cummins. It helps conceptualize the academic language demands English language learners face. The more direct and experiential the learning is, the less heavy academic language complicates it. In other words, for English language learners, more active, concrete, and experiential learning opportunities are preferable to more abstract, language-heavy, and often passive learning contexts. It can be adapted as a concrete lesson-planning tool that evokes the essence of experiential learning.

But *any* non-literacy-oriented and culturally disrupted learners will struggle with the heavy academic language demands of schooling, and therefore they will learn more

Figure 8.3 | Adapted Cummins Quadrants

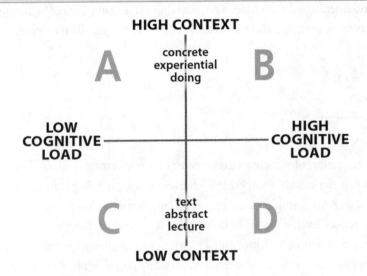

successfully if we can create more experiential learning opportunities for them. Experiential learning activities connect directly to episodic memory. So we can adapt Cummins Quadrants as a lesson planning tool that emphasizes movement within a lesson from more concrete/experiential (episodic) to more abstract knowledge (not just focusing on language use). It helps scaffold the learning of any student who struggles with the high language demand of school, and it also is more reliant on episodic memory than semantic memory as students learn, by building learning off episodic experiences.

The horizontal line indicates the level of complexity in the learning—its cognitive load. Learning can have a greater or lesser number of moving parts to keep track of. On the left of the diagram, the learning goal is simplest (the lowest cognitive load, the fewest moving parts), and on the right, the most complex (an intrinsically greater load, with more moving parts). For example, learning to recognize the word "I" in print would be on the simpler side, and reading a dense, technical paragraph in a textbook is on the more complex side. The inherent complexity of the subject cannot be altered.

The vertical "context" line indicates how concrete or abstract the learning task is: at the top, learning is the most direct, experiential, and concrete; and at the bottom, the most abstract and listening/text oriented. The following make things more "high context," and so more easily learned, and also more easily retrievable as episodic memories:

- Drama
- Student talk
- Visuals
- Experiments
- Projects

The intersection of these two axes creates four quadrants: A, B, C, D. Learning in Quadrant A is the easiest—something relatively simple is being learned in a concrete, experiential way. An example would be acting out a simple addition problem in 1st grade; at the high school level, it would be doing a test for acids and bases with litmus paper.

In contrast, learning in Quadrant D is the most challenging, being very complex concepts learned solely in the abstract and entailing dense, sophisticated language. For 1st graders, it would be reading two-step word problems; and at high school, it would be listening to a lecture on amino acids and taking notes. Quadrant D is the academic "death zone" at school for English language learners and other struggling students, particularly at the secondary level! Of course, by taking care not to overload working memory, we can break down complex material and give students sufficient processing time and facilitate the learning of more complex material—but we often can't make the material itself simpler.

Most of the time at school, learning will be relatively complex by definition. What we can control is whether we'll make it easier for students to learn (Quadrant B) or harder (Quadrant D), by creating "higher-" or "lower-" context lesson experiences. However, students are likely to be assessed in increasingly low-context formats as they get older. If we keep students always in the land of the concrete and experiential, we are not helping them be able to perform in lower-context activities. This application of Cummins Quadrants as a lesson-planning tool helps us frame a lesson (or a series of lessons) as moving from a high-context entry to more low-context assessments.

In one of Ken's trainings, a middle school math teacher created a wonderful lesson about mean, median, and mode using the quadrant model. A more traditional "Quadrant D" lesson on this topic might be

1. giving students the three different formulas with some explanation;
2. showing how they work on the board;
3. providing pencil-and-paper practices on a worksheet or in the text;
4. doing homework.

That's the way the authors, and likely most of you, "learned"—and if you're like us, promptly forgot it.

That teacher created the following lesson:

1. The students all weigh their backpacks (Quadrant A).
2. The backpacks are arranged on the floor from heaviest to lightest (Quadrant A).
3. The teacher leads the class in a discussion about what the "average" backpack is in terms of mean, median, and mode (Quadrant C).
4. In pairs, the students decide which would be the most appropriate measure for the backpacks and share their thinking (Quadrant B).
5. The teacher writes the formulas for mean, median, and mode on chart paper and posts them (Quadrant B).
6. The class figures out mean, median, and mode in a new backpack problem with different number data (than their class) (Quadrant C).
7. In pairs, students figure out the three different measures in a nonbackpack problem (Quadrant B [pair work] and D [pencil-and-paper problem]).
8. The whole class goes over the answers and how they got them (Quadrant B).
9. Homework: problems to find mean, median, and/or mode (Quadrant D).

Note the concrete experiences to start, and the scaffolded entry into more abstract recoding (into language and number systems). This lesson plan has the additional value of being based in something intrinsically motivating to the students—the weight of *their* backpacks and which of them has the "average" backpack in *their* class, depending on how average is figured. We may not always be able to start in Quadrant A, but at least we can get students grounded in Quadrant C.

But . . .

The good news is that all students easily create and retrieve episodic memories and we can harness that ability in our teaching. But in the end, academic learning is something that needs to be integrated into semantic memory. So even though we can scaffold student learning by creating episodic experiences as a bridge to semantic learning, some students still are largely limited to episodic long-term memory. And even though we can enhance their learning through our lesson design by creating more concrete learning experiences such as the backpack lesson, struggling students are still reliant on us doing something special for them; and if we don't, they'll struggle. Part of their "hidden curriculum" is to learn how to learn more independently through semantic memory.

It's quite possible that when, for instance, students seem to have no real recollection on Monday of what they'd seemed to have learned so well on Friday, just like the two Cambodian girls at the pond, they had been focused mainly on their episodic experience. They had not generalized their learning as a concept or information to store in semantic memory.

Teaching Point: Metacognitive Reflection

The big challenge is to help students who approach learning in a mainly episodic way to develop their capacity to generalize their learning. By generalizing, we can transfer learning to new situations, even if they bear little resemblance to the circumstances of the original learning. This is especially pertinent now that, under the Common Core, assessments will focus more on applying learning than regurgitating basic information.[11]

This need relates directly to the mediated learning factor of transcendence. In our mediated learning–compatible lesson plan (Chapter 3), one of the lesson segments relating to transcendence was to follow up each lesson with some kind of metacognitive reflection that connects that lesson's learning to the future. When we make time for this, we meet the needs of all learners, but of learners who rely on episodic memory in particular. We could think of this process as *the creation of knowledge representations that are available for future use.*

This can be accomplished in about three to seven minutes, depending on the activity, which is both good and bad: good, because it does not need to take long, and bad because it is easy to end up *not* doing it—because there is so much to teach and before we know it, the class is over. It is so important not to allow mediation of transcendence to get squeezed out of our lessons.

Reflection on learning can be about what was learned, as well as on the process of learning. The following are suggestions for reflective prompts:

- I learned that _____.
- What did you understand today that you think will be helpful tomorrow when we continue this unit?
- If you were the teacher, what would you test the class on? What would be a good answer for it?
- What did you do that helped you learn better today?
- How do you know you learned the material today?
- What did I do as the teacher that helped you learn better today?
- If the principal asks you what you learned today, what would you say?

Of course, these prompts lead to picking up the thread in the next class for individual students. For example, "Do you remember what you said you learned yesterday?" Or, "Why don't you look in your learning log and refresh your memory about what you said you did well in learning, so you can do it again today." Reflection can happen either in paired (Learning Buddy chat, Think-Pair-Share) or individual activities (learning log, sentence starters, exit tickets).

Culture and Episodic Memory

Culture impacts episodic memory in important ways. The kinds of experiences that students store in episodic memory and bring into our classrooms are, in large part, culturally based. Students from differing societies and communities bring a diverse range of experiences and worldviews. In Chapter 9, we take up culture in more detail when we explore autobiographical memory (which is based in episodic memory).

Culture also affects the interaction styles between caretakers and children.[12] The way a dialogue about a shared experience is constructed at the time of the event, and recoded in a discussion about episodic memories of the event afterward, strongly shapes what is remembered and how it is remembered. Over time, a child appropriates the social speech of his caretakers, and that strongly shapes the child's language and thinking; talking about shared events is one type of social interaction that generates a consistent type of recoding of episodic memories.

For example, in Europe and the United States, *elaborative* interactions are typical of mothers in recoding episodic memory.[13] It is our belief that this is probably also strongly influenced by different interaction patterns across social classes. Elaborative interactions are often child-centered events typically focusing on the characteristics of things, people, and events. That is, the focus is the child's experience, with the caretaker modeling those aspects of that experience that she thinks are valuable for the child to focus on. Over time, through many such recoding episodes, the child's personal memories of events also begin to focus on those similar aspects of experience highlighted by the mother. Research shows that East Asian mothers, in contrast, typically lead the recoding with a focus on social relationships, values, and obligations.[14] In the same way, children from that region begin to color their episodic memories of experience in the ways that their mothers have highlighted as important.

Thinking about a common writing task in American schools—narrative writing about personal experiences with a focus on linguistic accuracy and description—very much fits the worldview of children who have been trained to remember and recode episodic memories through elaborative memory interactions. They are automatically advantaged in such tasks over children from communities who employ a different style of interaction around episodic memories. In the classroom, we may assume that all students have to do is think of their personal experience, and they will be poised to be able to describe it well. But actually, students might not be remembering personal experiences with much of a focus on the descriptive characteristics of the people, place, and events.

Going back to Chapter 3 and the elephant-at-the-zoo scenarios, we now can imagine the kind of conversations about the experience that were happening at that moment in sharper detail. We can imagine the literacy-oriented family recoding the zoo experience on the car ride home, and then again at the dinner table that night: a child-centered interaction partially shaped by the parents around certain descriptive facets of the experience. We can also imagine in the other cultural context no further conversation at all by the parent and child about the day's experience. Which child would be positioned to write a better descriptive narrative of the trip to the zoo in the future?

It should be noted that vocabulary levels will increase with the amount of elaborative talk children engage in with parents, other adults, and more competent peers in the community. Indeed, there is ample research connecting parent-child talk to vocabulary level.[15] So children privileged in this way of relating to episodic memory not only get more practice in descriptive language and the kinds of things our culture values to describe, but also more vocabulary tools for doing it.

Although much research remains to be done in this area, there is beginning to be some indication that a student's proficiency with elaboration aids in story recall in some contexts.[16] If well-mediated learners from a literacy orientation are typically more often engaged by their caretakers in elaborative memory interactions, then it follows that when reading, students are more likely to attend to those same kinds of details. The stance we take as readers—more active versus more passive—and the details we focus on are connected to the ways that we have been trained to attend to and remember events through our interactions with others.

Well-mediated literacy-oriented students from cultures that prefer a low-elaborative maternal interaction style can likely adapt fairly quickly to the more high-elaborative expectations of an American classroom because they are well mediated, and because of their overall literacy orientation. However, students with less mediation in their background, and learners from a nonliteracy orientation, especially when culturally diverse, may find themselves disadvantaged in classroom settings party because of their lack of experience with elaborative memory interactions. We hope more research is done in this area, as it would be fascinating to see what it yields and how that might affect the kinds of support we offer struggling learners in school.

Episodic Grasp of Reality

Feuerstein et al. (2010) emphasizes that not all students are able, on their own, to generalize from experience and construct useful knowledge that can be applied to new contexts and challenges. He refers to this as "an episodic grasp of reality" and considers it one of the major characteristics of a lack of sufficient mediated learning experiences. Such learners do not weave their reality into a coherent whole, tied to past and future, tied to culture and history. Instead, life is experienced as a series of mainly isolated and disconnected experiences. Feuerstein et al. (2010) notes that such learners

- struggle to find connections between events;
- struggle to contextualize their experience into a broader perspective;
- struggle to create relationships between new input, events, and experiences, remaining passive toward them and so less able to learn from them.

While all learners can create rich episodic memories, many may need assistance from us in transforming that knowledge into the type of knowledge that is the goal in school. For students who have had fewer mediated learning experiences, they may become particularly stuck in the details of particular events that are not germane to the generalized learning goals we set or that are always implied in school learning. Beyond needing our support to generalize their learning from a particular lesson or activity, these students need mediation (of transcendence, alignment, and meaning) to help them learn how to more generally relate to experience with a broader perspective than just their own, how to catch patterns between events and their details, and how to weave their experiences into a more coherent whole.

Conclusion

Episodic memory is a powerful memory system. In contrast to semantic memory, it works the same way for everyone: every learner can remember individual personal experiences. Fortunately, we can intentionally make use of this ability all our students have as we plan and teach. However, we need to consider the complex ways that experience, memory, and knowledge are intertwined in the pursuit of academic learning.

Episodic memory, exquisitely rich with multisensory and contextual details, supports the ways we use the more abstract knowledge stored in semantic memory. In turn, semantic memory schemas help us make sense of our experiences and shape what we notice and encode in episodic memory. We sometimes rely on episodic memories to help us figure out what knowledge we need to solve a problem in everyday life.

Episodic versus semantic memory puts differing types of "knowing" into stark relief. The goal of modern education is centered around knowledge that is flexible and generalizable, so it can be applied to new situations and problems. Episodic memory retains a different type of knowledge that, while certainly valuable, is not the ultimate educational goal. Literacy practices draw upon both memory systems, but many students need significant teacher support to create the kind of abstract, generalizable knowledge that is so important for modern literacy practices and school learning.

But an understanding of the functioning of both episodic and semantic memory can help us design and implement lessons with our learning specialist hat on tight. We noted in multiple places that having applicable background knowledge is crucial to the process of learning. With our study of episodic memory, we can see the ways that cultural and experiential diversity affect background knowledge and the students' sense of themselves as school learners. While all students create episodic memories, these memories are not all equally valued at school or aligned with school curriculum and learning. How can we inquire into our students' lives and find ways to build upon their rich storehouse of memories in service to classroom learning? That's one of our main jobs as teachers.

In addition, culturally disrupted students can be stuck in what Feuerstein calls an "episodic grasp of reality," in which they do not automatically integrate their life and learning experiences into a coherent, historical whole. They may struggle in creating the kind of abstract knowledge so valued in schools. All students (without a specific neurological impairment) have the ability to do this, but some students require teacher mediation. Because helping the learner create a sense of cultural and historical continuity is one of the foundational consequences of mediated learning experiences, a lack of MLEs means less proficiency with this way of interpreting life and learning experiences. We need to intentionally help these learners develop the ability to store their learning in semantic memory as generalized representations that they can apply to future problems. When we support students in this way, we help them become more independent, more successful students.

1. Tulving (1993).
2. McRae & Jones (2013); Burianova et al. (2010).
3. McPhee (2013).
4. See Tileston (2004); Willis (2006); Armstrong (2008).
5. The importance of background knowledge and experience in learning shows up in every element of the memory system.
6. For example, giving mid-elementary students molasses cookies in a lesson on the Triangular Trade route between Africa, America, and Europe.
7. Tulving & Donaldson (1972); Tulving (1985).
8. Vygotsky (1986).
9. Miller (1956); Conway et al. (1997); See Tomasello's (1999) discussion of "representational redescription."
10. Cummins (1981).
11. For example, see the latest from PARCC (Partnership for Assessment and Readiness of College and Careers), one of the leading organizations responsible for creating Common Core assessments: http://www.parcconline.org/samples/item-task-prototypes#7.
12. Nelson (2007); Hedrick et al. (2009); Chiao (2009); Hayden & Ornstein (2009); Reese et al. (1993).
13. Nelson (2007).
14. Gutchess & Indeck (2009); Wang (2011).
15. Hart & Risley (1995; 2003).
16. Toyota (2004).

AUTOBIOGRAPHICAL MEMORY

The students at a vocational high school are over 90 percent low income, the large majority are Latino, and most struggle academically. Because it is a vocational school, of course, many students are there to learn a trade—but not all. Although the students are intelligent, they do not try much in academic classroom settings. They give up really quickly, try mightily to derail classes, and hardly ever do homework. They often say things like "I'm lousy at school," "I'm not really smart," "I couldn't give a sh*t about school," and "I'm bored." There are many things that have contributed to this over the years. But at this point in their school career, most now have an identity that is anti-school, that saps the desire to persevere or learn for the sake of learning if it's in a classroom. It's a chicken-and-egg syndrome: their identity undermines their motivation and confidence at school, and with a lack of motivation and confidence, they are likely to do poorly, which reaffirms their negative identity at school.

Autobiographical memory is a concept that is grounded in, but transcends, episodic memory. It is the information we remember about our personal lives, including specific remembered events, but it is more than just that. It is a synthesis of our experiences and includes our likes, dislikes, and preferences. It profoundly informs our sense of self; it is our identity,[1] which is to say, our identity is part of our memory system. The identities children develop at school become powerful components of their autobiographical memory, which in turn strongly affects how they function at school.

Our students' everyday experiences with classroom learning combine and generalize to help produce a sense of themselves as learners: *I'm a good writer. I hate math. I can't learn a foreign language.* As they enter any classroom task, they draw on autobiographical memory as they orient themselves to the learning situation, thinking of themselves as learners as well as their relationship to others they may be learning with. Working memory space can quickly get filled with thoughts and feelings of anxiety, concern, and inadequacy if our autobiographical memory positions us as "not good" in a given learning context. For Ken, that's anything that has to do with mechanical things. For Francis, it involves new technology. For our students, it could be whatever we happen to be doing in the classroom. Struggling learners often have a preponderance of unpleasant school learning–related autobiographical memories, which can affect their motivation, like the students in the chapter-opening scenario.

One of Feuerstein's[2] secondary elements of mediation—mediation of feelings of learner competence—is very often necessary with struggling learners. When a student has a low opinion of herself as school learner, it saps motivation and effort. So unless you directly address that issue with students, it's very challenging to get them to put out enough effort to persevere and overcome obstacles. Teacher mediation includes the transcendence piece of helping students see how having an "I can do it, even if it's a bit hard" script was helpful to them at some point in the past (in or out of school), how it could be helpful now, and how it probably also would be helpful in the future. We need to align ourselves with students' emotional challenges, taking an empathetic stance toward them as many times as needed until we see students beginning to form a new, more empowered sense of themselves.

Explicitly labeling and positively responding to their small successes ("Hey, Sam, I really like how you haven't given up, even though I know it's hard. Who's the man?!" or a whispered, "Liz, thanks for staying on task here even though your friends are trying to pull you away. I really appreciate it"), dialoging about difficulties we ourselves have had and ways that we overcame them, all help. When teachers sometimes say to us, "But I don't have time for conversations with kids during class time that aren't about the content— I have so much to teach!" our response is "For that student, that is the most powerful teaching you can do in that moment." And really, we can't *not* take the time for it if we want students to learn the content we are so pressed to teach, because they will *only* put forth effort if they think it's doable and worth doing. In these types of interactions, we are working directly with their autobiographical memory sense of self.

Not only do struggling students often have negative school identities, but they may even create active anti-school identities built upon years of frustration, humiliations, and failure. It is hard to imagine the emotional toll that attending school imposes on academically at-risk students who see themselves as academic failures. Students demonstrate real courage in just showing up in school and being willing to face the prospect of continued failure. They deserve our support, which requires spending quality time mediating students out of a negative relationship to school learning—at least in our own class.

Clearly, we want to help our students create identities of being competent and confident learners. The most effective way we can help students develop a stronger school identity is to provide lots of opportunities for them to experience success by building upon their background knowledge, avoiding cognitive overload, and conducting positive, respectful classroom interactions—and creating engaging, concrete, multisensory experiences that promote successful learning as a springboard to more academic learning.

Cultural Dimensions of Autobiographical Memory

As with all elements of memory that involve meaning making, culture profoundly affects the episodic memory system and, therefore, autobiographical memory. When we ask students to recall a personal experience related to something the class is about to study, we are more broadly asking students to call on their episodic memory of something that they did or that happened to them within a particular cultural context. In diverse classrooms, students will bring a wide variety of experiences and worldviews.

So, for instance, not all children have had the opportunity to go on summer vacation with their families, attend music or sports camps, or even visit the local museum or library. These kinds of experiential differences are usually easy to understand, but their effect on performance and self-image can also be rather subtle and surprising. So if we assign the very common writing task early in the fall of a new school year of writing about the "best time" students had in the summer, those students whose summers were filled with boredom because they didn't go anywhere or do anything will just end up feeling bad—even if the intent of our assignment was to ask everyone to access happy episodic memories.

The ultimate effect of that assignment is to put yet another layer of armor onto struggling learners' "*I'm lousy at school*" or "*I'm not like the 'good students'*" identity.

Because many of Ken's students hardly ever left their low-income apartment complex during the summer, he learned to assign writing tasks like "Write about the most boring day of the summer, and really make me feel just how bored you were when I read it!" Or, "You can choose to write a description of the best time you had during this summer or the worst time. If it's about the best time, make me feel reeeaaallly happy. If it's about the worst time, make me feel reeaaallly yucky!"

The cultural context of experiences deeply informs the frame we use to interpret our experiences and becomes part of our autobiographical memory. One example of this is a language-related example that Ken wrote about in his book *Beneath the Surface* (2008). There had been a big influx of children from Cambodian refugee families into his school. The many misunderstandings and mismatches that resulted were very instructive. One instance of cultural mismatch was when the teachers—like they did with all the students—responded to a student's answer by saying, "That's interesting, Phila! Why did you think of doing it that way?" While the middle-class, dominant-culture students understood that kind of utterance as a form of praise and a straightforward request for a reason that would get an interested, respectful hearing, the Cambodian children would look down and mumble, "I forgot . . ." The Cambodian paraprofessional at the school eventually explained that it was typical in his community for parents to use *why* questions mainly in a punitive sense, such as "Why didn't you put your clothes away like I told you!" Through specific unpleasant episodic memories of being asked *why* questions, they had formed a sense of *why*-questions as negative. So even though neither the teachers' tone nor intent communicated anything negative from the teachers' point of view—in fact, quite the contrary—the Cambodian children interpreted it that way.[3]

A third example is when a 2nd grade ESL-inclusion classroom Ken teamed in was doing a unit on the book *The Wizard of Oz*. At one point, they were going to watch the movie for comparison, and in preparation, the class had to write 10 things they'd take if they were running away from home. Most of the children wrote down dolls, toys, candy, and so forth.

But the Cambodian students, who worked with the Cambodian paraprofessional, generated a list with matches, rice, warm clothes, tents, and the like. That community's shared experiences of "running away" in Cambodia became part of the children's own schema, even though they had not directly experienced it themselves. Their performance in that task was elevated far beyond the other students' because of the appropriated episodic memories of their community, even though usually they struggled academically in relation to the other children at that school.

It is important to reiterate that episodic memory is composed of interpretations of our lived experiences, filtered through previous experience and knowledge (i.e., schemas stored in semantic memory). In a more subtle way, the cultural frame of our autobiographical memory and specific episodic experiences shapes our semantic knowledge, which then affects our interpretation of present experience. Say I am from a country that has a dictatorship, though the tightly controlled propaganda says it's a democracy—and indeed, some elections are held for local and provincial officials. But under this "democracy," friends and family members of opposition candidates are jailed or disappear. My frame for the concept "democracy" will be quite different from the frame of someone who only grew up in this country. My teacher may be having us read texts that extol the virtues of democracy, but my semantic knowledge and episodic and autobiographical memories, greatly shaped by my cultural experience, cause me to interpret the reading in a very different way than my teacher expects.[4]

We can't assume that students will interpret our classroom texts and activities in the ways we are expecting. Another powerful example of this is related by Raj Canagaraja, a Sri Lankan teacher of English.[5] His students' British textbook included stories of young men and women in England dating, socializing, and working. His students felt alienated from these stories as they contradicted many of the values and beliefs of their rural farming communities, and this autobiographical memory mismatch led to widespread resistance to learning from the textbooks. Students from diverse communities within the United States and the world, including many English language learners, enter our classrooms with a lifetime of experiences and memories that are profoundly challenged by the lifestyles, values, and beliefs embodied in our art, literature, and science. Bridging these cultural mismatches in ways that both honor our own traditions and respect those of our students, and their communities, is a key aspect of working successfully with struggling culturally and linguistically diverse populations.

Similarly, how we learn is affected by our cultural frame, which in turn affects our present learning experiences.[6] While there is individual variation within any culture, cultural learning patterns form along continua of learning styles. In some cultures making errors in public is a huge social shame to be avoided at all cost,[7] while in others, they are thought of mainly as fodder for more learning (even if no one likes making them). In some cultures, people tend to favor learning collaboratively, while in others, there's more of a focus on the individual.[8] In some cultures, people like to build their wall of learning brick by brick, while in others, the bricks get sketched in as you think about the whole wall, or sections of it. Ken once asked the Cambodian paraprofessional at his school, whom he relied on as a cultural informant, about why a lot of the Cambodian students seemed so shy about asking questions or giving opinions about academic topics even when encouraged to do so and even if not in front of the whole class. The para said that in Cambodian culture, children are just expected to learn the approved knowledge given to them by responsible adults, without question. For a Cambodian student to ask the teacher a question would mean one of two things: either they hadn't been paying attention well, which was bad; or they hadn't understood, which would be like telling the teacher, "You didn't explain it well enough, so take another stab at it," which would be horribly rude.

In a diverse classroom, we could imagine a student whose learning identity is passive until adult-directed, who has a low tolerance for errors, who expects to learn brick by brick, and who is not proactive about posing questions (either to the teacher or within him- or herself). How would that student look to us in our classroom? Maybe as a "slow learner" who has "special needs"?

Each student, then, brings personal preferences, likes and dislikes, a cultural learning frame, background knowledge, and feelings about being a student in their "bag" of autobiographical memory. In diverse settings, some or many of these factors may be mismatched to our teacher frame. When we see difference in any of these areas, a long-term process of dialogue and mediation is necessary to help students learn new ways of thinking, feeling, believing, and acting in a classroom setting.

Teaching Points: Struggling Students and the Cultural Roots of Autobiographical Memory

There are a number of things we can do to help bridge and minimize the "achievement gap" effects of cultural differences in autobiographical memory.

Dialogue Around Purpose and Meaning

As we have noted throughout this book, one of the key issues in orienting our memory systems to academic learning is whether we find meaning and value in the object of learning. As this pertains to autobiographical memory, we shouldn't assume that all our students share the same orientation to ways of thinking, using language, or school practices. Our willingness to ask and answer questions, or our proficiency in using descriptive language—in fact, nearly all uses of language and engagement in learning interactions—is a combination of both cultural and personal styles. When we see that students struggle to perform or produce language in the way or at the level we expect, rather than just assuming that they are misbehaving, inattentive, or a slow learner, we can engage students in a discussion about purpose, meaning, and value of what we're asking them to learn, and see where it takes us.

For example, say a student has a very difficult time writing much detail in descriptive writing. Asking him what he thinks the value of description is (if any) in reading and writing would be a good first step. Then, extending the conversation to giving the reasons that in school, and in life, learning how to describe well is a good skill to have would be a next step. Finally, we could break down what good description is and model what it looks like. And, of course, this student will also probably require a lot of vocabulary instruction.

Help Students Understand the *Whats*, *Hows*, and *Whys* of Our Classroom

Nearly every activity, way of using language, and way of thinking in a classroom is cultural. Different cultural groups go about organizing accepted processes of learning in different ways, according to their own cultural beliefs, traditions, and practices.[9] Sociolinguist James Gee speaks about how every group is governed by explicit and implicit cultural norms, and a classroom is a great example of this.[10] When we are members of the dominant group, we are aware of the implicit norms of that context, which includes the content and the language of interactions. But when we are "outsiders," we often cannot see those elements of interaction that are not made explicit. As cultural sites of learning by definition, classrooms enact a particular set of cultural norms. By definition, student diversity within our classroom means that some students will be aware of the implicit cultural norms of our classroom, but others will not unless they are explicitly shown what they are.

If we sense that somehow a student's autobiographical memories are mismatched to our expectations (the explicit *and* implicit norms of our classroom), rather than reactively assume anything negative about their personality, motivation, or intelligence, we can take a reflective, questioning stance: "What do I not yet understand about my student that led to this performance/communication breakdown, and/or what does the student not yet understand about the implicit norms of my classroom?" One aspect of this is trying to educate ourselves about our students' backgrounds and explicitly address any areas of mismatch that we find. We can also try to be proactive, surveying students' interests when starting with a new class.[11] We could give students reflective writing tasks that ask them about their past experiences at school or about their knowledge of a particular subject.

Inquire into Students' Backgrounds

An ongoing element of a reflective practice in a diverse setting should be inquiry into culture, including distinct communities within the United States, its impact on learning, and understanding our students through a cultural lens. As we have noted several times in this book, being able to connect to background knowledge is essential for learning. Especially when there are very different cultural experiences or knowledge bases, we may need to take an active role in helping students make the appropriate connections. But that means that we need to become more aware of our students' cultures. For example, a student's cultural background might explain why they are very reluctant (or don't know how) to become an independent learner, not reliant on constant, explicit teacher direction, or why they are so reluctant to speak in front of the whole class for fear of making mistakes. Fortunately, information about the cultural backgrounds of our students is readily available, through books and the Internet. We can also talk with students and gain a deeper understanding of the communities they come from and their personal experiences.

Another avenue for learning about our students' cultures is if we are lucky enough to have a "cultural informant" who works in our school or we know in the community. That is an invaluable resource—as long as we know that everyone can only give their perspective, not all members of a cultural group uniformly think and act alike, and many people don't like being looked upon as the spokesperson for an entire culture or race. But if we have this resource, and we go about it in a humble and open way, it's a great way to inform our inquiry and understand a perspective we might never hear otherwise.

Encourage Students to Work Toward Independence

One of the most important issues for struggling learners is helping them move from a position of needing teacher direction and evaluation to independence—in the way they approach learning tasks, solve problems, and ask proactive questions. As we noted in the chapter on executive functions, the ability to self-regulate is a key academic skill, and crucial to the ability to work independently in a classroom.[12] Self-regulation ties in closely with the ways that long-term memory and executive functions work together. In Chapter 5, we described a number of ways that mediation supports this process. As students develop more EF skills, their self-image as learners—their autobiographical memories—changes.

Conclusion

Autobiographical memory shares features of both episodic and semantic memory systems. On the one hand, it is grounded in the self and personal experience. On the other hand, it also can be, in part, more abstract and context-less as it synthesizes multiple experiences into hard-earned nuggets of personal truths: our identities, preferences, and opinions.

The act of naming and understanding autobiographical memory provides an opportunity for us to develop a new awareness of our role as classroom teachers. After all, that is the value of learning a new word; it raises our awareness of something in the world that we may never have noticed before but has been with us all the time. An understanding of autobiographical memory draws our attention to the ways that personal experiences become synthesized into durable features of students' view of themselves as learners. It also helps us see how disrupting negative student identities are, and helping students construct self-images that are more empowered, productive, and satisfying is a key mark of our effectiveness as teachers.

The hybrid nature of autobiographical memory, being part semantic memory and part episodic memory, helps us understand an important point about human memory: the clear boundaries that we have drawn between memory systems capture only a partial truth. The reality is that these systems are highly integrated. We have attempted in this book to highlight features of memory systems that appear to be most relevant to classroom learning, but the reality is that we have presented a selective slice of human memory research and theory. As the field of education learns more about the functioning of memory in classroom contexts, there will certainly be an expansion and deepening of our understanding of learning and teaching.

1. Fivush (2011); Fivush & Nelson (2004); Bloome et al. (2005); Pavlenko & Lantolf (2000).
2. Feuerstein et al. (2010); Mentis et al. (2008).
3. Bailey & Pransky (2005).
4. See Rose's (2005) discussion of the way that academic learning engages with student identity.
5. Canagaraja (1999). Canagaraja is a professor in applied linguistics at Pennsylvania State University.
6. Greenfield & Cocking (1994); Scollon & Scollon (1981).
7. Fu (2003).
8. Philips (1983); Rogoff (2003).
9. Au (1980); Lave & Wenger (1991); McKeon (1994); Spring (2011); Rogoff (2003).
10. Gee (1990).
11. Zacarian (2013).
12. Lantolf & Thorne (2006).

PRACTICE

10

Ken was working with a small group of 3rd and 4th grade culturally disrupted learners in reading. They had been working on fluency. In class, they showed they understood that fluency is making few mistakes, reading like they speak, reading words together that go together, and not reading too slowly. So Ken assigned the girls a passage for homework. It was a piece of text within their independent reading level, and they had not seen it before.

The next day, Ken asked if they had practiced reading for fluency. They all said yes. He then asked them to read—and not one of them read fluently at all. Yet they insisted they had practiced, and Ken was confident that they all had done some work with that text the night before.

In this book, we have traced the movement of new learning from its often fragile, ephemeral beginnings in working memory into the vast storehouse of one or another long-term memory system, where eventually it is permanently stored and integrated with other knowledge structures. At that point, we can be sure we've learned something that is available for future use. The one major element of this process we have only touched upon so far is how do we consolidate learning so it becomes more stable in our memory systems?

It's through practice. Practice causes the secretion of myelin around the axons of our neural connections and makes those connections more permanent. It's the turns of the screw that gets it flush with the wood. Without sufficient practice, much of our students' school learning is doomed to drop away, sooner or later—and for many struggling students, it's sooner rather than later. At whatever point we stop practicing before learning becomes permanent in long-term memory, that's where learning ends. Practice ties it all together.

Although everyone would agree that practice is important, if we look at the amount of time we actually devote to practice in our daily lessons—well, there's not always a lot. We and our students are constantly bombarded with the never-ending flow of the curriculum. Trying to get enough time for everything feels like trying to catch water in a sieve. Yet the reality is that students need enough practice to move learning into long-term memory. We can measure the amount of practice that is happening by student activity: practice is what *students* do. If our teaching takes up most of the classroom airtime, our students aren't practicing or learning much.

There are two basic kinds of classroom practice.[1] One is for the acquisition of discrete academic skills and knowledge, which serve some larger learning goals. For example, knowing math facts well is a skill we can use in problem solving. Spelling is a tool that enables us to communicate in writing more accurately. The practice that helps us learn that 4×5 is 20, how to spell "magic e" words, or 1066 is the date of the Norman invasion is *rote practice*. Learning in rote practice is the product of repetition with a focus on form.

It can be difficult to pin down when repeated rote practice engages semantic versus procedural memory. But for our purposes, the key is that the skills become as automatized as possible. What is essential is that students get enough practice, ideally to automaticity, so they can clear out space in working memory for the more important tasks of problem solving and content learning.

The second kind of practice emphasizes the integration of new information with existing schemas in long-term memory. It's sometimes referred to as "elaborative" practice. It's the kind of practice we need to internalize word meanings, describe the stages of the butterfly life cycle, or be able to explain the function of mitochondria. Students need ample practice opportunities to fully integrate new meaning into existing memory structures. Learning in elaborative practice is most often the result of extended performance in meaningful tasks, and the more we do it, the better we get. Sufficient meaningful practice with the content curriculum really should be the major goal of our instruction.

They Work Hand in Hand

There has been a battle raging for over 20 years in our field about the teaching of ELA and math. The forces array on the side of rote skills (i.e., emphasis on phonics or math facts/number crunching) or on the side of a big picture approach and concept building. Publishing companies make millions off this struggle, while we get whiplash as our districts swing from one side to the other. Most important, our students aren't well served. But once we understand how memory systems work, we realize that it's not an *either-or;* it's a *both-and.*

Students need to learn the mechanical tools that can be learned to automaticity as is grade appropriate (math facts, counting skills, formula recognition, etc.) so that they can be brought to bear quickly and easily to help working memory function in the service of creating concept knowledge, which is where instruction ultimately should be focused. But practice to automatize skills is not practice to internalize meaning, nor does the reverse hold true. That's why in organized sports, for example, there's always a lot of practice apart from playing the actual games, even though during games, all the skills are being used. Coaches realize that just playing the games is not enough. Conversely, just being good at dribbling doesn't automatically make one a good team player. Because we need to apply focused attention to engage in deliberate practice, discrete skills do not improve much simply in the process of being used, because our attention is being pulled to so many different things.

Here are some examples of elaborative practices that do not *automatically* lead to academic skill development:

- Early elementary: by engaging with books in school, young children do *not* automatically learn sound-symbol correspondences.
- Mid-elementary: by exploring the concept of equal-size groups in multiplication using a 100s chart, students are *not* practicing math facts to automaticity.
- Secondary: by reading about European monarchs in a 10th grade history text, students do *not* automatically retain all the important dates and names and information they need to keep everything straight.

Conversely, conceptual information cannot be learned sufficiently by rote practice of skills:

- By engaging in phonemic awareness practice, young children do *not* automatically develop reading comprehension skills.

- By practicing multiplication facts to automaticity, students are *not* learning the concept of equal-size groups in multiplication, nor are they necessarily any better off solving word problems where those facts need to be applied.
- By memorizing dates and names, students are *not* learning about the sweep of history, or what causes monarchs to rise and fall.

Both rote and elaborative practices are essential and will be described in more detail below.

The Practice Dilemma

While practice to mastery is a very good goal, what can teachers realistically be expected to accomplish? How can the deluge of conceptual information and skills students need to learn in math, reading, writing, science, social studies, and more *all* be practiced to mastery? There could be a halt to all new information, and we and our students would still grow old trying to practice everything to mastery. At the same time, practice is essential to learning. This is the dilemma: what do we take the time to practice to automaticity and deep integration in long-term memory, and what do we just work with temporarily, and then let drop when that lesson or unit is over?

Knowledge and skills that have a long-term payoff are the things students need to spend time practicing to mastery. In math, for example, number sense and basic computation concepts and skills need to be automatic. In reading, phonemic knowledge needs to be automatic[2] and strategizing skills need to be mastered. In science, the scientific method and creating hypotheses need to be practiced to mastery. The Common Core State Standards lay out a set of standards for teachers at each grade level in English language arts and math that could be used as the broad outline of what should be practiced to mastery.

But even when we establish what needs more practice, do we know how much is needed? Unfortunately, that answer will vary among individual students in a class, and even with individual students depending on the subject—a student might need just a small amount of practice in math, but a lot of practice in getting science terms down, for instance.

However, research suggests that a schedule of practice, spread out over time, beats one-shot practice.[3] The brain needs time to absorb new information. Think of it as similar to drinking water. When we're thirsty, we drink a glass or two. Then later on, we drink some more. At some point, we're not thirsty anymore. But drinking a gallon at a time just gives us a bellyache. We should try to avoid giving our students a brain bellyache. The more complex the learning, the more times we need to periodically drink, and the longer the period of time it will take.

One suggestion is to set up stations for periodic practice. In a biology class, with its bazillion vocabulary words to learn, we might have an "index card vocabulary game" station, a "label the picture" station, a "word sorting" station, and so forth. Then even when a particular lesson or unit is over, students can still practice what they need to until they have reached a level of mastery.

Practicing for High-Stakes Tests

In this era of high-stakes tests, we often find ourselves, unfortunately, needing to take time to have kids practice taking tests. Many of us work in schools where things grind to a halt before the standardized test schedule starts, and classrooms are given over to test-taking practice. But from a memory system point of view, considering how cognitively complex test taking is, and how much practice needs to happen, that's the bellyache approach!

Here are some in-sync-with-memory-system suggestions:

- Create formal test situations periodically *throughout* the year for whatever we're teaching, organizing the room as it needs to be set up for the standardized test.
- Discuss strategies for test taking with the class, practice them, and review them with the class before they take *any and all* formal assessments, whether practice standardized tests or our own end-of-unit assessments.
- Have students periodically evaluate which strategies they've been using, how they did with these strategies, and which strategies they'd like to get better at; *write strategies* up as scripts to practice.
- Throughout the year, take down or cover wall charts, environmental print, and word walls connected to the subject being tested, as per standardized testing, and have students jot down key things they had been using those charts for in the margins or on another piece of paper, before they start the test.
- Comb through the standardized testing at our grade level and cull meaty verbs ("analyze," "contrast," "explain") and academic phrases that recur (e.g., "according to the author…"); teach these words and phrases explicitly, *and* weave them into our own instructional language and assessments throughout the year.

Practice as Input Versus Practice as Retrieval

It seems counterintuitive, but retention is enhanced more through repeated acts of retrieval (testing) than merely studying (input) repeatedly.[4] In other words, information and skills are retained over the long term if they are periodically used and used in such a way that it requires effort to retrieve them. Testing in this sense is synonymous here with "effortful retrieval." This doesn't just mean lots of testing and assessment! We could use games, quizzes, centers, songs—*any activity that asks students to put forth effort to intentionally retrieve the information* we want them to retain.

Another example would be asking students to come up with information they've started to learn and scaffolding their answers, instead of merely giving input by repeating the information ourselves. So often, in the interest of time or maybe just because we're "built" this way as teachers, we tend to tell much more than we need to, instead of asking or eliciting information from students. It's like in Chapter 5, when we suggested periodically dropping out words from classroom scripts and eventually replacing the scripts with icons (retrieval), versus just repeating the same thing to students or having them read it, yet again (as input). The key is that students should be made to periodically retrieve skills and information we want them to retain for their own sake, with feedback discussion about strategies for retrieval.

This argues against a constant flow of new information, which we ask students to study and finally follow up with a single test at the end of a unit. It is more ammunition we can use to explain to administrators why we are a bit behind where they want us to be: we were helping students retain the information by slowing down the flow of new information to take more time for students to process and own it (as we explored in earlier chapters), but also taking time to "test" for it more frequently because research shows that aids in retention.

Practice and Social Justice

The reality is that regardless of how much classroom practice for skills we structure, many proficient learners from literacy-oriented homes will end up practicing them anyway. The rich get richer. How many of you, like the authors, practiced multiplication facts with your children to pass the time on long car trips, or read with your children hundreds of hours when they're young, before they ever went to school?

But other parents may not be able to help or may not be predisposed to participate in school-related practice in the home. Some parents will not have "played" with their children using formal counting games, ring stacks, and puzzles, which give young children many hours of practice with basic academic skills before they ever get to school, and which will pay off in spades when they finally do. We also have to remember that an older student may need to work nights and weekends to help support the family and have little time for academic work outside school. There are many other possible reasons for this reality of practice disparity. But regardless of the cause, we must not just perpetuate the unequal status quo.

Take reading as an example. From an evolutionary perspective, the brain was never designed to read.[5] In the process of learning to read, the learner has to rewire areas of the brain to rapidly connect visual processing areas to language processing areas.[6] In the process of developing this pivotal academic skill, with a brain that was not designed for the task, students need a lot of "prepping." Literacy-oriented students get many hours of this prepping in the home through the kinds of activities they do with parents, and the mediation they get, before they ever come to school. Many students walk into kindergarten reading, or are poised to launch into reading right away. In contrast, non-literacy-oriented students and culturally disrupted learners are unlikely to have had as many of those kinds of prepping experiences in the years before school; they are not usually readers or poised to launch into reading right away.

Interestingly, many schools have determined that the way to launch them is through a lot of practice with phonemic awareness, which constitutes very little, if any, of the literacy-oriented prepping that gets literacy-oriented students ready to read! Though no doubt some phonemic skill is essential to crack the code of reading, the following is what non-literacy-oriented and culturally disrupted learners *really* need to practice *a lot,* to get caught up with the "prepping" that literacy-oriented students get and allows them to read in the first place:

- Strong executive function skills—appropriate scripts, impulse control, flexibility, organization, goal setting (see Chapter 5)
- Strong metacognition skills (see Chapter 5)

- A belief that they are capable of doing it, confidence in their own ability to make it happen, and the ability to persevere when it becomes difficult
- Strong American Standard English language skills, especially vocabulary and grammar
- The ability to juggle well in working memory (see Chapter 4)
- The ability to solve problems independently

If public schools are designed to level the playing field of life, then it is our job to try to intentionally do something about it! One way we can disrupt the cycle of underachievement is through the kinds and amount of practice we structure for struggling students, based on what we know of them, in our role as learning specialists.

Automatized Skill Acquisition: Rote Practice

Rote practice often gets a "drill and kill" moniker. Why would we want students to focus on robotic, mechanical practice? However, the more automatized skills we have, and the less cognitive load it takes retrieving and using the skills, the more memory space is left for problem solving and learning. Conversely, the more conscious effort that must be applied when using a new skill, the more working memory workspace is used, and the less space is left for problem solving and learning. It's a straightforward, zero-sum game. Even if one believes deeply in a theory that students will learn the skills they need by engaging meaningfully with big ideas, it does not change the reality of students' brains: they need focused practice to master and integrate new information.

Students require opportunities to both practice academic skills to automaticity *and* engage in concept development. Remembering important names and dates in social studies, facts and formulas in math, spelling patterns and sound-symbol correspondences in reading, and symbols in science all need multiple iterations of form-focused practice for ease of recall.

Learning How to Practice

One mistake we often make is assuming that students know *how* to practice. Ken found two major practice-related issues with his struggling learners—really two sides of the same coin. One issue was that they didn't have a helpful process for practicing, partly because they lacked the necessary executive function skills, such as goal setting, shifting, and appropriate scripts. The other issue was that they were not metacognitively aware of whether their practice was successful or not. For example, Ken asked one of his 6th grade students—we'll call him "Miguel"—who struggled in math, and in particular struggled mightily to autonomize multiplication facts, to show him how he used a set of flash cards to study. Miguel looked at one, said it out loud, put it on the table, and then repeated the process for every card. Then he said, "That's it." So since 3rd grade, his teachers had asked him to study the math facts, and his method was to look at each card once. No wonder he never learned them well!

The flip side of the coin is that Miguel was not really paying attention to whether he had learned the facts or not. He was not focused on intentionally retrieving facts he may have already learned to some extent; instead, he was treating it as another input exercise by merely looking at each card again. Students remember better what they pay attention to, and one of the things students also need to pay periodic attention to is *themselves* as they learn. This is the attentional skill Miguel did not have. Teachers had asked him to practice them, and by gum, he obliged! But the mechanical, input-focused process he used yielded little if anything of value, although he had repeated it many times before.

The girls in the anecdote that begins this chapter told Ken how they'd practiced: they each said they read the passage once, except for one of the girls who'd read it twice. That was their "practice." But they had not monitored their performance at all, in spite of what they seemed to know about fluency during class, before the homework was assigned. They didn't own a metacogntive understanding of fluency, so when they practiced at home, it was not automatically available to them. They also didn't have access to the executive functions of goal setting, planning, and self-monitoring that night at home. Ken realized that he had not spent time on *how* to practice with them. They needed practice with how to practice.

So there are two challenges for us and our students: First, some students do not have a successful method to practice skills acquisition in math, or reading, or in any subject. Second, struggling students may go through the motions of practice without the attention and engagement required to actually activate their long-term memory systems. They do not have enough metacognitive skill to monitor their learning, or the independent goal-setting and planning skills needed, so their measure of "success" is the time they've taken, not the result they got. We need to figure out how to find time to address these issues in the classroom.

When we engage in what is called "deliberate practice,"[7] we are practicing optimally. The characteristics of deliberate practice come out of the research that looks at what contributes to expert performance. While we cannot expect students to become expert performers all the time in school (indeed, they could not, as so much practice and time is needed to make one an expert), there are several characteristics of deliberate practice that are useful for us to know as we design practice for students.

1. Someone must be motivated to engage in deliberate practice. Miguel was not really motivated to learn the facts, and time should have been spent helping him understand what value the practice would have for him, if he only put in that effort. Practice needs to be *aligned* to the learner, both in helping rouse effort and interest as well as in making sure the practice is something the student can do with instruction.

2. They need to exert effort, particularly attention. You can't practice deliberately on autopilot.

3. We should provide immediate feedback, or some mechanism should be in place for self-assessment. Ideally, this feedback includes not only an evaluation against a standard but also is tied to transcendence.

4. Finally, deliberate practice is repeated multiple times over a span of time.

Teaching Point: Requirements for Effective Rote Practice

The following strategy for training students to become more efficient learners when they have to practice a skill to automaticity builds off the characteristics of deliberate practice, the importance of retrieval effort in retention, and an understanding of learner struggles. Aside from the practice itself, each step in the list could be connected to scripts that students practice:

1. Talk to students about the importance of the skill you're asking them to practice.

2. Explicitly discuss with them the criterion that you will use to judge whether the student has reached the practice goal.

3. Explicitly teach students a method to practice a particular skill, and explain why you are asking them to practice that way.

For example, if students are using math facts flash cards, students should do the following:

a) Look at each and think about whether they can say the answer right away or not;

b) Confirm the right answer;

c) If correct, put the card on the table in one pile

d) If incorrect, or if they were correct but their response was not very fast, they put the card in another pile;

e) Go through all their cards in this manner, putting their cards in either pile;

f) Go through their incorrect-or-not-fast-answer pile, one at a time, looking at the fact and repeating it, covering it and repeating it, looking at it one more time and repeating it;

g) Mix all the cards together and go through them via steps a–e;

h) If there is still an incorrect-or-not-fast-answer pile, repeat steps f and g;

i) Report back to you, after in-class practice or homework, whether they were successful, how they know, and how they may practice even more successfully the next time.[8]

4. Model it, and maybe go through it with students once, giving immediate feedback.

5. Provide opportunities to discuss how the skill transfers to other situations and structure practice time for that transfer.

6. Periodically build some time for fun into classroom skill practice.

The more fun the practice is, the more students will do it. If students need to learn the symbols for the elements in chemistry, they could play Concentration, matching symbols (on one color index card) with the element name fully written out (on another color index card). Or they could do this with atomic weights and element names or element symbols. We could play 20 Questions in any subject at any grade. For example, in an upper elementary or middle school social studies class studying American history, it could be a series of statements: "I'm thinking of an important date. . . . It is pre-Revolutionary. . . . It involved the British Parliament." We could provide students with homemade board games—or students could make up their own—for practice.

Or students could write rap lyrics that the whole class can sing:

Yo, atomic symbols, some are ease-y
Like hydrogen is h, germanium's ge
Lithium is li, scandium is sc

Not too hard, it seems to me
But then there's a bunch,
They drive me craze-y,
Like Mercury's hg, and Silver is ag
If I don't learn them ease-y
It's not 'cause I'm laze-y

Rote practice to automaticity for skills development is a very important aspect of school learning, not because that's the main goal of learning—not by any means—but because automaticity frees up our working memory to engage with meaningful learning and problem solving. We need to provide some students the means to study, as well as the time and place during the school day if we don't think it will happen at home.

Elaborative Practice

When we want students to practice for meaning, we need to design elaborative practices. Elaborative practice often includes paraphrasing or restating; it is looking at something from multiple angles; it means connecting to and integrating new skills and knowledge into existing knowledge structures.

Bloom's taxonomy[9] can be a helpful guide for designing elaborative practice. It provides a framework for understanding higher-order thinking skills, which are related to elaborative learning activities. When we engage in elaborative practice, we are engaged in higher-order thinking. For those of us who need a refresher, Figure 10.1 shows the levels of Bloom's taxonomy, illustrating the revised version.

As one goes up the ladder, the cognitive skills that each level demands are increasingly complex. And though the boundaries between stages are not rigid or even completely hierarchical, it is generally true that the higher levels subsume the lower ones.

Anything that engages students beyond retrieving a fact or reciting a canned definition requires elaborative practice. The ability to analyze, evaluate, or compare requires us to draw upon multiple long-term memory schemas. It is the process of connecting new knowledge with old that makes higher-order thinking possible and allows students to transfer what they learn to new problems and contexts. If students only have a superficial understanding of a new topic, they will find it virtually impossible to connect the new learning with other knowledge structures in order to perform higher-order tasks.

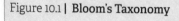

Figure 10.1 | **Bloom's Taxonomy**

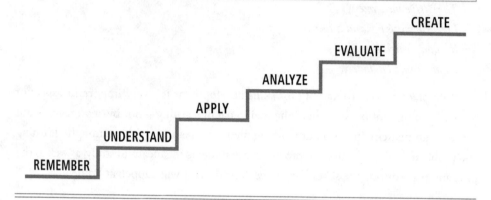

For example, many of us could quickly spit out "$E = MC^2$" in response to the question, "What is Einstein's most famous formula?" We've repeated it enough to screw it into our brain. If asked what it means, we might know that the speed of light is in there somewhere (even if we forgot exactly how fast that is, because we didn't have enough rote practice with that number), and that it's about mass and energy. That's the *remembering* level of Bloom's. It's a pretty sketchy schema. But if we were asked what C means in the formula or what the speed of light has to do with mass and energy, most of us wouldn't have a clue, even if we instantaneously could come up with the formula. That's because we lack sufficient elaborative practice with the core concepts toward creating a more developed, integrated schema about it. This is an example of the "empty verbalism" we discussed in Chapter 7. We shouldn't expect elaborative knowledge from rote practice.

A great instructional tool is Bloom's taxonomy verb wheel.[10] Figure 10.2 shows a generic, outline version, with a couple of specific examples in the *analyzing* section. The levels of Bloom's categories of knowledge are in the core. In the middle ring are the verbs we and our students can use when we are working with a particular type of understanding. The outer ring lists activities that students engage in that place them at that level of thinking. By structuring classroom activities at the different levels of Bloom's taxonomy, we are affording students elaborative practice time.

Figure 10.2 | **Generic Verb Wheel**

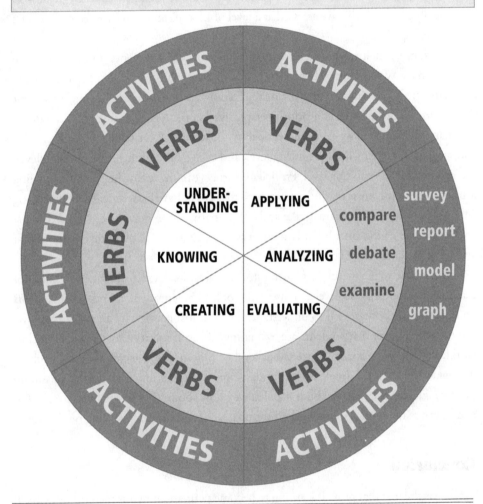

The practice we design should directly connect the learning goal(s) we set initially to our assessment in three ways: (1) the content has to match, but (2) the level of Bloom's taxonomy inherent in the objective and the assessment also have to match, and (3) the level of practice has to be at least at that level. For example, students practiced at the *knowing* and *understanding* levels, but we assess at the *analyzing* level. One reason we sometimes get fooled—for example, we think we've taught something really well, all the students seem to get it one day, and the next class we give a pop assessment and are shocked by how so few actually got it—is that we assessed at a level of Bloom's above the level of practice the students engaged in.

For example, if students were focused on identifying the events leading up to the Revolutionary War (naming them, being able to briefly describe them, knowing when they happened, knowing why they made the colonists or the British upset), an assessment like "Compare the colonial and British perspectives on the events leading up to the Revolutionary War in three ways" would probably not work well for struggling learners. We had students practicing at the knowing level, and even a bit into the understanding level, but assessed at the analyzing level. Proficient learners can make that jump, but struggling learners often can't. Instead, our practice activities could have had students (1) practicing comparison skills for their own sake and (2) preparing for a debate between a colonist and a member of the British Parliament (a synthesizing-level activity that assumes that analyzing must also have occurred).

But we have to be careful! Just having students with weak executive function skills, for example, work in analysis-level activities will not lead to a productive end. Or if students do not have the background to understand the task, just because it's an evaluation-level activity won't mean that students are evaluating. If the amount of material overwhelms working memory, it doesn't matter what level of Bloom's we're asking them to work at. The issues raised in this book are the fundamental underpinning of successful classroom practice. Elaborative practices built on what we know about what struggling learners need and how our memory systems work in the process of learning are the icing on the cake.

Conclusion

Practice is the fuel that propels learning to become permanent in our memory systems. If there's no fuel at all, it doesn't move. If there's too much, it stalls out. If it's the wrong kind of fuel, it sputters and does not work efficiently. Finally, by pouring fuel into our own vehicle, no one else's vehicle moves—what we do as teachers is *not* student practice, so the more we are doing, the less students are practicing. The art of teaching often consists of structuring the right kind and right amount of practice, based on what we know about our students.

The practice we provide for students also should connect our learning objectives to the *what* and *how* of our assessment, both the content of learning as well as the level of Bloom's taxonomy the learning (and assessment) requires. We may often find ourselves overlooking this reality and structuring assessment that matches the content, but not the level of learning that students were operating at. Or we may consistently connect objectives to assessments through practice, but at a low level of Bloom's, and then students are blown away by standardized test questions that require skill at higher levels of Bloom's than struggling students have practiced.

By being masters of practice, grounded in being learning specialists, we support student learning as best we can.

---

1. American Psychological Association (2013); Sousa (2011).
2. An entire chapter could be written on this subject alone. Students do not immediately need all phonemes, and should not learn phonemes in the order they appear in the alphabet. High frequency consonants should be automatized, and students should practice *strategizing maximally* with them. Ken found mastery of six or seven consonants to automaticity was often enough to springboard the independent learning of other consonants. W- d-n't n--d v-w-ls t- r—d —so we don't need to bog students down in much vowel practice. Making sure students get grounded in phonemic awareness, but treading lightly with it and always emphasizing what students can do with the phonemes they learn, in addition to systematic vocabulary practice, is key.
3. Medina (2008); Cepeda et al. (2006).
4. Roediger & Butler (2011).
5. Wolf (2007).
6. See Dehaene (2009) for a discussion of "neuronal recycling" in which a visual processing area used for identifying objects is adapted to rapidly process visual linguistic symbols.
7. Ericsson et al. (1991).
8. We might not initially assign students more than one set of facts at a time (e.g., the 2s until they have learned them well, the 3s by themselves until they're learned well, then the 4s); then have the students do all the 2s, 3s, and 4s together before they move on to the 5s.
9. Bloom (1956).
10. An Internet search for "Bloom's Taxonomy Verb Wheel" will yield hits, with different variations of this tool.

CONCLUSION

11

The evidence continues to mount:[1] in spite of all the educational movements and reforms designed to close the achievement gap, it continues to *widen* between income groups. There are, of course, many factors that affect academic performance, but we have come to believe that the performance gap between literacy-oriented learners and non-literacy-oriented and culturally disrupted learners is fundamental to understanding this academic gap. And we think most of you would also agree that at the same time that the performance gap is widening, teaching is getting increasingly burdensome under the weight of Academic Yearly Progress, high-stakes testing, and the public outing of "low-performing" schools and even teachers. So what is our field missing, year after year, well-intentioned decision after well-intentioned decision?

We are missing two crucial things, which together form the framework for this book. First, we are missing the reality of learning as a sociocultural process, and especially the symbiotic relationship between schooling and a literacy-oriented upbringing, mainly the province of middle-class and affluent families. If a student is lucky enough to be born into a literacy-oriented community, she wins. If not, the student loses, and she will be force-fed information at school, which will neither empower her as a learner nor enable her to achieve at a higher academic level. This issue will only be addressed by coming to grips with what this *really* means, and turning classrooms into places where the focus is on helping non-literacy-oriented and culturally disrupted learners *learn how to learn and use language* in literacy-oriented ways.[2] Squeezing the life and joy out of learning in the service of creating little child-scholars will not change the fundamental dynamic of the haves and have-nots. This is one of the most important social justice issues of our day.

Sadly, we feel the Common Core is sending us down yet another cul-de-sac, emblematic of so many trends in contemporary pedagogy.[3] While the Common Core somewhat reduces the quantity of content, it ratchets up the level of complexity of engagement with that content. It has designed the curriculum backward by first identifying the skills that students need for college, then deconstructing them back to the preK and kindergarten levels. That would ultimately be a very good thing except for one problem: it operates under two mistaken starting points.

First, the backward design philosophy of the Common Core must assume either one of two possibilities: (1) all students enter schools with relatively equal levels of school-ready skills, or (2) the school experiences of engaging with material in complex ways teaches all students the linguistic and cognitive skills they need to function *independently* at more sophisticated academic levels. After reading this book, we hope you understand how both assumptions are faulty.

Students are not entering our schools with equal levels of skill, and merely having students function in more complex learning environments does *not* automatically help them develop the level of academic learning skills they require to *independently* achieve at higher levels such as language skills, executive function skills, working memory skills, and so on. High expectations are great, and needed. But expectations have to be reachable to have the intended effect.

Second, the Common Core is stuck in the same rut our field seems to be stuck in since it forgot all about James Dewey: focusing on teaching more than learning. The Common Core seems to assume that the primary issue in achievement is what teachers do in relation to students' outside, not what struggling learners need for their learning on their inside, cognitively, emotionally, and autobiographically. Only by becoming learning specialists can we better address the realities of struggling learners. Only by understanding how memory systems operate in the process of learning can we teach in sync with the realities of the brain and better meet the needs of struggling learners. No Common Core lesson will ever do that for us!

Reality #1: Classroom Learning Is a Cultural Process

Diverse students represent diverse ways of thinking and learning. At one point it was fashionable and progressive to assume that all students were basically the same, with the same learning potential, provided they all received the same educational opportunities. This may have been an important step in our collective attempt to throw off the stupor of racism and sexism in our educational system.

However, the weight of the research in many fields—anthropology, education, psychology, linguistics—points to the conclusion that cognitive diversity goes hand-in-hand with cultural diversity. The human mind, largely through its memory systems, is designed to be sensitive to the linguistic, social, and physical environment. Not surprisingly, participation in differing types of social activity can result in differing forms of thought and learning preferences. For those of us teaching in classes with culturally and linguistically diverse learners, this will not be a shocking bit of news.

The challenge of educating our most vulnerable population of students will never be simple or easy. However, the hardest step will be the first, in which we identify non-literacy-oriented and culturally disrupted students as a priority and recognize that they require a curriculum that balances a focus on learning how to learn in school with what to learn.

Reality #2: Teachers Need to Become Learning Specialists

The more we teach in sync with these two realities—how the brain's memory systems are hardwired to operate in the process of learning, and that learning and memory systems are profoundly affected by culture—the more our students' learning will be enhanced. We then realize how fragile our students' memory systems are, and that the answer to the achievement gap is not to make classrooms increasingly complex learning environments, but to learn how to align ourselves with our struggling students' needs. Then we will be less likely to teach without

- activating relevant background knowledge;
- avoiding overloading students' working memories;
- affording students sufficient practice opportunities;
- clarifying the learning goal(s);
- aligning student practice with our goal(s) and assessment;
- building in a lot of active student talk time;

- graphically or visually representing the organization and meaning of the content;
- explicitly and systematically addressing executive functions in learning;
- reflecting on what we can do differently when a breakdown in learning occurs;
- taking into account the understandings of the novice learner;
- structuring appropriate mediated learning experiences that focus on learning how to learn for struggling learners.

This list synthesizes the main themes that organize the teaching suggestions we offer in this book, and it defines, to a greater or lesser degree, what is often missing in classrooms that ignore the academic advantages literacy-oriented students have in school and that define the pace of learning by what the *haves* can and should be able to do. Most of us intentionally do some of these things. Some of us do many of them. Few of us consistently do all of them. If we want to successfully teach all students, we have to shake free from a product-oriented approach to education and focus on the learning process—we need to become learning specialists.

As learning specialists, we will be more in tune with student struggles and design lessons to avoid causing those very struggles by teaching in synch with the brain's memory systems. We take on this role when we realize that good teaching is led by understanding our students, including the role that memory plays in classroom learning. And it's struggling learners who benefit the most when we teach while wearing our learner specialist hat.

What Else Can We Do?

Finally, it is important for us to prepare ourselves as learning specialists to become leading voices in educational policy and reform. Teachers are closer than anyone to their learners and the processes of classroom learning. So we must become advocates for meeting the real needs of our struggling learners. We believe it is in students' best interests for teachers who are open to becoming learning specialists to be empowered as leading decision makers in their own classrooms, schools, and districts.

One of the goals of this book is to provide support for how to focus the attention of administrators, school boards, parents, and community members on the distinctive educational needs of struggling learners. In order to be successful, we must ground our arguments not only on our lived experiences in the classroom but also on the vast research and theory that support a learner-centered approach to teaching diverse learners. Our hope is that this book's focus on memory and culture will provide support to all of you, as you advocate for an approach to education that acknowledges cognitive diversity and the unique needs of struggling learners.

---

1. Reardon (2013).
2. The reality is that the literacy orientation of schools is fundamental and will probably never change.
3. Bailey & Pransky (2005).

REFERENCES

Alloway, T. (2011). *Improving working memory: Supporting students' learning.* Los Angeles: SAGE.

Ambrose, S., Bridges, M., DiPietro, M. Lovett, M., & Norman, M. (2010). *How learning works: 7 research-based principles for smart teaching.* San Francisco, CA: Jossey-Bass.

American Psychological Association (2013). Practice for knowledge acquisition (not drill and kill). http://www.apa.org/education/k12/practice-acquisition.aspx?item=1

Armstrong, S. (2008). *Teaching smarter with the brain in focus.* New York: Scholastic.

Au, K. (1980). Participation structures in a reading lesson with Hawaiian children: Analysis of a culturally appropriate instructional event. *Anthropology and Education Quarterly, 11,* 91–115.

Baddeley, A. (2007). *Working memory, thought and action.* Oxford, England: Oxford University Press.

Baddeley, A., Eysenck, M., & Anderson, M. (2009*) Memory.* New York: Psychology Press.

Bailey, F., & K. Pransky (2010). Investigating the classroom discourse of mediation in a Feuerstein instrumental enrichment programme. *Classroom Discourse, 1*(2), 121–141.

Bailey, F., & Pransky, K. (2005). "Are 'other people's children' constructivist learners too? *Theory into Practice, 44* (1) 19–26.

Barkley, R. A. (2012). *Executive functions: What they are, how they work, and how they evolved.* NY: The Guilford Press.

Baumann, J. F., Jones, L.A., & Seifert-Kessell, N. (1993). Using think alouds to enhance children's comprehension monitoring abilities. *The Reading Teacher, 47,* 184–193.

Ben-Hur, M. (Ed.) (1994). *On Feuerstein's instrumental enrichment.* Palatine, IL: IRI/Skylight Publishing.

Best, J. R., Miller, P. H., & Naglieri, J. A. (2011). Relations between executive function and academic achievement from Ages 5 to 17 in a large, representative national sample. *Learning and Individual Differences, 21*(4), 327–336.

Bibok, M. B., Carpendale, J. I. M. & Müller, U. (2009, Spring). Parental scaffolding and the development of executive function." *New Directions for Child and Adolescent Development, 123,* 17–34.

Blair, C., Granger, D., Willoughby, M., Mills-Koonce, R., Cox, M., Greenberg, M., Kivlighan, K., Fortunato, C. & Family Life Project Key Investigators (2011). Salivary cortisol mediates effects of poverty and on executive functions in early childhood. *Child Development, 82*(6), 1970–1984.

Blair C. & Razza, R. C. (2007). Relating effortful control, executive function, and false belief understanding to emerging math and literacy ability in kindergarten. *Society for Research in Child Development, 76* (2), 647–663.

Bloom, B.S. (1956). *Taxonomy of educational objectives, handbook I: The cognitive domain.* New York: David McKay.

Bloome, D. & F. Bailey. (1992). Studying language and literacy through events, particularity, and intertextuality. In Beech's (Ed.) *Multiple Perspectives on Language and Literacy Research.* Urbana, IL: National Council of Teachers of English.

Bloome, D., S. Power Carter, B. Christina, S. Otto, and N. Shuart-Faris (2005). *Discourse analysis and the study of classroom language and literacy events.* Mahwah, New Jersey: Erlbaum Publishers.

Bodrova, E. & Leong, D. J. (2007). *Tools of the mind: The Vygotskian approach to early childhood education* (2nd ed.). Columbus, OH: Merrill/Prentice Hall.

Booth, J. N., Boyle, J. M. E., & Kelly, S. W. (2010). Do tasks make a difference? Accounting for heterogeneity of performance of children with reading difficulties on tasks of executive function: Findings from a meta-analysis. *British Journal of Developmental Psychology, 28,* 113–176.

Booth, J. N. & Boyle, J. M. E. (2009). The role of inhibitory functioning in children's reading skills. *Educational Psychology, 25* (4), 339–350.

Bower, G. (2000). A short history of memory research. In E. Tulving & F. Craik (Eds.), *The oxford handbook of memory.* Oxford, England: Oxford University Press.

Buckner, E. & Kim, P. (2012). Mobile innovations, executive functions, and educational developments in conflict zones: A case study from Palestine. *Educational Technology Research and Development, 60*(1), 175–192.

Burianova, H., McIntosh, A. & Grady, C. (2010). A common functional brain network for autobiographical, episodic, and semantic memory retrieval. *NeuroImage,* 49, 865 –874.

Cartwright, K. B. (2012). Insights from cognitive neuroscience: The importance of executive function for early reading development and education. *Early Education and Development, 23*(1), 24–36.

Canagaraja, S (1999). *Resisting linguistic imperialism in english teaching.* Oxford, England: Oxford University Press.

Cepeda, N. J., Pashler, H., Vul, E., Wixted, J. T., & Rohrer, D. (2006). Distributed practice in verbal recall tasks: A review and quantitative synthesis. *Psychological Bulletin, 132,* 354–380.

Chiao, J. Y. (2009). Clinical Neuroscience: a once and future discipline. *Progress in Brain Research, 178,* 281–304.

Clark, R., Nguyen, F., & Sweller, J. (2006) *Efficiency in learning: Evidence-based guidelines to manage cognitive load.* San Francisco, CA, Pfeiffer

Cole, M., Gay, J., Glick, J.A., & Sharp, D.W. (1971). *The cultural context of learning and thinking.* New York: Basic Books.

Cole, M., & Scribner, S. (1974). *Culture and thought: A psychological introduction.* New York: John Wiley & Sons.

Cole, M., & Scribner, S. (1977). Cross-cultural studies of memory and cognition. In R.V. Kail & J.W. Hagen (Eds.), *Perspectives on the development of memory and cognition.* Hillsdale, NJ: Erlbaum.

Collins, A., & Loftus, E. (1975). A spreading activation theory of semantic processing. *Psychological Review, 82,* 407–428.

Collins, J (1997). *Selecting and teaching focus correction areas: A planning guide.* West Newbury, MA: Collins Education Associates, L.L.C.

Conway, M., Gardiner, J., Perfect, T., Anderson, S., & Cohen, G. (1997). Changes in memory awareness during learning: The acquisition of knowledge by psychology undergraduates. *Journal of Experimental Psychology: General, 126,* 393–413.

Cutting, L. E., Materek, A., Cole, C., Levine, T. & Mahone, E.M. (2009). Effects of fluency, oral language, and executive function on reading comprehension performance. *Ann. of Dyslexia, 59,* 34–54.

Cummins, J. (1981). The role of primary language development in promoting educational success for language minority students. In *Schooling and Language Minority Students: A Theoretical Framework.* Los Angeles: Evaluation, Dissemination and Assessment Center, California State University, Los Angles

Davey, B. (1983). Think-aloud: Modeling the cognitive processes of reading comprehension. *Journal of Reading, 27*(1), 44–47.

Dawson, P. & Guare (2010). *Executive skills in children and adolescents.* New York: The Guilford Press.

Dehaene, S. (2009). *Reading in the brain.* New York: Viking Penguin.

Dehn, M. (2008). *Working memory and academic development.* Hoboken, NJ: John Wiley & Sons, Inc.

Delpit, L. (1996). *Other people's children: Cultural conflict in the classroom.* New York: The New Press.

De La Paz, S., Swanson, P. N. & Graham, S. (1998). The contribution of executive control to the revising by students with writing and learning difficulties. *Journal of Educational Psychology, 90*(3), 448–460.

Dewey, J. (1938). *Experience and education.* New York: Collier Books, Macmillan.

Draaisma, D. (2004). *Why life speeds up as you get older: How memory shapes our past.* Cambridge, UK: Cambridge University Press.

Egan, K. (1997). *The educated mind: How cognitive tools shape our understanding.* Chicago: University of Chicago Press.

Echevarria, J., M. Vogt, and D. Short (2008). *Making content comprehensible to English language learners: The SIOP model.* Santa Monica, CA: Pearson, Allyn & Bacon.

Ericsson, K., Krampe, R., & Tesch-Romer, C. (1991). The role of deliberate practice in the acquisition of expert performance. *Psychological Review, 100*(3), 363–406.

Fernald, L., Weber, A., Galasso, E. & Ratsifandrihamanana (2011). Socioeconomic gradients and child development in a very low income population: evidence from Madagascar. *Developmental Science, 14*(4), 832–847.

Fivush, R. & Nelson, K. (2004). Culture and language in the Emergence of Autobiographical Memory. *Psychological Science, 15*(9), 573–577.

Fivush, R. (2011). The development of autobiographical memory. *Annual Review of Psychology, 62,* 559–582.

Feuerstein, R., Feuerstein, R., Falik, L. & Rand, Y. (2006). *Creating and enhancing cognitive modifiability: The Feuerstein instrumental enrichment program.* Jerusalem: ICELP Publications.

Feuerstein, R., Feuerstein, R., & Falik, L. (2010). *Beyond smarter: Mediated learning and the brain's capacity for change.* New York: Teacher's College Press.

Feuerstein, R. & Lewin-Benhim, A. (2012). *What learning looks like: Mediated learning in theory and practice K–6.* New York: Teachers College Press.

Frawley, W. (1997). *Vygotsky and cognitive science: Language and the unification of the social and computational mind.* Cambridge, MA: Harvard University Press.

Fu. D. (2003) *Island of English: Teaching English in chinatown.* London, UK: Heinemann.

Gardiner, J., & Richardson-Klaehn, A. (2000). Remembering and knowing. In Tulving & Craik (Eds.), *The Oxford handbook of memory.* Oxford, England: Oxford University Press.

Gathercole, S. and T. Alloway. (2010). *Working memory and learning: A practical guide for teachers.* Los Angeles: Sage.

Garner, B. (2007). *Getting to "Got it!": Helping Struggling Students Learn How to Learn.* Alexandria, VA: ASCD.

Gauvain, M. (2001). *The social context of cognitive development.* New York: Guilford Press.

Gee, J. P. (1990). *Social linguistics and literacies: Ideology in discourses. Critical perspectives on literacy and education.* London: Falmer Press

Geertz, C. (1973). *The interpretation of cultures: Selected essays.* New York: Basic.

Giroux, H. (1983). *Theory and resistance in education: A pedagogy for the opposition.* New York: Bergin & Garvey.

Gluck, M., Mercado, E., & Myers, C. (2008). *Learning and memory.* New York: Worth Publishers.

Goswami, U. (2008). *Cognitive development: The learning brain.* New York: Psychology Press.

Grossman, M., & Koenig, P. (2002). Semantic memory. In V.S. Ramachandran (Ed.), *Encyclopedia of the human brain.* New York: Academic Press. The neural basis for categorization in semantic memory. *NeuroImage* 17, 1549–1561.

Gutchess, A.H., & Indeck, A. (2009). Cultural influences on memory. *Progress in Brain Research, 178,* 137–50.

Greenfield and Cocking (1994). *Cross-cultural roots of minority child development.* Hillsdale, NJ: Erlbaum.

Hart, B. & Risley, T. (1995). *Meaningful differences in the everyday experience of young American children.* Baltimore: Paul H. Brookes.

Hart, B. & Risley, T. (2003) The early catastrophe. *Educational Review, 17*(1) 110–118.

Harvey W (1628/1941) An anatomical disquisition on the motion of the heart and blood in animals. In F. Williams & T. Keys (Eds.), *Cardiac classics.* St. Louis, MO: CV Mosby Co 14–79.

Harrington, M. and Sawyer, M. (1992). L2 working memory capacity and L2 reading skill. *Studies in Second Language Acquisition, 14,* 112–21.

Hayden, C. A. & Ornstein, P. A. (2009). Research about telling about the past: The past, present and future. *Journal of Cognition and Development, 10*(3), 188-209.

Heath, S. (1983). *Ways with words: Language, life and work in communities and classrooms.* Cambridge, England: Cambridge University Press.

Hebb, D.O. (1949). *The organization of behavior: A neuropsychological theory.* Oxford, England: Wiley.

Herbers, J. E., Cutuli, J.J., Lafavor, T.L., Vrieze, D., Leibel, C., Obradovic, J., & Master, A.S. (2011). Direct and Indirect Effects of Parenting on the Academic Functioning of Young Homeless Children. *Early Education and Development, 22*(1), 77–104.

Hedrick, A.M., Hayden, C. A. & Ornstein, P. A. (2009). Elaborative talk during and after an event: Conversational style influences children's memory reports. *Journal of Cognition and Development, 10*(3), 188–209.

Himmele, P. & Himmele, W. (2011). *Total Participation Techniques.* Alexandria, VA: ASCD

Hochschild, J. L. (2003). Social class in public schools. *Journal of Social Issues, 59,* 821–840. doi: 10.1046/j.0022-4537.2003.00092.

Hughes, C. H & Ensor, R. A. (2009). How do families help or hinder the emergence of early executive function? *New Directions for Child and Adolescent Development, 123,* 35–50.

Hyerle, D (2008). *Visual tools for transforming information into knowledge.* Thousand Oaks, CA: Corwin.

Jerman, O; Reynalds, C. & Swanson, H. L. (2012). Does growth in working memory span or executive function processes predict growth in reading and math in children with reading disabilities? *Learning Disability Quarterly, 35*(3), 144–157.

Karpov, Y. (2003) Development through the lifespan: A Neo-Vygotskian approach. In A. Kozulin, B. Gindis, V. Ageyev, S. Miller (Eds.), *Vygotsky's educational theory in cultural context.* Cambridge, UK: Cambridge University Press.

Kaufman, C. (2010). *Executive function in the classroom: Practical strategies for improving performance and enhancing skills for all students.* Baltimore: Paul H. Brooks.

Kahneman, D. (2011). *Thinking, fast and slow.* New York: Farrar, Strauss and Giroux.

Kolb, D. (1983). *Experiential learning: Experience as the source of learning and development.* Upper Saddle River, NJ: Prentice Hall.

Kozol, J. (1992). *Savage inequalities: Children in America's schools.* Harper Perennial.

Kostopoulos, D. & Lee, J. (2012). A Naturalistic Study of Executive Function and Mathematical Problem-Solving. *Journal of Mathematical Behavior, 31*(2), 196–208.

Kozulin, A. (2011). Cognitive Aspects of the transition from a traditional to a modern technological Society. In P. Portes & S. Salas (Eds.), *Vygotsky in 21st century society: Advances in cultural historical theory and praxis with non-dominant communities*. New York: Peter Lang.

Lan, X., Legare, C., Ponitz, C., Li, S., Morrison, F. (2011). Investigating the links between the subcomponents of executive function and academic achievement: A cross-cultural analysis of chinese and american preschoolers. *Journal of Experimental Child Psychology, 108*(3), 677–692.

Lakoff, G. (1987). *Women, fire, and dangerous Things: What categories reveal about the mind.* Chicago, IL: The University of Chicago Press.

Lantolf, J. (Edt.) (2000). *Sociocultural theory and second language learning.* Oxford, UK: Oxford University Press.

Lantolf, J. & S. Thorne (2006). *Sociocultural theory and the genesis of second language development.* Oxford: Oxford University Press.

Lave, J. & Wenger, E. (1991) *Situated learning: Legitimate peripheral participation.* Cambridge: Cambridge University Press.

LeDoux, J. (1996). *The emotional brain.* New York, NY: Simon and Schuster.

LeDoux, J. (2002). *Synaptic self: How our brains become who we are.* New York, NY: Viking

Lewis, C., Koyasu, M., Oh, S., Ogawa, A., Short, B. & Huang, Z. (2009) *Culture, Executive Function, and Social Understanding. New Directions for Child and Adolescent Development, 123,* 69-85.

Levine, M. (2002). *A mind at a time.* New York: Simon & Schuster

Luria, A.R. (1976). *Cognitive development: Its cultural and social foundations.* Cambridge, MA: Harvard University Press.

Marcovitch, S., Jacques, S., Boseovski, J.J., Zelazo, P.D. (2008). Self-Reflection and the Cognitive Control of Behavior: Implications for Learning. *International Mind, Brain and Educational Society and Wiley Periodicals, Inc., 2*(3), 136–141.

Marzano, R.J., Pickering, D.J., & Pollock, J.E. (2001). *Classroom instruction that works: Research-based strategies for increasing student achievement.* Alexandria, VA: ASCD

Marzano, R., & Pickering, D. (2005). *Building academic vocabulary: Teacher's manual.* Alexandria, VA: Association for Supervision and Curriculum Development.

McKeon, D. (1994). Language, culture, and schooling. In F. Genesee (Ed.). *Educating second language children.* Cambridge: Cambridge University Press.

McPhee, J. (2013). Structure. *New Yorker Magazine, 14,* 46–55.

McRae, K., & Jones, M. N. (2013). Semantic memory. In D. Reisberg (Ed.) *The oxford handbook of cognitive psychology.* Oxford, England: Oxford University Press.

McTighe J. & Wiggins, G. (2013) *Essential questions: Opening doors to student understanding.* Alexandria, V: ASCD.

Medina, J. (2008). *Brain rules.* Seattle, WA: Pear Press.

Melby-Lervag, M & Hulme, C. (2012) Is working memory training effective? A meta-analysis review. *Developmental Psychology, 49*(2), 270–291.

Meltzer, L.(2010). *Executive function in education: From theory to practice.* The Guilford Press.

Mentis, M., Dunn-Bernstein, M. & Mentis, M. (2008). *Mediated learning: Teaching, tasks and tools to unlock cognitive potential.* Thousand Oaks, CA: Corwin Press.

Miller, G. (1956). The magical number seven, plus or minus two: Some limits on our capacity for processing information: *Psychological Review, 63,* 81–97.

Molfese, V. J., Molfese, P., Molfese, D., Rudasill, K., Armstrong, N., & Starkey, G. (2010). Executive function in 6-8 Year Olds: Brain and behavioral evidence and implications for school achievement. *Contemporary Educational Psychology, 35*(2) 116–125.

Nelson, K. (2007) *Young minds in social worlds: Experience, meaning, and memory.* Cambridge, MA: Harvard University Press

Newman, D., Griffin, P., & Cole, M. (1989). *The construction zone: Working for cognitive change in school.* Cambridge: Cambridge University Press.

Nisbett, R. (2003). *The geography of thought.* New York: Free Press.

Ortega, L. (2009). *Understanding second language acquisition.* London: Hodder Education.

Paradis, (2011). *Declarative and procedural determinants of second languages.* Amsterdam, The Netherlands: John Benjamins Publishing Company.

Plass, J., Moreno, R., & Brunken, R. (2010). *Cognitive load theory.* Cambridge, UK: Cambridge University Press.

Pavlenko, A., & Lantolf, J. (2000). Second language learning as participation and the (re)construction of selves. In Lantolf (ed.), *Sociocultural Theory and Second Language Learning.* Oxford: Oxford University Press.

Perry, K. (2012). What is literacy? – A critical overview of sociocultural perspectives. *Journal of Language & Literacy Education, 8*(1), 51–71.

Philips, S. (1983). *The invisible culture: Communication in classroom and community on the Warm Springs Indian Reservation.* New York: Longman.

Pinker, S. (1997). *How the mind works.* New York: W. W. Norton.

Plass, J., Moreno, R., & Brunken, R. (Eds.), (2010) *Cognitive load theory.* Cambridge, England: Cambridge University Press.

Pransky, K., & Bailey, F. (2003). To meet your students where they are, first you have to find them: Working with culturally and linguistically diverse at-risk students. *The Reading Teacher, 56*(4), 370–383.

Pransky, K. (2008). *Beneath the surface: The hidden realities of teaching culturally and linguistically diverse young learners.* Portsmouth, NH: Heinemann.

Pransky, K. (2009). There's more to see. *Educational Leadership, 66*(7), 74–78.

Purcell-Gates, V. (1995). *Other people's words: The cycle of low literacy.* Boston, MA: Harvard University Press.

Rasninski, T. (2010). *The Fluent Reader (2nd Edition): Oral and silent-reading strategies for building fluency, word recognition & comprehension.* NY: Scholastic.

Reardon, S. F. (2013). The widening income achievement gap. *Educational Leadership, 7*(8),10–17.

Reardon, S.F. (April 27, 2013). No Rich Child Left Behind. *The New York Times.* http://opinionator.blogs.nytimes.com/.

Reese, E., Haden, C. & Fivush, R. (1993). Mother-Child conversations about the past: Relationships of style and memory over time. *Cognitive Development* 8, 403–430.

Renkle, A. & R. Atkinson (2010). Learning from worked-out examples and problem solving. In Plass, Morenao and Brunker (Eds.), *Cognitive Load Theory*. Cambridge: Cambridge University Press.

Rodgers, C. (2002). Another look at John Dewey and reflective thinking. *Teacher's College Record, 104*(4), 842–866.

Roediger, H. L., & Butler, A. C. (2011). The critical role of retrieval practice in long-term retention. *Trends in Cognitive Sciences, 15*, 20–27.

Rogoff, B. (2003). *The cultural nature of human development*. Oxford: Oxford University Press.

Rose, M. (2005). *Lives on the Boundary: A moving account of the struggles and achievements of America's educationally underprepared*. New York, NY: Penguin.

Sadoski, M. & Pavio, A. (2001). *Imagery and text: A dual coding theory of reading and writing*. Mahway, NY: Lawrence Erlbaum Associates.

Sasser, T. R. & Bierman, K. L. (2012). The Role of Executive Function Skills and Self-Regulation Behaviors in School Readiness and Adjustment. Meeting of the Society for Research on Educational Effectiveness.

Schacter, D. (2001). *The seven sins of memory: How the mind forgets and remembers*. Boston, MA: Houghton Mifflin Co.

Schumann, J., S. Crowell, N. Jones, N. Lee, S. Schuchert, L. Wood (2004). *The neurobiology of learning: Perspectives from second language acquisition*. Mahwah, N.J. Lawrence Erlbaum.

Schleppegrell, M. (2004). *The language of schooling: A functional linguistics perspective*. New York, NY: Routledge.

Scollon, R. and S. Scollon (1981). *Narrative, Literacy and Face in Interethnic Communication*. Norwood, NJ: ABLEX.

Shank, R. and R. Abelson. (1977). *Scripts, plans, goals and understanding*. Hillsdale, N.J.: Lawrence Erlbaum Associates.

Shah, I. (1972). *The Exploits of the incomparable Mullah Nassruddin*. New York: E.P. Dutton. Spring, J (2011). *American education*. New York, NY: McGraw Hill.

Sousa, D. S. (2011) *How the brain learns*. Thousand Oaks, CA: Corwin Press.

Sodian, B. & Frith, U. (2008) Metacognition, theory of mind and self-control: The relevance of high-level cognitive processes in development, neuroscience; and education. *International Mind, Brain and Educational Society and Wiley Periodicals, 2*(3),111–113.

St. Clair-Thompson, H. L. (2011). Executive functions and working memory behaviors in children with a poor working memory. *Learning and Individual Differences, 21*(4) 409–414.

Smith, F. (1985). *Reading without nonsense*. New York, NY: Teacher's College Press.

Swain, M, P. Kinnear, L.Steinman. (2010). *Sociocultural theory in second language education: An introduction through narratives*. Bristol, UK: Multilingual Matters.

Swanson, H. L. (1999). Reading comprehension and working memory in learning-disabled readers: Is the phonological loop more important than the executive system? *Journal of Experimental Child Psychology, 72*(1), 1–31

Sweller, John, Jeroen J.G. van Merrienboer and Fred G.W.C. Paas (1998). Cognitive Architecture and Instructional Design. *Educational Psychology Review.* Vol. 10 no. 3., 251–296.

Taylor, J. (1995). *Linguistic categorization: Protoypes in linguistic theory.* Oxford: Clarendon Press.

Tennyson, R.D. & Cocchiarella, M.J. (1986). An empirically based instructional design theory for teaching concepts. *Review of Educational Research, 56*(1), 40–71.

Thomas, W.P., & Collier, V.P. (2002). *A national study of school effectiveness for language minority students' long-term academic achievement.* Santa Cruz, CA: Center for Research on Education, Diversity and Excellence, University of California-Santa Cruz.

Tileston, D. W. (2004). *What every teacher should know about Learning, Memory and the brain.* Thousand oaks, CA: Corwin Press

Toll, S. W., Van der Ven, S.H., Kroesbergen, E.H., & Van Luit, J.E. (2011). Executive Function as Predictors of Math Learning Disabilities. *Journal of Learning Disabilities, 44*(6), 521-532.

Tomasello, M. (1999). *The cultural origins of human cognition.* Cambridge, MA: Harvard University press.

Toyota, H. (2004). Effects of types of elaboration on children's memories of a story: interaction with academic performance. *Psychological Reports, 94*(1), 291–304.

Tulving, E., & Donaldson, W. (1972). *Organization of memory.* New York: Academic Press.

Tulving, E. (1985). Memory and consciousness. *Canadian Psychology, 26*(1), 1–12.

Tulving, E. (1993). What is episodic memory? *American Psychological Society, 2*(3), 67–70.

Tulving, E. (2002). Episodic memory: From mind to brain. *Annual Review of Psychology, 53,* 1–25.

Vanderhaeghen, P. & Cheng, HJ. (2010). Guidance Molecules in Axon Pruning and Cell Death. Cold Spring Harbor Perspectives in Biology 2(6), 1–18.

Vygotsky, L. (1986). *Thought and language.* Cambridge, MA: The MIT Press.

Vygotsky, L. (1978). *Mind in society: The development of higher psychological processes.* Cambridge, MA: Harvard University Press.

Wang, Q. (2011). Autobiographical memory and culture." *On-line Readings in Psychology and Culture, Unit 5.* www.scholarworks.gvsu.edu/orpc/vol5/iss2/2.

Wiggins, G. & J. McTighe (2005). *Understanding by design* (2nd edition). Alexandria, VA: ASCD.

Willis, J. (2006). *Research-based strategies to ignite student learning.* Alexandria, VA: ASCD.

Wolf, M. (2007). *Proust and the squid: The story and science of the reading brain.* New York: Harper.

Wong-Fillmore, L. (1985). When does teacher talk work as input? In Gass & Madden (eds.) *Input in Second Language Acquisition.* Cambridge: Newbury House Publishers.

Zacarian, D. (2013). *Mastering academic language: A framework for supporting student achievement.* Thousand Oaks, CA: Corwin.

Zwiers, J. & Crawford, M. (2011). *Academic Conversations: Classroom talk that fosters critical thinking and content understandings.* Portland, ME: Stenhouse Publishers.

Zwiers, J. (2007). Teaching practices and perspectives for developing academic language. *International Journal of Academic Language, 17*(1), 93–116.

INDEX

Note: Page references followed by an italicized *f* indicate information contained in figures. Information contained in end notes is indicated with an italicized *n* (for example, 66*n*13 means page 66, end note #13).

ABOUT THE AUTHORS

Francis Bailey is the Director of the Teaching English as a Second Language (TESL) Master's program at the University of Kentucky. Francis has a doctoral degree from the University of Massachusetts. His primary educational focus is on issues in teaching English language learners in and outside of the United States. He has conducted research on second language acquisition and the challenges faced by culturally and linguistically diverse students due to differences between home (and community) ways of learning and knowing and the academic and social demands of schools. Francis has become increasingly interested in the ways that the cognitive sciences can inform our understanding of classroom learning.

Francis has conducted qualitative research on classroom learning, both in the US and internationally. His publications include research on Feuerstein's Instrumental Enrichment program, topics on sociocultural perspectives on learning and teaching, and research on Nigerian primary school education. Francis attempts to bring a perspective on educational issues that is informed by research and theory on both the cultural nature of learning and the diverse cognitive processes of learners.

Ken Pransky has been working in the field of multicultural education for 35 years. He has taught K–12, at the college level, and to adults. He has taught as an EFL teacher overseas and for 20 years was an ESL teacher in the Massachusetts public schools, where he became increasingly interested in understanding, researching, and writing about what causes underachievement and academic struggle. Since 2008, he has been a full time teacher trainer and instructional coach through the Collaborative for Educational Services in Northampton, MA.

In addition to his teaching and training work, Ken has presented at national and international conferences. He has authored and co-authored several articles published in leading education journals, such as Theory into Practice, Reading Teacher and Ed Leadership, about working with underachieving students, and in 2008 published Beneath the Surface: The Hidden Realities of Working with Culturally and Linguistically Diverse Young Learners, with Heinemann.